Overseas Territories in World Affairs

Fred Constant

Overseas Territories in World Affairs

Linking up Subnational, National and International Politics

Fred Constant
University of the French Antilles
Schoelcher, Martinique, France

ISBN 978-3-031-64232-6   ISBN 978-3-031-64233-3   (eBook)
https://doi.org/10.1007/978-3-031-64233-3

Translation from the French language edition: "Géopolitique des Outre-Mer Entre déclassement et (re)valorisation" by Fred Constant, © Author has all English Rights 2023. Published by Le Cavalier Bleu. All Rights Reserved.

© The Editor(s) (if applicable) and The Author(s), under exclusive license to Springer Nature Switzerland AG 2024

This work is subject to copyright. All rights are solely and exclusively licensed by the Publisher, whether the whole or part of the material is concerned, specifically the rights of translation, reprinting, reuse of illustrations, recitation, broadcasting, reproduction on microfilms or in any other physical way, and transmission or information storage and retrieval, electronic adaptation, computer software, or by similar or dissimilar methodology now known or hereafter developed.
The use of general descriptive names, registered names, trademarks, service marks, etc. in this publication does not imply, even in the absence of a specific statement, that such names are exempt from the relevant protective laws and regulations and therefore free for general use.
The publisher, the authors and the editors are safe to assume that the advice and information in this book are believed to be true and accurate at the date of publication. Neither the publisher nor the authors or the editors give a warranty, expressed or implied, with respect to the material contained herein or for any errors or omissions that may have been made. The publisher remains neutral with regard to jurisdictional claims in published maps and institutional affiliations.

Cover credit: © Harvey Loake

This Palgrave Macmillan imprint is published by the registered company Springer Nature Switzerland AG
The registered company address is: Gewerbestrasse 11, 6330 Cham, Switzerland

If disposing of this product, please recycle the paper.

To the memory of my parents, Joseph H. B. Constant (1923–2009) and Marie-Thérèse F. Polyte (1929–2022) for whom, after all, I have always written.

Foreword

It is my pleasure to present the last book published by Fred Constant to the worldwide English-speaking readers. May I first point out that the initiative taken by the author is really courageous and should be welcomed, as there are very few works devoted to the topic of overseas politics: the concept appears so vague, confused, even contradictory that it deserves a serious investigation, especially as it is still at the very center of the French national obsessions. We only must watch the daily weather report at the French national TV for being convinced that showing every day all the French oversea settlement is a major and probably strategic concern! France should be presented as a permanent Empire, even after decolonization!

But, by the way, what does "oversea" mean? Regarding the invention and evolution of the territorial principle at a time when took place in Europe the state building process, the concept is somewhat blurring. How large the gap with the continent must be for interrupting or challenging the territorial continuity principle and granting a specific identity to an island? Why do Balearics would be an overseas possession rather than Corsica for France or Wight Island for the United Kingdom? What is the right measure and criterium of foreignness or exteriority when we consider the map of Nation-states? In any way, what does "exteriority" mean in geopolitics? It gets a relevant meaning when sovereignty does not match territorial continuity. Precisely, Robert Sack pointed in his time that territory is a substantial and functional basis of the state-building process, "an instrument by which a government tries to control a population, particularly by using delimitation and borderline".[1] Then, overseas becomes a contradiction or at least an exemption, a separate and an exceptional way of achieving sovereignty, joining as such the old colonial process that emerged during antiquity, taking on the old attributes of colonial settlements…

Such a vision is currently turned down in the present French political culture. Officially, "départements d'outre-mer" and "territoires d'outre-mer" are claimed to be integral parts of a 'unique" and "indivisible" Republic. But evidence is hardly given: beyond the territorial argument just mentioned, is history the same? Even if any kind of territory has been shaped by conquest, is this colonial conquest free of any project of enslavement, exploitation, cultural domination or even destruction? How can we conceptually deal with such an ambiguity? When Mayotte island was taken from Comoros that opted for its independence, what was the real meaning of such an initiative: dashing the territorial principle? Ignoring the cultural background of a nation?

This book opens brilliantly the debate…without being able to close it up, as it is obviously complex and hard! But it has also the merit to make this French exceptionality an operational variable in politics. We are grateful to Fred Constant to pave many ways through key questions: how to conceive post-colonial practices after colonialism? How to make status which would be compatible with our post-colonial law? What does citizenship then mean: how to conceive a citizen allegiance beyond the specific culture of each individual, their own traditions, their own geographical context, and even beyond their historical memory? All these interrogations raise an important question for a new political science: how to reinvent a new meaning to political identification beyond the old nationalism?

Behind this institutional dimension, overseas politics is also a laboratory of ideas and even of political and institutional inventions: how to build on diversity a real world of equality and social development? When sovereignty barriers are de facto removed, audacious inventions and initiatives become easier. We can even go further and handle the

---

[1] Sack, Robert, (2009), *Human Territoriality: Its Theory and History*, Cambridge, Cambridge University Press.

most crucial challenges of our global world, those challenges which are related to global issues and insecurities: climate, health, food… How to achieve such a perspective without passing through the Caudine Forks of inter-sovereign and transactional negotiations.

It is obviously in the international field that the most enigmatic questions are raised by the author. How can a state play close to the area of the others while its center is located far away, as it is the case in Indo-Pacific? Magically, France is present in South-Eastern Africa (Mayotte, Réunion), in Caribbean (Antilles), in North America (St Pierre et Miquelon), in Oceania (Nouvelle Calédonie, Wallis et Futuna, Polynesia), even in Antarctic… What does it exactly mean? Is it a real projection of a real power? Of an effective law, perceived as such by the local players? A right to voice or a colonial reminiscence? A challenge to traditional geopolitics or an attempt to reactivate the old one?

In fact, more than considering material capacity, we should talk about prestige, rank, symbolic hierarchy, so many features inherited from the Westphalian tradition. As an uncertain power involved into a fluid and instable world, French government tries to implement an overachieved power by highlighting its territorial overseas possession. With a double risk: a lack of efficiency when social dynamics do not follow; a lack of credibility in a world, as Susan Strange[2] pointed out thirty years ago, overestimating the territorial relevance in a time of globalization (Strange, 1994).

The great virtue of the Fred Constant's book is to open the floor to these most relevant questions, while the topic has been marginalized by the present literature. We are grateful to him for what he preciously brings not only to the scientific community, but also to all those who are interested in the new directions of modern politics.

Bertrand Badie
Emeritus Professor
of International Relations at
Sciences Po, Paris, France

---

[2] Strange, Susan, (1994), *States and Markets*, London, Pinter.

ACKNOWLEDGEMENTS

If social sciences and my life as a political scientist have taught me anything, it is that no one can write a book alone even if writing is a very personal endeavor. Many people and institutions played a role in bringing *Overseas Territories in World Affairs* into being, and I am privileged to express my gratitude and appreciation to all of you. First and foremost, I would like to pay tribute to the work of previous scholars who strived, over decades, to make the so-called "overseas territories"[1] a worthy object of study.[2] Among these pioneers, I should mention Gordon K. Lewis (University of Puerto Rico, US), David Lowenthal (University College of London, U.K.), Harry Hoetink (University of Leiden, the Netherlands), Jean Benoist (University of Aix-Marseille, France), Robert Aldrich (University of Sydney, Australia), John Connel (University of Sydney, Australia), Rose-Mary Allen (University of Curacao, the Netherlands), Jean Crusol (University of the Antilles and Guyane, France),

---

[1] Many scholars accept the pre-notion of "overseas territory" without discussing it seriously. Instead, they take it for a granted category of governance as if it were natural. Far from being neutral, it carries in most cases a colonial imagery and still conveys imperialist overtones. In Chapter one, I challenge common uses of the term and attempt to provide a heuristic definition in line with the scientific questioning underlying this book.

[2] Even today in most countries, the overseas territories are not a regular or standard object of scientific research despite considerable progress in scholarship. To many respects, they remain outside the mainstream of international and national research programs.

Richard Price (University William & Mary, US), Alban Bensa (Ecole des Hautes Etudes en Sciences Sociales, Paris, France), David Milne (University of Prince Edward Island, Canada), Michel Giraud (CNRS, France), Aaron G. Ramos (University of Puerto Rico, US), Claude-Valentin Marie (INED, Paris, France) and Paul Sutton (London Metropolitan University, U.K.). Members of a younger but no less prolific generation include Philippe Lesseyne (French Ministry for Defense), Gert Oostindie (University of Leiden, the Netherlands), Justin Daniel (University of the Antilles, Martinique, France), Helen Hintjens (International Institute of Social Studies, The Hague, the Netherlands), Fred Réno (University of the Antilles, Guadeloupe, France), Godfrey Baldacchino (University of Prince Edward Island, Canada), Jean-Pierre Sainton (University of the Antilles, Guadeloupe, France), Jean-Christophe Gay (University of Côte d'Azur, France), Stéphanie Mulot (University of Toulouse, France), Carlyle Corbin (University College of the Cayman Islands, U.K.), Christian Lechervy (French Ministry for Foreign Affairs), Francio Guadeloupe (University of Curacao, the Netherlands), Nathalie Mrgudovic (University of Aston, U.K.), Sémir Al Wardi (University of French Polynesia, France), Jack Corbett (University of Southampton, U.K.), Audrey Célestine (University of New York, US), Wouter Veenendaal (University of Leiden, the Netherlands), Syliane Larcher (Northwestern University, US) and Cédric Audebert (CNRS, France). A special mention is due to Daniel Immerwahr (Northwestern University, US) whose *How to Hide an Empire*[3] has been a fantastic source of inspiration and emulation as I was starting my own draft. At the end of the day and retrospectively, I feel very lucky to have had the opportunity to build on their scholarship and moreover to have met some of them who became friends over time. Of course, the usual disclaimers apply: any imperfection of any kind is my sole responsibility.

In a similar vein, I was fortunate to benefit from the generosity of dozens of persons who accepted to share with me their experience of overseas politics and especially to reflect on the international dimension of these offshore territories. Among them are career diplomats, military officers, civil servants from various ministries, national and local politicians, businessmen and women, think tank and foundation members, and

---

[3] Immerwahr D. (2019) *How to Hide an Empire? A History of the Greater United States*, New York, Farrar Straus and Giroux.

most importantly, citizens at the grassroot level. Their perceptions of what 'overseas territory' means in *theory* and in *practice*, were often ambivalent or even contradictory, but they always conveyed what appeared most important to them in a given context. What struck me the most was their ability to scale up in their own ways, depending on the issues and challenges involved in our discussions. Without their inputs, the book would not have been the same. For that, I would like to thank them collectively and warmly.

My gratitude goes also to my own institution, the University of the French Antilles and the Caribbean Laboratory for Social Sciences (LC2S) in Schoelcher, Martinique. Thanks to the director of the latter, Jean-Raphaël Gros-Desormeaux, the research program this book is based on, was awarded a financial grant (BQR 2023 – AAP of Research Committee). With the support of Myriam Moïse and Jaime Aragon-Falomir, it was also funded by the European Commission under the project *Connected Worlds: The Caribbean, Origin of Modern World* (H2020-MSCA-RISE). This European subsidy was very helpful for my fieldwork but also for the translation into English of the original version published in Paris in 2023. I would like to express my appreciation to my French editor, Marie-Laurence Dubray, who has made the whole project possible. Likewise, I am indebted to Sally Stainier who worked tirelessly to translate and adapt the manuscript for English-speaking readers. Alike, I am beholden to my executive editor at Palgrave Macmillan, Dr. Anca Pusca who welcomed the book proposal and guided me throughout the editing process, as well as to Karthikeyan Kalahasthi who supervised the technical production of the book. My recognition is also directed to the two anonymous peer reviewers for their helpful comments and valuable suggestions.

Finally, as always, I want to thank my friends and family. In their own ways, they have always stimulated me. For this, I am very appreciative to Jean-Yves Lacascade, Bertrand Badie, Yves Mény, and to my graduate students at the University of the French Antilles. I have been privileged to give presentations of early versions of chapters of this volume at several institutions such as the French Parliament (Delegations of the Senate and of the National Assembly for the Overseas Territories), the French Ministry for Overseas Territories, the University of Paris-Pantheon-Assas, the University of Paris Panthéon-Sorbonne, the University of the French Antilles (Guadeloupe and Martinique), Sciences-Po Bordeaux.

Above all, I am grateful to my wife, Rita Mazzapica-Constant, and my stepson, Matthéo. Throughout the years Rita has done all she could to support my research, including accepting with humour and dedication my frequent travels for conferences and fieldwork. It has not been easy every day and I know for sure that I owe her a lot. As for Matthéo, who may wonder in silence what I spend most of my time on, I hope that this book will one day provide him with a convincing answer. Last but not least, this volume is dedicated to the populations of these so-called "overseas territories" who seldom receive the consideration they deserve from their administering powers.

Fred Constant
Fort-de-France, Paris,
Saint-Raphaël
April 2024

Map of the Overseas Territories covered

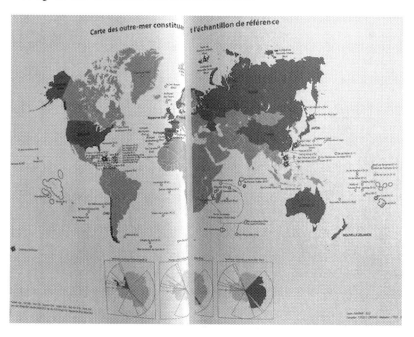

Overseas territory	Geographic location	Surface area	Population (official national sources)
Australia			
Christmas Island	Indian Ocean	52 mi2	1,843 (2021)
Cocos Islands	Indian Ocean	5.40 mi2	654 (2018)
Antarctic territory	Antarctic Ocean	2,362,874.939 mi2	No permanent population
Chile			
Isla Salas y Gómez	South Pacific	0.193 mi2	Uninhabited
Desventuradas Islands	South Pacific	1.54441 mi2	Uninhabited
Easter Island (*Rapa Nui*)	South Pacific	63.32 mi2	7,890 (2018)
People's Republic of China			
Hong Kong	China Sea	426 mi2	7,629,181 (2022)
Macau	China Sea	127 mi2	680,000 (2020)
Paracel Islands (dispute with Vietnam and Taiwan)	China Sea	130 islets adding up to 58 mi2	1,500 Chinese civilian and military personnel
Senkaku/Diaoyudao Islands (administered by Japan but claimed by the PRC)	China Sea	2.7 mi2	Uninhabited
Spratly Islands (multiple disputes)	China Sea	1.93 mi2	Uninhabited
Denmark			
Faroe Islands	North Atlantic	540 mi2	49,000 (2022)
Greenland	Arctic/Atlantic	836,330.48 mi2	57,000 (2022)
Spain			
Canary Islands	East Atlantic	2,991.13 mi2	2,153,389 (2020)
Balearic Islands	Balearic Sea	1,927.42 mi2	1,219,404 (2021)
Ceuta (claimed by Morocco)	Mediterranean coast of Northwest Africa (the Maghreb)	7.72 mi2	84,700 (2022)
Melilla (claimed by Morocco)	Mediterranean coast of Northwest Africa (the Maghreb)	4.63 mi2	86,487 (2020)
United States			
Puerto Rico	Caribbean Sea	3,515 mi2	3,252,000 (2022)
Virgin Islands	Caribbean Sea	132.8 mi2	104,425 (2022)
Hawaii	North Pacific	10,941 mi2	1,455,530 (2020)
Guam	South Pacific	212 mi2	168,800 (2021)
Samoa	South Pacific	76.8 mi2	55,000 (2017)

(continued)

(continued)

Overseas territory	Geographic location	Surface area	Population (official national sources)
Northern Mariana Islands	Philippine Sea	180.3 mi2	58,308 (2022)
Midway Atoll	North Pacific	2.39 mi2	40 (2018)
Palmyra Atoll	Central Pacific	4.63 mi2	No permanent population
Baker Island	Central Pacific	0.58 mi2	No permanent population
Howland Island	Western-Central Pacific		No permanent population
Jarvis Island	South Pacific	1.74 mi2	Uninhabited
Johnston Atoll	North Pacific	1.04 mi2	Uninhabited
Kingman Reef	Central Pacific	0.046 mi2	Uninhabited
Wake Island	Western Pacific	2.51 mi2	Uninhabited
Navassa Island (dispute with Haiti)	Caribbean Sea	1.93 mi2	Uninhabited
France			
Guadeloupe	Caribbean Sea	648.65 mi2	400,020 (2021)
French Guiana	South America	32,373 mi2	294,146 (2021)
Reunion Island	Indian Ocean	970 mi2	857,800 (2021)
Martinique	Caribbean Sea	417 mi2	354,800 (2021)
Mayotte	Mozambique Channel, Indian Ocean	144 mi2	279,507 (2021)
New Caledonia	Coral Sea, Pacific Ocean	7,164 mi2	271,407 (2019)
French Polynesia	South Pacific	1,609 mi2	275,918 (2020)
Saint Pierre and Miquelon	North Atlantic	93.43 mi2	5,794 (2020)
Saint Barthélemy	Caribbean Sea	8.11 mi2	9,877 (2021)
Saint Martin	Caribbean Sea	36.68 mi2	75,000 (2020)
French Southern and Antarctic Lands (TAAF)	Antarctic and Indian Oceans	169,758 mi2	No permanent population
Wallis and Futuna	South Pacific	54.83 mi2	11,558 (2020)
Japan			
Minamitorishima/ Marcus Island	North Pacific	0.58 mi2	Uninhabited
Kuril Islands (dispute with Russia over 4 of the northern islands)	Sea of Okhotsk	4,092.68 mi2	17,000 (2012)

(continued)

(continued)

Overseas territory	Geographic location	Surface area	Population (official national sources)
Ogasawara/Bonin Islands	Philippine Sea	38.61 mi2	Uninhabited
Ryūkyū Islands	China Sea	849.4 mi2	1,050,000 (2015)
Senkaku Islands (dispute with the PRC)	China Sea	2.7 mi2	Uninhabited
Norway			
Bouvet Island	Antarctic Plate	18.92 mi2	Uninhabited
Svalbard Archipelago	Arctic Ocean	23,561 mi2	2,504 (2022)
Jan Mayen Island	Arctic Ocean	145.56 mi2	No permanent population
New Zealand			
Cook Islands	South Pacific	93.05 mi2	17,756 (2021)
Niue	South Pacific	100 mi2	1,650 (2021)
Tokelau	South Pacific	3.86 mi2	1,373 (2021)
Netherlands			
Aruba	Caribbean Sea	69.11 mi2	107,755 (2022)
Bonaire	Caribbean Sea	113.51 mi2	21,000 (2021)
Curaçao	Caribbean Sea	171.43 mi2	158,665 (2019)
Saba	Caribbean Sea	5.02 mi2	1,915 (2019)
Sint Eustatius	Caribbean Sea	8.11 mi2	3,200 (2019)
Sint Maarten	Caribbean Sea	14.28 mi2	43,938 (2022)
Portugal			
Azores	North Atlantic	896.53 mi2	236,657 (2021)
Madeira	Central Atlantic	308.88 mi2	254,368 (2018)
United Kingdom			
Anguilla	Caribbean Sea	35.13 mi2	15,288 (2022)
Ascension Island	South Atlantic	33.98 mi2	816 (2018)
Bermuda	North Atlantic	20.46 mi2	61,777 (2022)
Cayman Islands	Caribbean Sea	101.93 mi2	68,706 (2022)
Falkland Islands	South Atlantic	4,710.44 mi2	3,700 (2022)
Gibraltar	European Continent	2.58 mi2	33,669 (2022)
Montserrat	Caribbean Sea	39.38 mi2	4,972 (2022)
Pitcairn Islands	Pacific Ocean	18.14 mi2	45 (2018)
Saint Helena Island	South Atlantic	46.72 mi2	6,116 (2022)
South Georgia and the South Sandwich Islands	South Atlantic	1,506.95 mi2	No permanent population

(continued)

(continued)

Overseas territory	Geographic location	Surface area	Population (official national sources)
Tristan da Cunha	South Atlantic	79.92 mi2	238 (2018)
British Antarctic Territory	Antarctic Ocean	660,003 mi2	No permanent population
British Indian Ocean Territory	Indian Ocean	23.16 mi2	2,500 (varies)
Turks and Caicos	Caribbean Sea	237.83 mi2	47,726 (2022)
British Virgin Islands	Caribbean Sea	59.07 mi2	31,305 (2022)
Russia			
Kuril Islands (territorial dispute with Japan)	Sea of Okhotsk, Pacific Ocean	4,093 mi2	17,000 (2012)
New Siberian Islands	Arctic Ocean, Laptev Sea, East Siberian Sea	11,544.45 mi2	No permanent population
Novaya Zemlya/Nova Zembla Islands	Barents Sea, Kara Sea, Arctic Ocean	35,000.16 mi2	2,421 (2012)
Sakhalin	Sea of Okhotsk, Sea of Japan	29,498.20 mi2	500,000 (2012)
Franz Joseph Land	Barents Sea, Arctic Ocean	6,229.37 mi2	No permanent population

Contents

1	**Introduction**	1
	Linking up Subnational, National and International Politics	7
	On Comparatism: Scope and Standpoint	9
	Case Selection and Data	11
	Structure of the Book	14

Part I Inventing the Overseas Territories

2	**Expansionist Dynamics**	19
	Introduction	20
	Wars	21
	Colonial Conquests	23
	Annexations	24
	Purchases	25
	Retrocessions	26
	Conclusion	27
3	**The Diversity of Post-colonial Statuses**	29
	Common Law Statuses	31
	Special Statuses	34
	Direct Administration Models	37
	Conclusion	40
4	**Geopolitical Assignments in the Post-war Era**	41

Advanced Security/Defence Outposts	42
Vehicles in the Fight Against Communist Ideology	45
Flagships of a Liberal and Pluralist Democratic Model	48
Conclusion	52

Part II Geopolitical Virtues in a Globalised World

5	**Levers for Maritime Power and Sovereignty**	55
	Exclusive Economic Zone Multipliers	56
	Sovereignty Conflicts and Maritime Disputes	58
	The Proliferation of Regional Affiliations	62
	Conclusion	65
6	**Security/Defence Assets**	67
	Pre-positioning and Display of Conventional Forces	68
	At the Forefront of Nuclear Deterrence	71
	Space and Cyber Defence	75
	Conclusion	77
7	**Vectors of Influence and Prestige**	79
	Significant Geo-economic Resources	80
	Exceptional Geoenvironmental Resources	85
	Remarkable Geocultural Resources	86
	Conclusion	88

Part III Local Checks on Geopolitical Assignments

8	**From Citizenship Deficits to Demands for Real Equality**	93
	Puerto Rico, Hurricane Maria and a Faint-Hearted Federal Administration	94
	Guadeloupe, French Guiana, Martinique, Reunion Island: From Popular Mobilisation Against "Pwofitasyon" to the Desire for Idiosyncratic Recognition	97
	Greenland/Kalaallit Nunaat and Faroe: Dual Power, Frustrations and Resentment	100
	Hong Kong, the Pro-democracy Movement and Resistance to China's Political Scrutiny	103

	Conclusion	106
9	**From Environmental Issues to Health Scandals**	107
	The Radioactive Liabilities of Nuclear Powers	109
	Chemical Contamination of Island Ecosystems	113
	Conclusion	117
10	**From Memory Conflicts to Reparation Claims**	119
	The War on Statues: Heroes or Executioners?	120
	From Population Displacement to Land Redistribution	122
	Territorial Identities as a Power Struggle	125
	Conclusion	129

Part IV An Ambivalent Status on the International Stage

11	**Diverse Forms of International Interaction**	133
	A Growing Presence in Regional and Multilateral Organisations	134
	Differentiated Partnerships with the European Union	139
	The Exponential Rise of Bilateral Agreements	142
	Conclusion	145
12	**Relays of Hardly Mutual Interests**	147
	Brexit: An Opportunity (for "Global Britain") or a Step Backwards (for Overseas Territories)?	148
	Transport of Nuclear Waste: Riskless Strategic Activity or Major Environmental Threat?	150
	Cooperation with China: Mutually Beneficial or Potentially Dangerous?	152
	Conclusion	157
13	**Vulnerability as a Political Resource**	159
	The Lobbying Initiatives of Europe's Outermost Regions (ORs)	160
	The Battle for Ocean Protection	163
	Is There any Political Alternative to Autonomy?	165
	Conclusion	167

Conclusion 169

Epilogue 173

Bibliography 179

Index 191

Abbreviations

ACS	Association of Caribbean States
AOSIS	Alliance of Small and Island States
BAT	British Antarctic Territory
BIOT	British Indian Ocean Territory
BOT	British Overseas Territories
BUMIDOM	*Bureau pour le développement des migrations dans les départements d'outre-mer*
BVI	British Virgin Islands
CARICOM	Caribbean Community and common Market
CARIFESTA	Caribbean festival of Arts
CEDA	Caribbean Export Development Agency
CEP	*Centre d'expérimentation du Pacifique*
CIA	Central Intelligence Agency
CIOM	Inter-Ministerial Council devoted to the Overseas Territories
COFA	Compact of Free Association
CSG	*Centre spatial guyanais*
CSNU	Conseil de sécurité des Nations unies
C24	The United Nations Special Committee on Decolonisation
EC	European Commission
ECLAC	Economic Commission for Latin America and the Caribbean
EEZ	Exclusive Economic Zone
EDF	European Development Fund
ERDF	European Regional Development Fund
EU	European Union
FESPAC	Festival of Pacific Arts & Culture
FIPIC	Forum for India-Pacific Islands Cooperation

FLNKS	*Front de Libération Nationale Kanak et Socialiste*
FSAL	French and Southern Arctic Lands
GDP	Gross Domestic Product
GNI	Gross National Income
GNP	Gross National Product
HK	Hong Kong
IOC	Indian Ocean Commission
MCES	Micronesian Chief Executives Summit (MCES)
MSG	Melanesian Spearhead Group
NA	Netherlands Antilles
NATO	North Atlantic Treaty Organization
NGO	Non-government Organisation
NSGT	Non-self-governing territory
NL	Netherlands
NZ	New Zealand
OAS	Organization of the American States
OCTA	Overseas Countries and Territories Association
OCT	Overseas Countries and Territories
OECS	Organization of Eastern Caribbean States
OFC	Offshore Finance Centre
ORs	Outermost Regions
OTs	Overseas Territories
PC	Pacific Community
PIF	Pacific Islands Forum
PLG	Polynesian Leaders Group
PNG	Papua New Guinea
POTUS	President of the United States
PRC	People's Republic of China
RFI	Radio France Internationale
ROC	Republic of China (Taiwan)
SAKIFO	Musik Festival (La Reunion Island)
SAR	Special Administrative Region (People's Republic of China)
SIDS	Small Island Developing States
SPC	The Pacific Community (officially, South Pacific Commission)
SNIJ	Subnational Island Jurisdiction
TAAF	French Southern and Antarctic Lands
TCI	Turks and Caicos
TCP	E.U. Territorial Cooperation Policy
UK	United Kingdom
UKOT	United Kingdom Overseas Territories
UNESCO	United Nations Education, Scientific and Cultural Organisation
US	United States of America
USVI	United States Virgin Islands
WHO	World Health Organization
WTO	World Trade Organization

CHAPTER 1

Introduction

Abstract The process of decolonization through formal sovereignty that marked the post-World War II period, has left out former colonies which did not opt for independence. In most cases, they became overseas territories (OTs) and are likely to stay as such in the near future since the push for independence remains weak. Accordingly, they are politically linked to a larger metropolitan power under specific, asymmetric power-sharing arrangements. Ranging from Puerto Rico to Hong Kong; from Mayotte to Faroe; from Eastern Island/Rapa Nui to Sakhalin, they include many other islands in the Atlantic, Pacific and Indian Oceans, the Caribbean, the Mediterranean and the South China Sea. These "out-of-sight and out-of-mind" jurisdictions deserve much more academic, high-level political, diplomatic, and media attention because they are magnifying mirrors of issues linking up subnational, national and international politics. Some are occasional flashpoints of international crises (for instance, over Senkaku/Diaoyu, the Kuril Islands or the Chagos archipelago), of island/mainland's political and cultural conflicts (for example, Greenland, Curacao or Martinique), of outbreaks of violence related to the quest for independence (New Caledonia). Others are at the forefront of illegal migration (for example, Mayotte) or climate change (for instance, French Polynesia). In their own ways, OTs provide an original angle to address strategic issues of the twenty-first century.

© The Author(s), under exclusive license to Springer Nature
Switzerland AG 2024
F. Constant, *Overseas Territories in World Affairs*,
https://doi.org/10.1007/978-3-031-64233-3_1

Keywords Overseas territories · Decolonisation · Subnational Island jurisdictions · Linkage politics · Geopolitics · Postcolonial politics · Cultural identities · International territorial disputes · The power of the powerless

> *The challenge at hand is to place small jurisdictions at the centre of research and critical inquiry. With so many small states in the world today, and many more small subnational jurisdictions developing their own international presence and paradiplomatic practices, the absence of a sustained interest in their behaviour, in their social, economic and political character, in their development trajectories, in their relations with other powers and amongst themselves, is palpable.*
> Godfrey Baldacchino (2018: 4).

The process of decolonization through formal sovereignty that marked the post-World War II period was a major geopolitical rupture (Fabry 2010: 147–179). The proliferation of nation-states that followed, however, left out some former colonial territories which did not opt for independence (Connell Aldrich 1998: 2–9). In the vast majority of cases, they became overseas territories (OTs) and are likely to stay as such in the near future since the push for independence remains weak[1] (Oostindie *alii*. 2020: 44–45). Accordingly, they are politically linked to a larger metropolitan power under specific, asymmetric power-sharing arrangements. These alternative forms of decolonisation through secession are very often based on a continuum of "shared rule versus self-rule" that is at the centre of "mainland-island" power relations (Baldacchino 2010: 23). In the scientific literature, these non-self-governing political units are referred to as non-sovereign jurisdictions (Fabry 2000), subnational governments (Kaizer 2002) or sub-national island jurisdictions (Baldacchino 2010).[2] They are commonly defined as "*(..) bilateral*

---

[1] With a couple of exceptions such as New Caledonia/Kanaky, Greenland/Kalaallit Nunaat, French Polynesia, the Faroe Islands.

[2] I use these terms interchangeably as well as offshore territories. Yet, it should be noted that in France, the designation of OT is periodically debated because of its alleged

systems of self- and shared-rule (..) with a much larger state. (..) Their jurisdictional powers are principally a result of bilateral negotiations between island political elites and a (..) metropole. This bargain is struck against the backdrop of a particular colonial inheritance, a local 'sub-nationalist' culture, and the varying ambitions of local elites to win jurisdictional powers to advance 'sub-national' territorial interests" (Baldacchino, Milne 2006: 487). As such, they display an evolving array of jurisdictional capacities, from the most restricted to full but unofficial sovereignty in multiple sectors.

Depending on the sources[3] and criteria used, their numbers vary from 119 (Stuart 2008: 176) to 66 (Rezvani 2014: 12), 55 (Oostindie and *alii*. 2019: 4–5) to 58 (the CIA World Factbook 2024 online). Ranging from Puerto Rico to Hong Kong; from Mayotte to Faroe—including islands in the Atlantic, Pacific and Indian Oceans, the Caribbean, the Mediterranean and the South China Sea—these Sub-National Island Jurisdictions (SNIJs) deserve much more academic (and political) attention not only to get a better understanding of what their people stand and struggle for, but also and above all to clarify how they cope with an increasingly complex and uncertain world.

These extracontinental territories that have flanked the world since the modern era, considerably broaden the geographical base and international scope of their administering countries. Far from being confined to a mainland, they benefit from these assets under different statuses and to varying extents around the globe. This state of affairs applies to the two main world powers—the United States and the People's Republic of China (PRC)—the other permanent members of the United Nations

---

colonial overtones. According to Patrick Chamoiseau, laureate of the Goncourt Prize, *"To use the terms "overseas", "metropolis" and "ultra-peripherals" without caution is to keep a colonial paradigm active"* (2022). For linguist Corinne Mencé-Caster, *"The colonial order is somehow extended into a form of neo-colonization when we use metropolis. It's never by chance that you keep a word. It always says something about an order that has not been totally abolished"* (2023). In May 23rd 2023, an amendment was voted by the French national Assembly to banish the word "metropole" in official documents and to replace it by Hexagone.

[3] The Sub-National Island Jurisdiction Database merits to be singled out. Conceived by Godfrey Baldacchino at the University of Prince Edward Island (Canada) in 2007, it is a valuable scientific outcome of a research program of an unprecedented international scope. For more on the "Jurisdiction Project", refer to Baldacchino (2008: 21–31).

Security Council (UNSC)—Russia, France and the United Kingdom—and other member states of the European Union (EU)—including Spain, the Netherlands, Denmark, Portugal, Finland or third countries like Norway. Such is also the case of nations in other continents: Africa, with South Africa or Tanzania; South America, with Argentina and Chile; and Oceania, with Australia and New Zealand. Vast or small, populated or uninhabited, managed by local councils or a central government; these offshore territories are often construed as oddities that elude conventional framings due to seemingly intractable specificities. Regardless of whether they are—or not—a colonial legacy, economically autonomous or dependent, a geostrategic asset (as part of a global military scheme) or a geoeconomic destination (as in, an exclusive economic zone) crystallising domestic policy issues or international disputes (especially geostrategic ones); they play a full part in the power strategies of the nations that have sovereignty over them. Who could deny the pivotal role played by Guam, despite being twice smaller than Martinique, in the United States' military presence in the Pacific Ocean? Or that of the Paracel islands for the PRC, which turned the South China Sea into a matter of national concern? Not to mention French Guiana's part in the strategic autonomy of both France and the EU in the space industry?

Thanks to these footholds, the administering powers enjoy extensive access to the world's seas and oceans. They cover the Atlantic, Indian and Pacific oceans. Some are also present in the Arctic and Antarctica. Others are present in the Mediterranean Sea, the East China Sea, the Caribbean Sea, the Greenland Sea and the Mozambique Channel. These sometimes-long-established outposts are invaluable assets when it comes to controlling trade routes and the ensuing power struggles. Scattered across the Earth, they add a global flavour to the nations they are attached to, providing them with outer borders in several parts of the planet. France's largest land border lies not in Europe, but in South America, where it runs 453 miles along French Guiana's frontier with Brazil. Similarly, its smallest border is not located on the mainland but on the island of Saint-Martin, where it shares sovereignty with the Netherlands under the Treaty of Concordia (1648). Ignored or all too rarely highlighted, these relics of colonial history continue to offer windows of opportunities to their respective administering countries, which do not always acknowledge this fact. Yet the same countries readily deploy heavy diplomatic and military resources to defend their sovereignty over those offshore assets, when challenged by their peers—as in the Anglo-Argentine war over the Falklands.

Paradoxically, they get little attention in the field of geopolitics as in any subfield of mainstream political science. Overseas territories appear as a blind spot or only in passing. Beyond scientific constructs, this situation mirrors the ambivalent perception of overseas territories in mainland societies, where they fail to make an impression on the mental maps of the elites and the general population alike. How many US citizens are actually capable of listing their overseas territories? How many of their French or British, Spanish or Portuguese counterparts? The full history of these OTs is scarcely taught in most mainland countries including the US, the UK and France, and so it is not surprising that few people in either country know much about these more or less "remote" territories. Until recently, however, the populations of many of these offshore island jurisdictions were no more cognizant of this history. Take the example of Martinique, homeland of the twentieth century's most lucid theorists of anti-colonialism (Aimé Césaire, Frantz Fanon, Edouard Glissant), where one would expect basic education to provide much better knowledge about at least France's overseas constituencies than the (very poor) one given to me in mainland France. In that sense precisely, the story of the OTs remains *untold* and therefore, mostly ignored from the general public. Knowledge regimes say a lot about regimes of power[4] (Foucault 1969). How could the OTs be regularly and indiscriminately included in mainstream educational programs when they have been kept out of the logo map of the country to which they officially belong, sometimes for several centuries? As Daniel Immerwahr put it: "*(..) The logo map carries a cost for mainlanders too. It gives them a truncated view of their own history, one that excludes part of their country. It is an important part. (..) a lot has happened in the overseas territories, occurrences highly relevant to mainlanders. (..) Only by including them in the picture do we see a full portrait of the country – not as it appears in its fantasies, but as it actually is*" (2019: 19).[5]

Along with others scholars, I have been struggling to get them taken seriously scientifically i.e. politically. In France, my native country, the

---

[4] By considering what he called the "legal-political matrices", Michel Foucault demonstrated not only that knowledge depends on these "legal-political matrices" but also that it contributes to their constitution.

[5] My emphasis.

national elite finds it so difficult to face up to the country's colonial history and to consider these postcolonial territories as a part of *true France*, and their residents as full citizens (Pattieu, Sibeud, Stovall 2022, Keaton 2023). As a result, claims from overseas populations are often viewed with a mixture of misunderstanding and indifference by mainland political authorities who try to force upon them—openly or by the back door—decisions that do not match their expectations. In such a political context where double-standard policy tends to prevail, OTs cannot be fully integrated in mainstream, national scientific research programs.[6] Which is a pity. I strongly believe that studying them is very stimulating for social scientists because they lie at the intersection of many evolving issues—especially decolonization, self-determination, post-colonialism, globalisation, climate change, ecological and energy transition, patterns of innovative governance. Moreover, they offer occasional "hotspots" for analysing international rivalries, conflicts related to illegal migration and disputes pertaining to the delimitation of exclusive economic zones (EEZ). In addition, they also provide fascinating case-studies to grasp the interplay of international factors in sub-national domestic politics and the feedback of the latter in the national—if not international—politics of the administering powers. Indeed, some OTs are fully involved in world affairs even if they continue to be perceived as pawns on the international chessboard opposing the Great Powers. Common views on nations and their global standings usually overlook them. The comparative advantages countries reap from them in asserting their politics of power and influence, are still poorly known and hardly acknowledged. Building on the existing scholarship and my own previously published work, this book that I started writing at the beginning of the Covid-19 pandemic, is a global comparative analysis of non-sovereign territories, some of which are not included in similar endeavours. It

---

[6] In some countries, the lines are moving in a positive direction. In 2003, a Canada Research Chair in Island Studies was created at the University of Prince Edward Island. A research program "Patterns of Sub-National Autonomy amongst the World's Islands" was completed under the supervision of Dr. Godfrey Baldacchino who was awarded the Research Chair. An *Island Studies Journal* was then created with an interdisciplinary approach to islands, archipelagos, and the water that surround and connect them. In 2018, he initiated an Islands & Small States Institute at the University of Malta where he founded an online *Small States and Territories Journal*. In France, a Chair in (French) Overseas Studies was created at Sciences Po Paris in 2019 but has not yet changed the fate of the OTs in the national research landscape.

unfolds from a twofold perspective: the standpoint of national authorities in the "mainland" and the point of view of local authorities in the "islands". More to the point, it aims at combining both optics to examine common issues while accounting for the power games that are their corollaries.

Linking up Subnational, National and International Politics

My argument is threefold: (*i*) the relations between the administering powers and the OTs are characterised by cooperation, conflict and competition; (*ii*) these "mainland/island" relations are shaped by a set of Subnational-National–International linkages; (*iii*) the politics of the administering powers toward their OTs are related to domestic and international factors while the politics of the latter toward the former depend on the extent to which they are *perceived* as mutually beneficial.[7] From this argument stems a set of three propositions: (*i*) whenever the interests of an administering power converge with those of a subnational island jurisdiction according to their respective perceptions, relations of cooperation prevail over relations of conflict or competition; (*ii*) whenever the interests of an administering power diverge from those of a subnational island jurisdiction, relations of competition, mistrust or conflict prevail over relations of cooperation; (*iii*) However, the power play is somehow complicated when SNIJs belonging to the same national political entity have opposing views on a national policy applied to them. In any case, the local perception of a national policy is highly contingent and varies in time and space according to evaluation criteria specific to each level of governance, and often depends on the relations between majority and opposition parties, locally and nationally.

Stated differently, the need to take into full account *linkage politics*, refers here to the dramatic changes experienced by most OTs which, under the combined action of globalisation, the emergence of a less predictable international arena as well as internal reforms implemented by the administering countries, are much more involved in international

---

[7] Of course, an administering power can impose its views upon a subnational jurisdiction but it usually comes with a political cost such as international disapproval campaigns and huge local protests such as those sparked by nuclear testing in French Polynesia in the 1990s (Fisher 2013).

matters than over the last century. Many of them became associate or full members of regional and international organisations, and have over time acquired a level of expertise that has enabled them to expand their portfolio of external relations with sovereign countries in their regional or even in some cases, extra-regional environments. Most of these subnational jurisdictions enjoy a relatively high level of internal autonomy that allows them to make decisions for themselves in some areas. As a result, they happen to oppose more frequently their respective central authorities, turning their vulnerability into a political resource. Hence, it does not seem possible to fully comprehend the political rationales at work in subnational jurisdictions without using the right prism; namely a multi-level system of governance. Similarly, understanding the political logics of their administering powers means taking into account subnational, national and international determinants. In making this claim, I draw from scholarship on *linkage theory* and from a recent surge of literature on small states and subnational island jurisdictions. On linkage theory, I build on and extend James Rosenau's pioneer work. In his essay "Toward the Study of National–International Linkages" (1969: 44–63), he examines the interplay between domestic and global dynamics, focusing on how these two systems intersect and influence each other. To describe and account for this phenomenon, he proposes the concept of linkage *"as a basic unit of analysis, defining it as any recurrent sequence of behaviour that originates in one system and is reacted to in another"* (1969: 45). According to him, *"Polities are increasingly dependent on their environment and interdependent with each other in the sense that, increasingly, what transpires at home would unfold differently if trends abroad were different"* (1969: 47). For my analysis of the relationship between cooperation, conflict and competition between OTs and their sometimes faraway metropolitan powers, I take up this analytical framework but complement it at the subnational level. As noted above, one can hardly grasp the feedback loops of the relationship between OTs and their administering power without highlighting how a macro-level change can impact micro-level dynamics (and vice-versa). These *linkage politics* may sound easy to formulate but they are not easy to research. Here, I turn again to James Rosenau who warned us about this challenge at the time: *"(..) by definition linkage politics involve subtle processes of influence that can be extremely difficult to trace and measure."* (1969: 14).

Yet, the scholarship researching small states and non-sovereign territories is quite resourceful. Over the past twenty years, it has expanded tremendously. I engaged with it in two ways: by drawing on the literature related to the geopolitics of the OTs and by taking a stand in the debate over the costs/benefits of being a non-sovereign territory in the international arena. On the first point, I approach the issue from the perspective of the strategic shift of the US and its allies towards the Indo-Pacific zone. Here, I attempt to assess its consequences for the OTs: does it trigger a process of "downgrading" those located in the Atlantic and in the Caribbean? Or does it, on the contrary, generate a process of revaluation for those situated in the Indo-Pacific area? On the second point, I hold a balanced stance between those who support the thesis of "power of the powerlessness" (Rezvani 2014, Prinsen 2017) and those who promote the thesis of the vulnerability of the subnational jurisdictions (Connell Aldrich 2020). The former argue that a non-sovereign or partially independent status is the political arrangement which best serves their interest in the international arena. The latter argue, on the contrary, that it does not provide any shelter to escape the consequences of international decisions beyond their control. I am neither overly optimistic nor pessimistic about the ability of the OTs to exploit their vulnerabilities in a variety of ways in order to achieve their goals. The book's empirical core shows that it is all about contingency in the sense that it depends on the conjunction of several parameters, chief among them being coincidence or conflict of interests between the "mainland" and the "island». Therefore, my argument is that when a strategic issue is at stake, the administering power will impose its views upon its subnational jurisdiction no matter what the political cost might be. When it is not, there may be room for the latter to manoeuver.

On Comparatism: Scope and Standpoint

Unsurprisingly, I take inspiration in the aforementioned James Rosenau's volume, and in the more recent works of scholars studying small states and territories. In their essay edited by the former, Robert Holt and John Turner rightly identified the limitations of their attempt to try out the linkage politics matrix on insular polities: "*In exploring the question of whether the fact of insularity has any effect on the characteristics of the interface between the domestic polity and the international system, we must concentrate upon the characteristics of that intersection that are shared by the insular polities we are examining. (..) But once we have discovered some common characteristics, we have only reached a halfway mark. As a next* step we need to compare the insular politics to the "noninsular" polities., because some characteristics that these two sets have in common could not be related to the factor of insularity. Unfortunately, this second – and most crucial – step in the comparative analysis lies beyond the scope of this discussion" (1969: 203–204). Obviously, our comparative study is no exception. It could hardly engage in an explicit comparison with subnational "non-insular" jurisdictions.[8] Rather, it focuses on a limited set of issues located at the intersection of the international system, the nation-states, and the subnational insular jurisdictions. It is aimed at elucidating the interactions at the heart of this postcolonial multi-level system of governance which at the same time harbours and nurtures an evolving debate over decolonisation, sovereignty, autonomy and self-determination.

Here I am indebted to the scholarship of many but specifically to Godfrey Baldacchino (2010), John Connell et Robert Aldrich (2020) and James Corbett (2023). The former is certainly the most talented advocate of the heuristic virtues of small state and territory studies. Not only did his work confirm my early intuition that the OTs are magnifying mirrors of international relations but his empirical comparative method paved the way for my initiative. He proved that comparing many SNIJs had limitations, called for scientific precautions, but was not impossible. In the same vein, the latter have remarkably documented the variety of ways by which non-sovereign insular jurisdictions are caught up in global changes far beyond their shores and the extent to which they are able or not, to take some advantages from them for themselves and/or for their administering power. Again, their empirical approach to comparative research has proven to be effective for the study of OTs geopolitics, connecting international challenges to local issues. From them, I borrow the idea that it is more fruitful to conduct a comparison based on a case study that best illustrates the subject matter rather than doing so from a complex matrix that could not account for each and every case. With Jack Corbett, I share the interpretivist standpoint according to which "*(..) the state is never complete or finished. It is a story that actors tell. The task of political science is to uncover theses narratives to explain actions*" (2023: 6). Likewise, I approach the ongoing debate over "political emancipation" in the same way, as its content is highly contingent and varies across space and times. This conceptualisation echoes anthropologist Clifford Geertz's

---

[8] Claudia N. Allevaneda and Ricardo Bello-Gomez have edited a nice collection of essays on "continental" subnational jurisdictions in 2024.

argument to put "local knowledge" first in our understanding of societies, which invites us to decrypt the meaning that actors give to their actions and understand the way in which they interpret their environment and its changes. From this viewpoint, my comparative research deals with conflicting narratives at the international, national and subnational levels over issues located at their intersection. For instance, the PRC's continental and oceanic Road and Belt policy is construed very differently in the "mainlands" as opposed to the "islands". Inevitably, this leads to conflicts that alter their relationship, with the former trying to impose its views upon the latter.

Case Selection and Data

In *Statehood à la carte in the Caribbean and the Pacific*, Jack Corbett's case selection was aimed at "*considering enough variation in experience to shed new and penetrating light on the research puzzle*" (2023: 19). In this volume, my objective is also to favour diversity in order to showcase the variety of the geopolitical uses of OTs by their administering countries as well as the range of their responses to them. As far as possible, I place the cursor of the analysis at the meeting point between the former's views and the latter's perspectives, holding both ends of the explanatory chain.

Yet for practical reasons, I have distinguished two categories of empirical references: on the one hand, those more numerous that I merely mention to illustrate my point without further extensive analysis and on the other hand, the fewer ones which are subject to a more in-depth analysis. Around fifty territories fall in the first category, including inhabited jurisdictions and others without any colonial history. These OTs are scattered around the world, in the Arctic Ocean (3), the Atlantic Ocean (6) and the Caribbean (15), the Indian Ocean (6) and the Pacific (18) but also in the South China Sea (2), the Mediterranean (2) and the Antarctic Ocean (1). They are politically related to a total of 13 metropolitan powers: Australia (3), Chile (2), Denmark (2), France (9), Japan (2), Netherlands (4), New-Zealand (1), Norway (3), PRC (2), Russia (2), Spain (2), United Kingdom (10), United States (10). Of these fifty territories, thirty fall in the second category, including the largest and the smallest ones, some of which are the subject of international territorial disputes pending before the International Court of Justice. They are distributed all over the world, in the Pacific Ocean (8), the Caribbean Sea (6), the Atlantic Ocean (5), the South China Sea (5), the Indian Ocean

(1) but also in the Okhotsk Sea (3), the Balearic Sea (1) and the Barents Sea (1). They are politically related to 12 metropolitan powers: Chile (1), Denmark (1), France (5), Japan (2), Netherlands (2), New-Zealand (2), PRC (2), Russia (2), Spain (2), United Kingdom (5), United States (3), disputed territories (5).

These thirty jurisdictions form the empirical core of the book. They appear to be the most relevant examples for the purpose of probing and discussion. They are listed below in no particular order or hierarchy: Easter Island/Rapa Nui (Chile), Greenland/Kalaallit Nunat (Denmark), Guadeloupe, French Guiana, Martinique, Reunion Island, New Caledonia, Polynesia (France), Hong Kong, Macau (PRC), Canary Islands, Balearic Islands (Spain), Puerto Rico, Guam, Hawaii (US), Ryūkyū (Japan), Cook Islands, Niue (New Zealand), Curacao, Sint Maarten (the Netherlands), Azores, Madeira (Portugal), Bermuda, Falkland, BIOT, Cayman Islands, Turks and Caicos (United Kingdom), Novaya Zemlya/Nova Zembla, Sakhalin, (Russia), disputed territories (Paracel Islands, Diaoyu/Senkaku, Kuril Islands).

Despite their extraordinary diversity, my belief is that these SNIJs deserve the collective examination allowed by their commonalities. Firstly, they are all offshore territories, more or less distant geographically but above all culturally and even psychologically, from their metropolis. For instance, Hong Kong is geographically close to continental China but is not so much in political or ideological terms. Secondly, they are all subordinate political units—without any formal sovereignty—although some are more subordinate than others. For example, the Cook Islands enjoy an impressive devolution of power including in international matters while Wallis and Futuna is mostly administered by a local representative of the French central government. Thirdly, most of the cases selected are not economically self-reliant with only a few exceptions. For instance, Macao does not rely on the financial benevolence of the PRC whereas Greenland still does depend on Denmark's despite its outstanding resources. Fourthly, all are extremely vulnerable to natural hazards and to the backlash of climate change. Seven years later, Puerto Rico has yet to fully recover from Hurricane Maria and Saint-Martin is still under reconstruction after Hurricane Irma. Finally, and fifthly, most of them harbour cultural and memory conflicts over the legacy of slavery and the colonial past.

Processing so many subnational jurisdictions within a relatively short volume comes with a cost, and may be found somehow unsatisfying.

Of course, the broader the coverage, the less depth the case studies can provide. What you gain on one side, you may lose on the other. Some may expect further development, others may ask for less empirical references. In any case, my approach is linked to one of the book's foremost objectives, that is giving evidence of the "universal" character of non-sovereign jurisdictions across the world. They are much more widespread than it is usually stated, and merit to be considered as valuable research topics like any other.

In terms of data, I have drawn information from the following sources: secondary literature, public sources, and interviews. Despite an uneven bibliography, it includes quality academic work that provides substantial food for thought, overall. If most researchers on small states and territories have worked on domestic politics, they have obviously paved the way for international comparison. This is especially true of France (Connel Aldrich 1992, Doumenge 2000; Gay 2021), the US (Roberts, Stephens 2017; Immerwahr 2019), the U.K. (Cawley 2015, Clegg 2018)) and the Netherlands (Oostindie 2006, Veenendaal Oostindie 2018). But this is less true for Russia, PRC, Japan or Chile where it remains difficult to get reliable information and inquiries. I compensated as much as possible with press articles and some archival documents but I acknowledge, however, that I have not been able to obtain the same level of information as for other OTs. Within these limitations, I have presented a brief updated state of the art, on every major topic treated in the book. I neither reviewed nor discussed that literature in systematic fashion but only when it happened to be necessary. Regarding public sources, abundance coexists with scarcity, depending on the overseas territory. Obviously, it is easier to find any kind of report on Puerto Rico, Curaçao, Reunion Island or even Greenland than to get access to the same documentation for the Kuril Islands, Pitcairn, Tokelau or the Nova Zembla archipelago. Additionally, the quality of the data varies tremendously across space and time. As far as possible, I conducted interviews[9] with resource-persons (political leaders, business persons, diplomats, senior civil servants or journalists) to collect first-hand accounts on specific events or circumstances. Unfortunately, I was not able to go everywhere and especially in the Russian overseas territories or in the South China Sea where atolls and sand blocks are subject

---

[9] Over a period of 5 years, I conducted fifty-five interviews of resource-persons, including former colleagues of the diplomatic corps. I am very grateful to all of them.

to territorial disputes. Yet, I could visit almost two thirds of them, some on several occasions.

Structure of the Book

The book is divided into four parts. Each part is composed by three chapters. Every chapter comes with a conclusion. *Part One* comprises Chapters 2, 3, and 4. It focuses on the historical invention of the overseas territories, the diversity of their postcolonial statuses and their geopolitical assignments during the Cold War. *Chapter 2* looks back at the imperial and colonial rationales that presided over the "conquest" of these offshore outposts which were in some cases literally created by Western Powers. Emphasis is placed on the fact that they were set up to satisfy the needs and fantasies of the latter. This congenital extroversion will never stop weighing on their distinct fates. *Chapter 3* focuses on the reasons that led local and national leaders to reject decolonisation through secession in favour of postcolonial (non-sovereign) arrangements proving more or less "decentralised". Of course, it echoes and reflects on the frustrations generated by the ambiguities of a situation where the former colonial State is sometimes also the postcolonial State. *Chapter 4* reviews the geopolitical assignments of the OTs in the aftermath of World War II and the various ways they were managed to best serve the strategic interests of their "motherland" in the context of a bipolarised world.

Part Two comprises Chapters 5, 6 and 7. It deals with the geopolitical virtues attributed to OTs in the era of globalisation and examines how the "Asian pivot" has been impacting their previous assignments. *Chapter 5* focuses on how these outposts are used by their administering countries as levers for maritime power and sovereignty around the globe, regardless of the practical consequences for their inhabitants. *Chapter 6* highlights the extent to which most of these offshore SNIJs were integrated into security and defence schemes, according to the interests of their national political authorities. *Chapter 7* addresses how the "Asian pivot" has been diversifying the geopolitical vocations of OTs, especially those located in the Atlantic Ocean and in the Caribbean.

Part Three comprises Chapters 8, 9 and 10. It looks at the "resourcefulness of jurisdiction" (Baldacchino, Milne 2000) as it is managed by the local elites to secure the "protection and benevolence of the mainland" or on the contrary, oppose its adverse decisions. *Chapter 8* sets the scan cursor on the politics of *equaliberty* (Yvon van der Pijl and Francio

Guadeloupe 2022: 4–5) and for *true equality* (Gert Oostindie and *alii*. 2020: 45). *Chapter 9* takes up the same analysis in the field of ecology and public health where many OTs are suffering from large scale chemical pollution and the related medical consequences. *Chapter 10* focuses on memory conflicts related to the colonial past and on the reparation claims addressed to postcolonial States.

Part Four comprises Chapters 11, 12 and 13. It brings the discussion back to the international arena. *Chapter 11* evaluates how the OTs are diversifying their international interactions in order to raise additional resources sometimes for their own purpose. *Chapter 12* focuses on situations where the local interests of OTs clash with those of their administering country. *Chapter 13* revisits the debate over "decolonisation", "sovereignty", "self-government" and "national identity". It argues that their meaning varies according to the geopolitical context, the political issues at stake, and the level of frustration of the insular population.

The *Conclusion* provides a brief synthesis of the main findings and of the overall discussion. It outlines some of the main challenges and dilemmas that the SNIJs' elites have been handling so far and their attempts at redefining their "autonomy" in theory and in practice. However small these insular jurisdictions might be, they harbor—just as in larger political units—debates over how best their territories could be managed to satisfy their populations' expectations. It is the reason why their study is so fascinating and engaging, as it cuts across subnational, national and international politics.

PART I

Inventing the Overseas Territories

> « *Empire might be hard to make out from the mainland, but from the sites of colonial rule themselves, it is impossible to miss (..) These tiny specks – Howland Island and the like – are the foundations of the U.S. world power. They serve as staging grounds, launchpads, storage sites, beacons, and laboratories. They make up what I call a pointillist empire (..) Today, that empire extends all over the planet.* »
> Daniel Immerwahr (2020: 15–18)

For want of a *universal* definition of the overseas territories to reflect their astonishing diversity, this section will briefly outline their historical genealogy, showing the different ways in which they became parts of larger political entities. Western expansionism will be emphasised, with its imperial and colonial rationales and the wars ignited in pursuit of its goals. Next, we will look at the consequences of decolonisation, by shedding light on the geopolitical calculations that nailed down the status of present-day overseas territories. Finally, we will show how this new spatial organisation of global powerhouses gave offshore territories new scores on the stock exchange of strategic assets. Yet they still lie on the fringes of the nations to which they are politically attached. *Mental* maps fail to match the official maps of the nations involved: *mainland* parts constantly overshadow their offshore counterparts. These skewed self-perceptions, which continue to prevail in many cases, have far-reaching impacts on collective views. Overseas territories are still regarded as peripheral oddities, more or less remote and exotic, to be looked upon with wonder and curiosity but not as integral components of the national entities they are legally a part of. And yet their fates have been intertwined with the latter's throughout a shared history and according to political guidelines induced by events outside of their borders. Colonialism's enormous impact on the trajectories of most OTs is now common knowledge but what we do not know—or wish to recognise—is just how much these former colonies have been contributing to the making of their former colonial and—in most cases—postcolonial State. Here, we draw inspiration from the scholarship of Frederick Cooper and Ann Laura Stoler. They were among the first social scientists to call on the necessity of rethinking colonialism. In a book they coedited (1997: 1-56), they rightly urged us to approach colonial history as a dialectic process bringing together the Colonizers and the Colonized; Metropolis and Colonies. Here is a brief overview of that Mainland/Island general history, that is usually unknown beyond the narrow circle of academics and experts.

CHAPTER 2

Expansionist Dynamics

Abstract Today's overseas territories are *by*-products of the expansionism that led rival nations to spread their borders beyond oceans and seas. This movement, which dates back to the seventeenth century, was driven by an eagerness to serve their own economic interests and to promote their political and religious beliefs. The seas have embodied that power struggle from the beginning. Controlling the seas was essential to wielding lasting influence across the globe. Logistical support points and power hubs were absolutely crucial. The British, Spanish, Portuguese, French and Dutch competed, colluded and battled to establish their territorial strength. Some lands were conquered by force (for instance, Gibraltar, the Balearic Islands or the British Virgin Islands). Others were voluntarily retroceded (for example, Macao, Hong Kong). Some were sold and experienced a change in sovereignty (for instance, US Virgin Islands, Saint Barthelemy or Senkaku Islands). Others were even annexed (among others, the Faroe Islands, French Polynesia or Novaya Zemlya). From the very beginning, these offshore territories were set up to satisfy the needs and fantasies of their colonial power. This colonial legacy is becoming common knowledge but the OT's huge contribution to the making of their former colonial and postcolonial State, remains to be properly acknowledged.

Keywords Expansionism · Imperialism · Colonialism · Slave trade and slavery · Geopolitical rivalries · Colonial conquest · Annexation · Retrocession · Colonial legacy

Introduction

Today's overseas territories are *by*-products of the expansionism that led rival nations to spread their borders beyond oceans and seas. This movement, which dates back to the seventeenth century, was driven by an eagerness to serve their own economic interests and to promote their political and religious beliefs. The seas have embodied that power struggle from the beginning. Controlling the seas was essential to wielding lasting influence across the globe. Logistical support points and power hubs were absolutely crucial. The British, Spanish, Portuguese, French and Dutch competed, colluded and battled to establish their territorial strength. Some lands were conquered by force. Others were voluntarily traded. Some were sold and experienced a change in sovereignty. Others were even annexed. Trading companies flourished, such as the British East India Company, the French West India Company or the Dutch West India Company. In the background, the slave trade, colonialism and imperialism merged their ruthless philosophies. Just as human right declarations seemed to triumph across Europe, a pernicious ideology rationalised the merciless marginalisation of enslaved populations to the fringes of humanity. The slave trade came along with racial prejudice, dehumanisation, anti-Blackness (Kiple 2012: 293–311; Lockley 2012: 336–356). Colonialism led to the large-scale exploitation of people forcibly reduced to the state of free manpower. Imperialism resulted in the takeover of huge territories and their inhabitants in order to quench a few dominant nations' thirst for power (Singaravélou 2023: 7–17). In his last book,[1] Tyler Stovall remarkably documented the interwoven histories of racism and freedom in France and the United States. In these pioneering nations, freedom as an ideology was defined in racial terms and liberty was conceived as a characteristic and privilege of Whiteness. Moral qualms and political values yielded to the feverish pursuit of highly profitable expeditions to faraway lands. European nations competed in a race to grab land and resources all over the world—regardless of the grandiose ideals that flourished in their capital cities. In Britain, several influential leaders such as William Pitt, Robert Clive or Warren Hastings contributed to the establishment, expansion and administration of the British Empire. According

---

[1] Tyler Stovall (2021) *White Freedom. The Racial History of an Idea*, Princeton, Princeton University Press.

to Lawrence James, "(..) the possession of an empire profoundly influenced the ways in which the British thought of themselves and the rest of the world. British character was changed by the empire (..) It encouraged a sense of superiority (..) that frequently bordered on downright xenophobia. It also fostered racial arrogance. And yet at the same time, deeply-rooted liberal and evangelical ideals produced a powerful sense of duty and mission. The empire existed to civilize and uplift its subjects, or so its champions claimed." (1997: xiv). In France, among other political leaders, Jules Ferry, member of the French Parliament, justified these ventures unreservedly before the National Assembly: "*(...) What our large-scale industry lacks is outlets. Competition, supply and demand, free trade, the influence of speculation, all these things spread out in a circle that stretches to the ends of the earth. Now this agenda is linked to colonial policy (...) A navy like ours cannot do without solid shelters, defences and supply facilities across the seas (...) There is another point I must address (...) Superior races (...) have a duty to civilise inferior races*" (Speech of 25 July 1885). The lust for overseas lands was thus driven by the call of the sea. The methods used to secure them were closely intertwined: wars, colonial conquests, annexations, purchases and handovers.

Wars

Armed conflicts are the basic framework for land grabbing. Whether overt or covert, they have set the pace for the conquest, trade, annexation and handover of colonial territories. Among other countries, Spain, England and the United States have played major roles in this troubled history.

The Spanish empire was for the most part acquired by force (Maltby 2008: 52–73) as illustrated by its current overseas territories, remnants of the Spanish crown's "grandeur." The Balearic and Canary Islands as well as the two North African enclaves of Ceuta and Melilla were won in a long-ranging military venture. In mediaeval times, these territories were under Muslim rule and Christian monarchs decided to reconquer them. They thus launched the *Reconquista* to free the Iberian Peninsula from the grip of the Umayyad Caliphate of Damascus. Military campaigns started in 722 and continued until the conquest of Granada in 1492. The Balearic archipelago was reclaimed in two separate stages (Majorca in 1229–1231; Minorca in 1287) before its annexation by the Crown of Aragon in 1349. In 1479, it was the Canary Islands' turn; the archipelago became a regular battleground between the Spanish and the Portuguese due to its strategic location on the sea routes to Africa, America and Asia. The Treaty of Alcáçovas granted Castile sovereignty over the Canary Islands, while Portugal gained Guinea, Madeira, the Azores and Cape Verde. After the fall of Granada in 1492, the Catholic kings of Spain attempted to set up military posts along the North African coast to prevent attacks from Barbarian pirates. As a result, Melilla fell under Spanish sovereignty in 1497, and Ceuta in 1580. These two tiny enclaves are flanked by a handful of rocks (*los peñones*): Alhucemas, Vélez de la Gomera and the Chafarinas islands near the Algerian border. Most of the visitors crowding the beaches of these offshore Spanish territories every summer are unaware of this distant past, which explains why these *Plazas of soberanía* (as they are called in Spain) remain under Spanish sovereignty.

The British Empire owes a great deal to the English navy's supremacy. It played a vital part in its expansion all around the globe (Jackson 2013: 53–70. As a maritime superpower, Britain was able to rule over half of the globe for almost four centuries. British Sea Power allowed her to persist, conquer and expand remarkably its empire. Military superiority made possible by cutting edge technology, propelled British leaders to manage the world largest empire. Naval power laid the foundations for the nation's imperial ambitions. Even so, British hegemony was contested, internally, by the claims, resistance and revolts from colonized people and externally, by other European countries such as France or Germany. Among today's British Overseas Territories, the Virgin Islands (BVI) and Gibraltar still bear its mark. The former were conquered following the Anglo-Dutch naval wars to control trade, which placed them under British sovereignty in 1672. In 1704, the Rock of Gibraltar, which Spain had turned into a stronghold, came under British jurisdiction. Spain, diplomatically isolated and militarily weakened, refused to budge despite the Treaty of Utrecht of 1713, which ratified the transfer of sovereignty. In 1727, the Spanish launched an attack, but the English thwarted the siege of the city. Spain still did not give up. In 1966, Franco forced a blockade—which was lifted in 1985 when Spain joined the European Economic Community. Brexit, latest avatar of bilateral tensions and widely rejected by the people of Gibraltar, is now pushing the British authorities to seek a *modus operandi* with their Spanish counterparts, so as not to isolate this strategic micro-territory. Shared sovereignty, however, seems very unlikely (Duke 2019: 60).

The use of violence was also central to the expansion of the US empire. Against a backdrop of religious messianism (Manifest Destiny 1845), but above all under the influence of Alfred Thayer Mahan's theories (*The Influence of Sea Power upon History 1660–1783*, 1890), the United States intended to control the seas to guarantee free trade, spread its political paradigm and assert the civilising mission of the Anglo-Saxon White race (White Man's Burden). On 25 April 1898, it went to war against Spain—which still had many colonies in Africa, Asia and America—, with the Cuban War of Independence as the pretext. In Washington, it was viewed as an opportunity to increase the United States' influence in its own backyard. The fighting was short-lived. Spain surrendered in August 1898. The Treaty of Paris of 10 December enshrined Cuba's sovereignty and the cession of several Spanish colonies to the United States—the Philippines, Puerto Rico and Guam for a settlement of twenty million dollars. In 1901, under the Platt Amendment, Cuba was placed under the protection of the United States which established a naval base in Guantánamo Bay. In 1903, a bilateral treaty consolidated its legal status but failed to make it a US overseas territory. Leased to the Cuban authorities, it constitutes a *sui generis* territory where the US Constitution does not apply. In 2001, the Bush administration deliberately set up an offshore detention centre there, as part of its war on Islamic terrorism. In defiance of international law, several hundred people have been held in that facility indefinitely, interrogated under torture and denied access to legal counsel. Unlike Guantánamo, the Philippines—until 1946—, Hawaii, Guam and Wake Island are all official US overseas territories. It was their bombing by the Japanese air force that triggered the United States' entrance in World War II. In his "Infamy Speech" to Congress, President Roosevelt deliberately chose to only mention Hawaii in order to gain Congress approval and his fellow citizens' support more easily. Unlike the other overseas territories that had also been attacked, Hawaii was the only one considered by the American public as an integral part of the national territory, due to its large population of mainland US citizens (Immerwahr 2019).

Colonial Conquests

Historically, the inception of the overseas territories is rooted in colonial conquests, which are closely tied to the wars and annexations that often arose in their wake. In fact, most of today's offshore territories stem from that form of territorial expansion. Apart from a few exceptions, the countries in charge of administering them are both the former colonial state and the post-colonial state. Denmark colonised the Faroe Islands before turning them into an autonomous entity within the Danish kingdom; France did the same with Polynesia and New Caledonia, Portugal with the Azores and Madeira, and Russia with Novaya Zemlya. Many overseas territories were colonised as early as the seventeenth century, including Bermuda in 1612, Anguilla in 1650, Montserrat in 1632 and Cayman in 1670. France took possession of Guadeloupe and Martinique in 1635, Reunion Island in 1642 and French Guiana in 1654. At the same time, the Netherlands grabbed Sint Eustatius in 1632 and Curaçao in 1634. Two years later, Aruba and Bonaire also came under Dutch sovereignty. In 1640 and 1648, it was Saba's turn, followed by Sint Maarten's. Contrary to popular belief, the Danish Crown was also involved in the colonisation of the Antilles. It claimed St. Thomas and St. John in 1672 and 1683 respectively. In 1733, the Danish Crown purchased St. Croix, which was under French sovereignty at the time. These three islands were later sold to the United States. Denmark had previously colonised Greenland. Erick the Red was the first to establish a settlement there in 982, which endured until the fifteenth century. In 1721, Hans Egede, a pastor of Danish origin, founded a town named Godthab which would later become the capital, *Nuuk*. In the eighteenth century, Greenland—or *Kalaallit Nunaat* in the Inuit language—experienced spectacular economic growth thanks to its fishing resources, which profited all Scandinavian countries. Under the Treaty of Kiel, Denmark retained control of Greenland when it separated from Norway in 1814.

Annexations

Defined here as the incorporation of an offshore territory into a "mainland" territory, annexation can be the outcome of long-term occupation, or a penalty stipulated in any treaty aimed at terminating an armed conflict. Portugal annexed the archipelagos of Madeira and the Azores in 1418 and 1432 respectively. Uninhabited at the time of their discovery, both these territories became supply hubs for ships en route to the West Indies, before specialising in agriculture and livestock production. Madeira produced sugar cane and wine, while the Azores focused on livestock farming and market gardening. Denmark had already claimed the Faroe Islands in 1380, when it annexed them in 1814 under the provisions of the Treaty of Kiel signed with the United Kingdom, while Norway was assigned to Sweden. As for France, it gradually annexed Polynesia by establishing an evolving protectorate with Queen Aïmata Pomaré IV, who ceded all the territories under his jurisdiction in exchange for keeping his royal attributes and receiving financial compensation. The Protectorate was replaced in 1880 by the *Établissements Français d'Océanie* (French Establishments in Oceania) until 1958, when Polynesia officially became an overseas territory. In Wallis and Futuna, France shared power with local monarchs and the leaders of a very influential Catholic Church as part of a protectorate, until the overseas territory status was adopted by referendum in 1959. The United States did the same with the Baker Islands in 1857, Midway Atoll in 1867 and Hawaii in 1898. Chile annexed Easter Island/*Rapa Nui* in 1888, under a treaty brokered by a naval officer with a *Rapanui* customary chief. This led to the marginalisation of the indigenous population and subsequent collapse of their ancestral traditions. This discriminatory situation prevailed until 1966, when the *Rapanui* were granted Chilean citizenship and regained their freedom of movement. In the far north, the Svalbard archipelago came under Norwegian sovereignty in 1920, as provided by the Spitsbergen Treaty which converted it into a free and demilitarised economic zone. Signatory countries (Denmark, Norway, Sweden, the United States, France, Italy, the Netherlands, Great Britain and Japan) all enjoyed fishing quotas, but Norway was the only country still producing coal in the area. A year later, Jan Mayen Island became an open-air scientific laboratory for short-term research assignments. In the South Atlantic, Norway annexed Bouvet Island in 1927. With no permanent population, it became a wildlife reserve in 1971 and is now listed as an international ecopolitical hotspot.

Purchases

France, the United States and Japan purchased some of their overseas territories. The former acquired the Mayotte islands in 1841 and Saint-Barthélemy in 1877. Mayotte fell under French sovereignty amid fierce competition between the "battling sultans" over control of the Comoros archipelago. To escape the domination of his Anjouan counterpart, the sultan of Mayotte sold his island to a French naval officer for a lump sum of 1,000 piastres. A few years later, the sultans of Grande Comore, Mohéli and Anjouan also requested protection from

France, which administered them collectively as a protectorate. In 1946, the Comoros became a French overseas territory while all the other colonies were being decolonised. Saint-Barthélemy followed a different path. France bought the island in 1674 but swapped it in 1784 for warehouse rights in the port of Gothenburg. King Gustav III of Sweden inherited the island and turned it into a prosperous free port until its destruction by a hurricane in 1852. Having lost its value, the island was sold back to France in 1877 for a token price. In 1917, the United States bought the Virgin Islands from the King of Denmark for 25 million dollars. For the Danish monarch, the islands had lost their value with the abolition of slavery, but they were an obvious geopolitical asset to the United States. For the record, the US had purchased Louisiana from France for 15 million dollars in 1803, and Alaska from Russia for 7 million dollars in 1867. The Senkaku islands were acquired by Japan to counter the People's Republic of China's covetous dispute over their sovereignty. After being returned to the Japanese empire in 1972 by the United States, which had administered it since 1945, the archipelago was then privately owned by a Japanese manufacturer. To curb Chinese pressure, the Japanese government decided in 2021 to buy it back from its rightful owners. For the Japanese authorities, this transaction simply amounted to a transfer of ownership over land that already was considered integral to the national territory. The Chinese government, however, given its eagerness to achieve supremacy in the China Sea, viewed it as a form of defiance.

Retrocessions

With Macau and Hong Kong, the PRC boasts two overseas territories that have been retroceded. Macau, a former trading post turned Portuguese colony that has become a mecca for the gambling industry, was handed back to the PRC in 1999. Prior to Portuguese colonisation, it was a full-fledged part of the Middle Kingdom. The Portuguese, who landed in China in the early sixteenth century, fought for control of the territory until World War II, when it fell under Japanese rule. After gaining national sovereignty, the PRC did not directly call for the retrocession of Macau, which was still being administered by Portugal. The handover took place after the Carnation Revolution, which marked the start of an unprecedented decolonisation campaign. Hong Kong, formerly a trading post and then a British colony but also a hub for the opium trade and now one of the world's largest financial centres, reintegrated the People's Republic of China in 1997 at the end of a 99-year lease signed with the British Empire. Colonised by the Chinese under the Han Empire, Hong Kong experienced a commercial boom from the seventh century onwards, thanks to the Silk Road. Its growth caught the eye of Great Britain in particular, which made considerable profits from the opium trade. The wars that followed resulted in Hong Kong being ceded to the British Empire. In 1984, the PRC entered into negotiations to regain control of Hong Kong, which the United Kingdom accepted on condition that its political and economic model be maintained for the next fifty years. The transfer was celebrated in a grandiose ceremony broadcast on world television.

Conclusion

This second chapter sought to present concise but explanatory illustrations of the historical making of overseas territories. It highlighted a couple of events at the intersection of subnational, national and international politics in order to examine the extent to which these former colonies were very often—disregarded—*boosters* for the political and economic expansion of their then colonial powers. From the early beginnings, metropolises and colonies were bound by an intimate history—despite national narratives that exclude the latter in most cases. Yet, this historical overview, however selective, has gone to show how both sides have built (from) each other. It underlines at the outset how costly a truncated view of history has been for the colonisers and the colonised alike. Indeed, whatever their post-colonial political status might be—as independent States or non-sovereign territories—this silenced past continues to haunt relations with the former colonial power in postcolonial times (Trouillot 1995).

CHAPTER 3

The Diversity of Post-colonial Statuses

Abstract The demise of colonial empires gave way to alternative forms of decolonisation through integration: total incorporation (such as Saba, La Reunion or Hawaii) or partial incorporation (such as Wallis and Futuna, Puerto Rico or Aruba) into the politico-administrative framework of the former colonial state; and direct administration by the postcolonial state's central authorities (for instance, Midway, Pitcairn Islands or the Archipelago of Svalbard). The first variant involves the application of common law statuses, while the second entails special statuses. The third option involves direct management by the national government. These alternative paths to decolonisation through independence were more appealing for a set of former small colonies than full sovereignty. But their implementation did vary according to political and administrative traditions, as well as geopolitical considerations. Its implementation depends on two variables: strategic interest and overall cost for the metropolitan power. By strategic interest, we refer to its added value in military, economic or political terms. By overall cost, we mean the spending associated with the strategic gain—such as military infrastructure and the human resources needed to operate it—as well as the expenses incurred in administering the local population, i.e. public services and governance. Far from being optimal, these postcolonial (non-sovereign) arrangements generate in most cases periodic conflicts with subnational and national authorities, some of which are intertwined with international politics.

© The Author(s), under exclusive license to Springer Nature
Switzerland AG 2024
F. Constant, *Overseas Territories in World Affairs*,
https://doi.org/10.1007/978-3-031-64233-3_3

Keywords Alternative forms of decolonisation · Postcolonial politics · British Overseas Territories · US Overseas Territories · French Overseas *collectivités* · Dutch Overseas Territories · Danish Overseas Territories · Special Administrative Regions · Island/mainland's power-sharing · Regionalism · Autonomy · Proto-nationalism

Remnants of Western and Asian expansionism, contemporary overseas territories are also a *post-colonial* creation. The disintegration of colonial empires which led to the proliferation of new independent states, gave way to alternative forms of decolonisation based on integration. Integration can take at least three forms: total or partial incorporation into the politico-administrative framework of the former colonial state; and direct administration by the postcolonial state's central authorities. The first variant involves the application of common law statuses, while the second entails special statuses. The third option involves direct management by the national government. These alternative paths to decolonisation are not as widely known or even acknowledged; yet they are included in the Declaration on the Granting of Independence to Colonial Countries and Peoples, adopted on 14 December 1960 by the General Assembly of the United Nations. For a small territory, being attached to a large political entity is usually more appealing than sovereignty. But the choice does vary according to political and administrative traditions, as well as geopolitical considerations. Its implementation depends on two variables: *strategic interest* and *overall cost*. By strategic interest, we refer to its added value in military, economic or political terms. By overall cost, we mean the spending associated with the strategic gain—such as military infrastructure and the human resources needed to operate it—as well as the expenses incurred in administering the local population, i.e. public services and governance. As Jean Crusol (2007:17) puts it: "*(...) the crucial question for powers is the ratio between the cost and the benefits derived from a strategic position. The lower this ratio, the greater the attractiveness of a strategic position. Islands are particularly attractive because they are small, sparsely populated and scattered across the oceans. Their indirect strategic cost is generally low, compared with the strategic advantages they provide.*" Consequently, the more an administering power values a strategic position and the lower its overall cost, the more it will favour the option of integration under common law. The higher the overall cost in relation to the expected benefits, the more it tends to prefer partial integration under specific statuses. Clearly, independence is the go-to option when the overall cost dismisses the option of decolonising through integration.

Common Law Statuses

This type of status involves an administrative framework, a legislative system and local powers that are identical or close to the common law enforced in the country to which the territory is attached. However, these common law statuses vary in terms of administrative frameworks. Below are a few case examples.

France took this innovative route in 1946, with the *départementalisation* of Guadeloupe, French Guiana, Martinique and Reunion Island. This was an unprecedented form of integration-based decolonisation, long advocated by local elites, against the historical and seemingly irresistible flow of independence movements among colonial peoples. There are several reasons for this counter-cyclical reform, designed to turn these former colonies into replicas of the French *départements*. First, stood the promise of French republican equality which carried the hope for a drastic change in the populations' living conditions, based on the extension of welfare laws and the gradual alignment of standards of living with those of mainland France. Secondly, it recognised the French overseas' contribution to the liberation of France during World War II.

Thirdly, it was the culmination of a centuries-old policy of assimilation aimed in theory at making them full-fledged French citizens. Finally, the strategic cost/benefit equation was extremely favourable, with limited public expenditure in relation to the benefits reaped in terms of strategic footholds and influence. However, the new status was enforced but sparingly. The economic and social progress touted by the government proved slow to materialise, while the matter of territorial identities burst into the political debate. Aimé Césaire adamantly questioned the government before the French National Assembly: "*Are we full citizens or fully apart?*" Overseas, impatience turned to anger. The unrest triggered by the feeling of being second-class citizens set the pace for political and social progress. Standards of living did improve, but still failed to catch up with mainland levels. Under pressure from locally elected representatives, laws were gradually extended to these new *départements* when they should have been automatically enforced. Despite these setbacks, Saint-Pierre-et-Miquelon embraced the same status in 1976 before willingly becoming a *sui generis* collectivity in 1985 to escape European Community law, which would have penalised its economic trade with Canada. In 2011, Mayotte took the opposite route. Its constituents voted in favour of *départementalisation*, enshrining a long-standing political demand motivated by the rejection of any potential return to the Comoros, and by a burning desire to boost local development. In this overseas territory located in the Indian Ocean, which is by far the poorest in France, the challenges are considerable: overwhelmed public services, a very dynamic demography, which feeds on massive immigration, a very limited labour market and growing insecurity. However, the departmental status remains very attractive for the vast majority of Mahorais who put pressure on the French authorities to ensure that it is implemented more quickly.

In the United States, similar considerations have shaped statutory developments. While President Truman led the Philippines to independence, he chose to incorporate Hawaii and Alaska into the Union. The cost/benefit ratio for these two overseas territories was clearly favourable to their inclusion in the federal state, given their strategic value for national security and their relatively small populations. However, such a status change was far from obvious, given the racial prejudice that prevailed in Congress. There were two opposing factions: on the one hand, those who refused to incorporate territories which did not have a majority White population; on the other, those who saw it as an opportunity to advance the United States' political values. The former feared cultural differences beyond assimilation, while the latter argued the exact opposite. In the end, Congress passed a majority vote in 1959 to establish the 49th and 50th States of the Union. With the Cold War in full swing, their added value to the United States' security came into sharp focus. This historic decision also rewarded their populations' loyalty and participation in national defence. Lastly, it served as a political seal on the national integration of their economies and the acculturation of their native peoples. The United States now had two states that were not contiguous with its mainland, both of which were home to a minority White population. Alaska and Hawaii benefit from the full protection of the federal Constitution, the same political institutions and all the laws of the federation. Their populations take part in national elections just like citizens of the other States. Alaska elected Ernest Gruening, a former Democratic Governor in the vanguard of the fight against racism, to the Senate. Hawaii sent Hiram Fong, of Chinese descent, and Daniel Inouye, who was to become the first *pro tempore* president of Japanese descent. To date, no other offshore territory has joined them in the Union. Yet, Puerto Ricans voted massively (97.3%) in favour of statehood in a 2017 plebiscite. Free association/Independence received only 1.52% of the votes. Puerto Rico's current territorial status got a mere 1.35% of votes. The US Congress and the President of the United States did not take the will of the majority of Puerto Ricans electors into consideration. They decided to maintain the *status quo ante* as they are entitled to under the Federal Constitution.

Two decades later, the return of democracy in Spain and Portugal enabled the conversion of their overseas territories into local authorities under ordinary law, as part of an unprecedented policy of decolonisation that helped restore the Iberian peninsula's international reputation. Spain undertook this process for the Balearic Islands and the Canary Islands in response to the pressing demands of local trade unions and political organisations, which were eager to reappropriate the public administration of island affairs. The organic laws of 10 August 1982 and 25 February 1983 granted their wishes and made them autonomous communities with the same powers as the rest of Spain, thereby entrusting them with the levers of local development and the promotion of their island identities. The Azores and Madeira followed a similar path. They changed status after a long history of conflict with the central government of Portugal, especially under the Salazar dictatorship. In 1974, the Carnation Revolution engendered a twofold political process: at the international level, the last colonies were emancipated; at a domestic level, the status of the Azores and Madeira was normalised. Under the new Constitution adopted in 1976, the Azores and Madeira were granted internal autonomy, allowing them to freely administer their internal affairs except for matters of sovereignty. In 1995, Ceuta and Melilla were granted the status of autonomous cities. Attached to the provinces of Cadiz and Malaga, they form the EU's external borders. This increases their strategic significance at a marginal cost to the budget considering the European investments required to manage exponential migratory flows.

Special Statuses

This type of status features administrative and legislative systems, as well as local powers that derogate from the ordinary law in force in the country of incorporation. The institutional set-up, the applicable laws and the powers vested in the local authorities all reflect a clearly defined territorial approach. These specific statutes provide for systems of internal autonomy that reflect partial incorporation into national political groupings. Rather than an exhaustive review, the following section presents a number of distinct examples.

Right after the war, as the British colonial empire unravelled, a dozen or so British Crown colonies were left on the sidelines. These colonies did not aspire to become independent states due to their limited resources and small territories. However, the British authorities had no intention of turning them into local authorities under ordinary law. Instead, they took an intermediate route that involved keeping a bond with the post-colonial state while increasing their internal autonomy. There were two stages to this process: in 1981, with the creation of British Dependent Territories (BDT), and then in 2002, with their conversion into British Overseas Territories (BOT). The overarching principle of this status is self-government; the overseas territories that enjoy it are not eligible for national public policies, but subject to special legislation. Each of them has a constitution, a parliament and a government headed by a Prime Minister or Chief Minister. Drawing on the Westminster model, parliament is the cornerstone of local democracy. General elections are held every four years. A Governor represents King Charles III, who is the Head of State. Local populations hold British Overseas Territory Citizenship, which does not grant them the same rights as British Citizenship. As a result, the financial burden of administering these territories remains much lower than the strategic benefits that some of them bring to the United Kingdom, which can therefore continue to exert its sovereignty over them at minimal cost, as is the case with Gibraltar. However, the British authorities freely intervene in the public management of local affairs when it is subject to major abuses. Among other occurrences, the UK seized back control of Turks and Caicos in 2009 over allegations of widespread corruption. Michael Misik, Premier of the government, resigned after a UK parliamentary committee and a commission of enquiry found a high probability of systemic bribery. Local government was suspended for almost two years while the governor was empowered to set local affairs back on tracks (Jones 2009).

The United States has four overseas territories with comparable statuses: Puerto Rico, the US Virgin Islands, Guam and the Northern Mariana Islands. These *unincorporated, organized territories* are not intended to become States of the Union like Alaska or Hawaii. The Federal Constitution only partially applies to them, and their local institutions are independent from the United States Congress. They do not elect representatives or senators to Congress, but do have a delegate with an advisory vote. Citizens of these territories do not take part in presidential elections. They do not enjoy the full protection of the Constitution or of all federal laws. For the US authorities, this halfway house between independence and incorporation into the Union offers several advantages in terms of costs and benefits. Federal spending is lower than in a federal state, and the laws in force are less restrictive in economic, social and environmental terms. On the other hand, these territories are extremely useful when it comes to defence and certain offshore economic activities. Puerto Rico has been home to as many as twenty-five military facilities and bases where experiments involving weapons, including chemical ones, have been carried out with full impunity. Several mainland companies transferred their environmentally harmful industrial activities to the island in order to evade the federal environmental code and profit from cheap labour. Guam, which has become a pivotal platform for the security of the United States, is experiencing a form of development driven by military concerns that have nothing to do with the aspirations of its civilian population. Just like their elected counterparts in Puerto Rico, Guam's representatives are keen to influence decisions that affect their territory. But the federal Congress continues to reject their aspirations in the name of a *status quo* that favours US interests at minimal cost to the national budget. However, the political debate goes on in both islands despite the US federal authorities' indifference. In Guam, the government planned to hold a non-binding political status vote for native residents, which was to allow them to state their preference for the island's future relationship with the US. But the initiative was rejected in 2011 by a ruling of Guam's district court, on the grounds that the definition of a *native resident* was discriminatory to US citizens living on the island (Limtiaco 2023). In 2016, a very interesting initiative took place. A debate was organised in the island's high schools over the comparative merits of Statehood, Free Association and Independence. Prior to the debate, the 800 students were polled. Statehood garnered 51% of the votes, Free Association 30%, Independence 19%. At the end of the debate, the students were polled again. Statehood got 48%, Free Association 16%, Independence 34% (Office of the Governor, 2016). Whatever the interpretation of these results, the status quo does not seem like a sustainable option to the youth, that is: the future of this US overseas territory.

Some of the French overseas territories face a similar situation when it comes to rights and duties of citizens. Although full-fledged nationals, their residents cannot claim the entire benefit of national laws. For instance, the social security system differs from that in mainland France: the risks, benefits, rates and conditions of eligibility are different and vary from one territory to another. Each of them is regulated by an organic law that sets out the scope of legislation, the division of powers, the organisational and operational framework for institutions and the electoral system for deliberative assemblies. The powers vested in these local authorities evolve according to local political dynamics. Saint-Pierre-et-Miquelon, Saint-Barthélemy and Saint-Martin have their own specific motion of no-confidence mechanisms. In Wallis and Futuna, where the state representative continues to act as the executive body of the territorial assembly, the Organic Law recognises the role of customary kingdoms in the running of local institutions. French Polynesia displays a very high level of internal autonomy, with a government that reports to a territorial assembly and is in charge of taxation. New Caledonia's institutions, which have no equivalent in France, include a Congress that votes on the country's budget and laws, a collegiate government accountable to Congress, a Customary Senate that is the guardian and defender of Kanak identity, and an Economic and Social Council that serves as an advisory body. As far as France is concerned, these *à la carte* statuses provide a combination of political and economic benefits: under cover of transferring powers to local assemblies, they proportionately reduce state expenditure in these territories. By promoting territorial identities, they also help preserve French strategic interests at little cost. No matter the level of autonomy enjoyed by these subnational jurisdictions, it remains a disputed feature, subject to periodic debate and amendments, because it lies at the heart of the mainland/island's complex relationship.

As compensation for their retrocession, the People's Republic of China turned Hong Kong and Macau into special administrative regions (*tèbié xíngzhèngqū*). This was the political price to be paid for their return into the national fold, because of their strategic value for China's national security. At first glance, the short-term cost may seem high, but it is outweighed by a considerable economic and financial added value and, in the longer term, the possibility of freely disposing of these assets. Under the "one country, two systems" doctrine, Hong Kong and Macau continue to enjoy a democratic and pluralist form of governance, their own currency, a judicial system based on common law; and various standards inherited from British and Portuguese colonisation, that contribute to their distinctive lifestyle. This special administrative region status, which is based on a fundamental law adopted in 1990 for one and in 1993 for the other, essentially guarantees their internal political autonomy and lucrative economic models until 2047 and 2049 respectively. It grants them extensive powers to manage their internal affairs, apart from matters relating to defence and foreign affairs. In theory, Hong Kong enjoys a relatively more democratic governance model than Macau. Every four years, its population elects by direct universal suffrage a legislative assembly and a government headed by a Chief Executive. In Macau, on the other hand, the Chief Executive is appointed by a college of four hundred voters, and half the members of the Legislative Assembly are elected by indirect universal suffrage or appointed by the Chief Executive. In both cases, however, public freedoms—in particular the right of association, the right to strike and the right to protest—are actually monitored on a case-by-case basis by the Chinese government. Local populations do not shy away from asserting their rights, but the Chinese authorities closely supervise local political life in order to bend its course. Will they one day go so far as to put an early end to the internal autonomy of these regions and administer them directly? (More about Hong Kong in Part III).

Direct Administration Models

Direct administration of overseas territories encompasses a variety of practical approaches. From one country to another, it ranges from centralised to decentralised forms that can be entrusted to a single body or to several ministerial departments. In any case, the state holds a monopoly. This administration model offers a very attractive cost/benefit ratio, as it applies to territories that are almost always uninhabited, for the most part very isolated and sometimes inhospitable; spread across the Pacific, Indian, Arctic and Antarctic Oceans and the Mediterranean Sea. Some of these territories are used for military purposes, while others are protected natural areas.

Most of them are administered by the United States: Palmyra, Jarvis, Wake Island, Baker, Howland, Johnston, Kingman, Midway and Navassa. Apart from the last, which is located in the Caribbean, they all lie in the Pacific Ocean. Among them, Palmyra Atoll is the only *incorporated unorganized territory*. This 7.45 mi2 atoll is a protected natural area administered by the federal government. It is fully subject to the US Constitution and to the principle of inalienable US sovereignty. All the others are unincorporated and unorganised territories that are not bound by the federal Constitution. According to the official terminology, they form a group known as the US Minor Outlying Islands. Seven of them (Baker, Holland, Jarvis, Kingman Reef, Midway and Wake) are uninhabited but are home to protected natural sites and have a surface area of less than 6.21 mi2. Johnston Atoll, the eighth one, is a military base. American Samoa is the ninth and last unincorporated and unorganised American territory. They are administered by the federal government, but have unilaterally set up local institutions (a House of Representatives and a Senate) that are not recognised by Congress. The population does, however, count with a non-voting delegate. Despite the small size (124 mi2) and population (43,000) of their island, Samoans have been claiming for a change of status to have a say in the management of local public affairs. Line-Noue Memea Kruse, a native researcher, argues convincingly that the current form of insular governance is undemocratic and unchecked: "(..) without an Organic Act or legal instrument to guide (..) the Navy became the executive, legislative, and judicial overseer. Too much power was vested in the Commandant-Governor." (2018: 194). Furthermore, she demonstrates the inequitable power relations between Native Samoans and the military, the erosion of vernacular pillars of culture (communal land) and calls for a democratisation of insular governance.

The UK boasts five directly administered overseas territories: the British Indian Ocean Territory (BIOT), the British Antarctic Territory (BAT), Akrotiri & Dhekelia in the Mediterranean Sea, the Pitcairn Islands, South Georgia and the Sandwich Islands in the Pacific Ocean. Stretched over 1,062,544.739 mi2, the BAT is the largest one. With 26.7 mi2, the Pitcairn Islands are the smallest. The BIOT and Akrotiri & Dhekelia are home to military bases; while the other three are protected natural sites with no permanent population. The Indian Ocean base at

Diego Garcia is operated by the US Navy; while the military facilities on Cyprus are managed by the British Army. The BAT was officially established in 1962, after the United Kingdom ratified the Antarctic Treaty (ATS). The British authorities hold two research stations on that territory, which periodically host scientific expeditions. It is administered by the Foreign, Commonwealth and Development Office (FCDO). The Governor of the Falkland Islands is in charge of the South Georgia and Sandwich Islands, which are a wildlife sanctuary and protected natural area.

France applies this management method to its Southern and Antarctic Lands (TAAF), which are scattered across the southern hemisphere. They form a *sui generis* collectivity established by law in 1955 and comprised of the Scattered Islands (Bassas da India, Glorioso Islands, Tromelin, Juan de Nova, Europa), the Austral Islands (Amsterdam & Saint-Paul, Crozet Islands, Kerguelen Islands) in the Indian Ocean and Adélie Land in Antarctica. A prefect based in Saint-Denis, Reunion Island, is in charge of this colossal nature reserve, which is also a sanctuary for biodiversity. Chile and Norway are in the same position. Chile has sovereignty over the Juan Fernandez Islands and the Desventuradas Islands off the South American coast. These micro-territories are attached to the region of Valparaíso. They were declared a national park by the Chilean government in 1955 to preserve their endemic flora and fauna. Norway administers Bouvet Island in the South Atlantic, Jan Mayen Island in the Greenland Sea and the Svalbard Islands in the Arctic Ocean. The first two, which are uninhabited, are run by Nordland County, while the Svalbard archipelago is run by a governor with the assistance of a community council. An autonomous, neutral and demilitarised territory, Svalbard is not included in Norway's official surface area. Like the other two overseas territories, it is nonetheless an international flagship of Norway's commitment to preserving endangered species.

Whether huge or tiny, populated or uninhabited, directly or autonomously governed; overseas territories are integral to the international presence of the countries that have sovereignty over them—and to their global ambitions. The distribution of their geopolitical positions shifts according to the strategic interests of their mainland countries and to changes in the international landscape.

Conclusion

This chapter focused on the reasons which led postcolonial states and former colonies to explore alternative forms of decolonisation through secession, in a context marked by the end of World War II and early stages of the Cold War. It identified the geopolitical rationales that fostered a counter-cyclical process of decolonisation through integration. Then, it highlighted the driving subnational and national forces at play in the evolving debate over decolonisation, sovereignty, autonomy; one that lies at the heart of mainland/island relationships. Finally, it unveiled how the overseas territories provide ideal grounds for exploring the ways in which internal dynamics intersect with external ones. More than other territories, they embody what Edouard Glissant called a poetics of Relation that "links, connects, relays, relates"(1990: 40).[1] They are places where worldviews meet, clash and collide. After consideration of how decolonisation paved the way for innovative political avenues, it is now time to assess the impacts of another major post-war political breakthrough on the OTs' geopolitical assignments.

---

[1] *Poétique de la Relation*, Paris, Gallimard, 1990, p. 40.

CHAPTER 4

Geopolitical Assignments in the Post-war Era

Abstract The Cold War led to the bipolarisation of the international arena, with the "free world" and the Communist Bloc battling it out to expand their spheres of influence. The Cuban Revolution and the missile crisis were the high points of this strategic rivalry between the United States and the Soviet Union. Overseas territories stood at the forefront of their respective mainland's geopolitical agenda. Most of them fell into line behind the United States. Great Britain embraced its own relative decline. France asserted its national sovereignty policy. The Netherlands and Portugal chose to come under NATO's protection. Spain did not join, but provided the United States with access to several military bases. Denmark and Norway rallied to the West, but maintained a "good neighbour" stance towards the USSR. These developments gave Western overseas territories a threefold geopolitical function: as outposts in the containment policy orchestrated by the world's leading power, as relays for the fight against Communist ideology and as windows on the democratic and liberal model. These various ways OTs were managed to best serve the strategic interests of their "motherland", remain little- known outside a narrow circle of academics and experts. Yet, they have tremendously contributed to the security and defense of their administering countries, in the context of a bipolarised world.

Keywords Cold War · Bipolarisation · USSR · NATO · Offshore military outposts · General de Gaulle · John F. Kennedy · Guantánamo ·

© The Author(s), under exclusive license to Springer Nature Switzerland AG 2024
F. Constant, *Overseas Territories in World Affairs*,
https://doi.org/10.1007/978-3-031-64233-3_4

Cuban Revolution · Hawaii · Guam · Puerto Rico · Luis Munoz Marin · French Polynesia · Nuclear experiments · Nuclear deterrence · Missile crisis · McCarthyism · Red Scare · OJAM · Aimé Césaire

The Cold War led to the bipolarisation of the international arena, with the "free world" and the Communist Bloc battling it out to expand their spheres of influence. The Cuban Revolution and the missile crisis were the high points of this strategic rivalry between the United States and the Soviet Union. Overseas territories stood at the forefront of their respective mainlands' geopolitical agendas. Most of them fell into line behind the United States. Great Britain embraced its own relative decline. France asserted its national sovereignty policy. The Netherlands and Portugal chose to come under NATO's protection. Spain did not join, but provided the United States with access to several military bases. Denmark and Norway rallied to the West, but maintained a "good neighbour" stance towards the USSR. These developments gave Western overseas territories a threefold geopolitical function: as outposts in the containment policy orchestrated by the world's leading power, as relays for the fight against Communist ideology and as windows on the democratic and liberal model.

Advanced Security/Defence Outposts

Overseas territories boast a myriad of comparative strengths. Many are small territories, sometimes isolated, sparsely populated, that enjoy some measure of political stability and are often located in communication hubs where military activities can flourish. Depending on their geographic location, they contribute to securing communication and maritime trade routes, pre-positioning conventional forces and military equipment, enabling air and sea surveillance and rapid intervention, as well as conducting nuclear and space research and experimentation.

Ensuring secure lines of communication is paramount to supplying Western economies. To carry out this crucial task, the United States strengthened and extended the network of military bases built during World War II in the overseas territories of its NATO allies. Their purpose was to guard the straits and channels from the Soviet threat. In the North Atlantic, the United States converted the Azores base of Lajes into a major military and logistical hub for Western air forces. Ideally located between the North American and European continents, it accommodated up to twenty thousand military aircraft a year and employed almost one thousand five hundred soldiers. In Central America and the Caribbean, the United States has a military foothold that is controlled by a network of naval and air facilities. This network runs north to south: from Cuba, which is home to the Guantánamo offshore base, to the Chaguaramas offshore base in Trinidad and Tobago—in addition to the Vieques and Culebra military stations in Puerto Rico and the Aruba, Bonaire and Curaçao military stations off Venezuela. This network extends into the Eastern Caribbean with Coolidge Airfield in Antigua, Beane Field in St. Lucia and further north with the Andros Naval Base in the Bahamas and the Kindley Air Force Base in Bermuda. Coordinated from Florida and Puerto Rico, they helped keep the US mainland secure by deterring Soviet submarine incursions into its backyard. On the eve of the Cuban revolution, the United States controlled the "Caribbean Mediterranean" except for the French overseas territories.

France began modernising its military assets and its forces took part in allied army exercises sponsored by the United States. In the Indian Ocean, they played a part in monitoring the routes used for the vital transport of hydrocarbons and strategic raw materials. Freedom of navigation is just as crucial for military vessels as it is for merchant ships. The Diego Garcia naval air base provides key logistical support for military surveillance, intelligence and defence operations in an area roamed by oil tankers from all over the world. It still employs 1,500 soldiers and has the infrastructure to support several types of air (B52 bombers, C5 cargo planes, KC-135 in-flight refuellers) and naval (ships and submarines) vehicles. France rounds out this network with Reunion Island, home to its Armed Forces of the Indian Ocean (FAZOI) and a number of French Navy vessels. In the Pacific Ocean, both powers rely respectively on Hawaii and Guam, and French Polynesia together with New Caledonia. Pearl Harbor returned to being the main logistical hub for US forces and a strategic base to counter Soviet manoeuvres. Located at the junction of the Philippine Sea and the Pacific Ocean, the Guam military base (i.e. the Andersen Air Force Base) served as its main relay station. As the only European country to hold permanent military assets in the Pacific, France leverages its armed forces in French Polynesia (FAPF) and New Caledonia (FANC)—in collaboration with the United States, Australia and New Zealand—to help keep the seaways secure in this vast ocean zone.

The pre-positioning of conventional forces and military assets overseas enables the Allied Powers, starting with the United States, to take swift action whenever their interests are threatened. Hawaii, Guam and Puerto Rico have served as launching pads and preparation platforms for numerous military operations abroad: from the Korean War (1950–1953) to Vietnam (1955–1975); from the Bay of Pigs invasion (1961) to the military intervention in the Dominican Republic (1965). These offshore territories also provide sites for nuclear, space and satellite research and experimentation. Under a bilateral agreement with Denmark, the United States enjoys a dual military presence in Greenland. The Thule air base, located less than 1,242 miles from the North Pole, is designed to pre-position bomber aircraft carrying nuclear warheads and to conduct aerial surveillance of Soviet defences. Camp Century, in the far northwest of Greenland, was built entirely in the ice cap and engineered to bring nuclear missiles as close as possible to Soviet territory. This secret underground base, which has never been used but did require massive investment, is a good measure of the extent of US-Soviet strategic rivalry.

An ally of the United States, France under General de Gaulle still strived to acquire the nuclear resources needed to secure its national autonomy. Following Algeria's independence, the Head of State chose French Polynesia as the location for the *Centre d'expérimentation du Pacifique* (CEP or Pacific Test Centre) because its fragmented geography made it possible to test nuclear weapons with allegedly no risk of harm to the local population. Founded in 1962, the CEP has a command centre based in Papeete and operations centres located on the atolls of Hao, Mururoa and Fangataufa. Considerable resources were dispatched from the mainland throughout the construction phase and testing campaigns. The CEP became the territory's gravitational centre, the mainstay of the island's partisan relations and a bone of international discord. Pouvanaa Oopa Tetuaapua, an autonomist Member of the French Parliament and leader of the anti-nuclear movement, was imprisoned on trumped-up charges. Australia, New Zealand and the Oceanian micro-States, fearing the environmental impact of nuclear experiments, harshly criticised French policy. Still, the Cold War pushed ahead with its agenda—including in space, where it gained a whole new momentum. France was not willing to let either the United States or the USSR have the monopoly. After the secession of Algeria, General de Gaulle decided to transfer space activities to French Guiana because of its geostrategic location and low population density. Established in the municipalities of Kourou and Sinnamary, the Guiana Space Centre (CSG) opened in 1968, and became the territory's epicentre, perplexing a local population that was initially completely left out of it. Four years earlier, General de Gaulle had visited Cayenne where he had addressed the population on *Place des Palmistes*, a square located at the centre of the city. He mentioned France's great plans for French Guiana but did not disclose any information about what was actually going to come out of it. Retrospectively, it sounds incredible that the French president did not deem necessary to inform even local officials, some of whom were his political allies. Nevertheless, the CSG grew to become the cornerstone of the local economy and the driving force behind the territory's appeal. Space research developed quickly, turning the CSG into a world-class launch facility.

In the Pacific, Hawaii contributed to the exploration programmes of the United States National Aeronautics and Space Agency (NASA) with its spacecraft tracking station (satellites, rockets), the use of ships based out of Pearl Harbor to retrieve space capsules at sea, as well as its astronaut training centre. But the space element in the Cold War should not be allowed to divert the spotlight from the political propaganda campaigns waged by the West versus the East (and vice versa), which were also echoed overseas.

Vehicles in the Fight Against Communist Ideology

This ideological battle against the USSR and its satellite countries, which came to the forefront of the general public's awareness, crystallised domestic policy issues of variable intensities, depending on the country or offshore territory involved. Those administered by the United States faced the same "witch-hunt" atmosphere that raged in the mainland at the time in association with McCarthyism (1950–1954). There was both a profound aversion to a demonised Soviet regime and an obsessive fear of ideological contagion. All those likely to be engaged in or sympathetic to communism (i.e., Un-American activities) were shunned or prosecuted by the local authorities. Puerto Rico was not spared from that fear of the "Red Scare." The communist party (*Partido Comunista Puertorriqueño*), the socialist party (*Partido Socialista Puertorriqueño*) and the nationalist party (*Partido Nacionalista de Puerto Rico*), which had existed in Puerto Rico since the interwar period, were all the more targeted by the federal government because of their open support for independence. Their leaders and supporters faced harsh repression from the US authorities, which were intent on preserving the island from Soviet influence as it was gaining ground across Latin America in the wake of the Castro revolution. Under federal anti-communist legislation (the Smith Act) and a Puerto Rican law (the *Ley de la Mordaza*), popular protests were brutally crushed, pro-independence activists arrested and leaders imprisoned—sometimes without trial. In 1954, a commando of Puerto Rican nationalists carried out an attack on the House of Representatives in Washington to expose this political crackdown. They were arrested and sentenced severely. In British territories, the anti-Soviet sentiment took a less obsessive turn but still met with strong resistance. This shift stemmed from the changing political socialisation of island elites, who tended to be reformist rather than nationalist. Local Labour parties were more interested in improving living conditions for workers than in overturning capitalism. The alternation of power reflects the renewal of elites rather than that of public policy. The British authorities were chiefly concerned with preserving their Caribbean offshore territories from any potential contagion effect from the Cuban revolution.

The French overseas territories displayed a very different political situation. The French Communist Party (PCF) has been firmly established in Reunion Island, Guadeloupe, Martinique and French Guiana since the inter-war period, when it spearheaded the *départementalisation* process. In 1945, it won 26% of the national vote, while its local federations controlled several major cities in overseas France. Communist ministers joined the government and demanded sovereign ministries. General de Gaulle resisted them and then left power. An advocate of French autonomy, he was a sharp critic of the PCF, which in his view was subservient to the USSR. Back in power in 1958, he asserted his solidarity with the Western bloc while at the same time rejecting the very "bloc" mentality. He supported the United States during the Cuban crisis of 1962 and ensured that the Castro revolution had no sway in the French overseas territories. Activists from anti-colonial, communist and local autonomist parties were kept under close surveillance by French intelligence services. In 1959, riots broke out in Fort-de-France, leading to a deadly shoot-out. In an Order issued on 15 October 1960, Michel Debré's government empowered prefects to deport anyone "whose behaviour was likely to disrupt the public order". A number of public servants with openly communist and anti-colonial views were automatically removed to France. Among them was Alain Plénel, schools inspector and vice-rector in Martinique, who was recalled to Paris in 1960 and dismissed by presidential decree in 1965. He was guilty of exposing, in an official speech, the combination of violence, injustice and racism that had claimed the lives of three secondary school students. At the same time, the sugar industry continued to plummet, leading to massive unemployment. The youth was idle. Strikes were on the rise among farm workers. So were student rallies and protests. They were severely repressed. In 1962, a group of young activists from the *Organisation de la Jeunesse Anticolonialiste Martiniquaise* (OJAM—Organisation of the Anticolonial Youth of Martinique) were arrested and imprisoned in Fresnes, in mainland France. In 1963, Michel Debré created the *Bureau pour le développement des migrations dans les départements d'outre-mer* (BUMIDOM—Bureau for the development of migration in the overseas departments). The mass departure of unemployed young people to mainland France became a safety valve for local socio-political unrest. (Constant 1987) The French authorities made no concessions to the demands of the autonomist parties, which they accused of promoting Castro's revolutionary ideology.

Meanwhile, in the Dutch overseas territories, populations were growing frustrated with increasingly degraded living conditions, racial discrimination and the colonial structure of local government. Riots broke out in Curaçao on 30 May 1969. The khaki green uniforms and slogans of the Antillean activists led the Dutch authorities to fear that Cuban activists had been infiltrating the Caribbean to spread Soviet propaganda. The army was sent into the capital and many people were arrested. In Suriname, the political arena was split between the pro-independence and pro-autonomy factions, with tensions running between communities. The Dutch authorities were torn between their desire to disengage and their concern with being replaced by a regime hostile to the West. When they finalised the country's accession to independence in 1975, they made sure to hand over the reins to a government sympathetic to the Western bloc. Five years later, a military coup brought Desi Bouterse to power, who against all odds turned to the USSR, Cuba and North Korea. The Dutch government suspended bilateral cooperation, while Suriname sank into deep political and economic turmoil (Oostindie G. Klinker I. 2003).

In the overseas territories administered by Spain and Portugal, the battle against Sovietism and its ideological offshoots took no chances whatsoever. Under the rule of ruthless dictators, anti-communism led to an outright rejection of all leaders of the opposition. Nationalists, socialists and communists were hunted down indiscriminately, and frequently arrested and imprisoned. During Franco's reign, nationalist and communist groups in the Canary Islands and the Balearic Islands were forced underground or into exile. The People's Communist Party of the Canary Islands (PCPC) and the Movement for Self-Determination and Independence of the Canary Islands (MAIB) went into "hibernation" until the country's democratic transition. The Socialist (PSOE) and Communist (PCE) parties in the Balearic Islands, which are local federations of the national parties, were subjected to the same repressive measures under the supervision of Spanish secret services. In Portugal, the Salazar regime banned left-wing autonomist and/or communist parties along with the national progressive parties they were affiliated to. In the Azores and Madeira, the local sections of the Portuguese Communist Party (PCP) drastically scaled down their operations, but nevertheless continued to wage a clandestine battle against Salazar's dictatorship. This repressive state of affairs prevailed until the "Carnation Revolution" of 1974, which legalised and normalised their existence.

Denmark's overseas territories add further nuance to this general overview. Like Norway, Denmark maintained good neighbourly relations with the USSR for geopolitical reasons. Their political authorities had not forgotten the part played by Soviet troops in freeing their country during World War II. They were also grateful for the prominent role played by local communist parties in the resistance against Nazi occupation. However, the Cold War placed them unambiguously in the Western camp. A secret anti-communist resistance network (Gladio), supported jointly by the United States and NATO, was established in both countries. At the time, Communist parties were heavily criticised and lost many supporters. Even in Greenland and the Faroes, where there were none, a pro-West campaign undermined the rival Soviet model.

Flagships of a Liberal and Pluralist Democratic Model

Despite the imperfect implementation of the rule of law, individual freedoms and the market economy in overseas territories, they continue to be subjected to a variety of propaganda methods: from government rhetoric to media manipulation (especially on the radio); from school books filled with "political catechisms" to religious proselytism; from the partisan shaping of the public opinion to the advocacy of voluntary associations (Freemasons in particular). The high-profile official visits that represented the high points of this era left a lasting mark on people's minds in territories where they remained the exception rather than the rule. On 15–16 December 1961, President Kennedy visited Puerto Rico as part of an international tour aimed at strengthening economic cooperation with South America. On this occasion, he praised the merits of the Puerto Rican Commonwealth, which he presented as a source of inspiration for the South American continent: "Puerto Rico is an admirable bridge between Latin America and North America. I believe you have made it easier for us to understand each other, so it's very important (…) that we come here first (…) What we are trying to do with the Alliance for Progress has already been achieved to a remarkable scale in Puerto Rico. What the people of Puerto Rico have accomplished by turning goals of economic and social progress (…) into tangible realities, is undeniable proof to all citizens of the Americas of the strength and creativity of democratic ideals." (JFK Library Archives). Luis Muñoz Marin, Governor of Puerto Rico, took the opportunity to request President Kennedy's support for federal agencies to speed up the implementation of the territory's new status. In his view, there was no more effective strategy for promoting the US political model and disqualifying the Puerto Rican independence movement. In the same spirit, he persuaded him to put on hold the Department of Defense's plan to evict the populations of Vieques and Culebra in order to expand the existing military bases, on the grounds that it would inevitably reinforce anti-American sentiments on the island.

Given its "special" relationship with the United States, the United Kingdom has leaned on the Commonwealth of Nations (an intergovernmental organisation made up predominantly of the British Empire's former colonies) more than on its overseas territories (which are also members of that organisation) to spread its political vision. However, as both the Head of State and Head of the Commonwealth, Queen Elizabeth II has paid them numerous official visits during her international tours. Regardless of appearances, her visits have always carried a political undertone. They served to highlight British sovereignty over these territories, and to nurture their links with the mainland. They strengthened shared values of democracy, human rights and separation of powers. While they do not interfere directly in international relations, these territories are part of the UK's diplomatic influence. Accompanied by Prince

Philip, the Queen thus presided over a number of formal events and often came to inaugurate new facilities. In these small, often remote and isolated communities, the monarch's presence alone was a political event. Each visit reaffirmed their loyalty to the British crown and their belief in the local variant of the Westminster model. Such was the case when she visited Bermuda in 1953, just after her coronation, on her first tour of the Commonwealth. On that occasion, she took part in the celebration of the 333rd anniversary of the Bermudian Parliament, which held its first session in 1620. In her speech, the Queen of England emphasised the local population's strong attachment to the British parliamentary monarchy and its core values. In her view, Bermuda was a model of stability and smooth development. She visited the island again in 1975, 1976, 1994—and in 2009, to celebrate the 400th anniversary of the founding of Bermuda. In the meantime, she would have visited almost all of the British Overseas Territories, from those closest to England (Gibraltar) to those farthest away (Falkland Islands, St. Helena, Montserrat, Turks and Caicos Islands, the Virgin Islands, etc.).

Like the British monarch, Queen Juliana travelled several times to the offshore territories controlled by the Kingdom of the Netherlands. She visited Curaçao in 1955 to formalise the new status of the federation of the Netherlands Antilles. She took that opportunity to express her attachment to the principle of self-determination of peoples and to democratic values. She held talks with the Governor and local political leaders before chairing a series of formal events. That first visit helped her seize the weight of colonial legacies, social inequalities and racial discrimination. Two years later, it was Princess Beatrix's turn to tour all six Caribbean territories, where people regularly voiced their discontent. Despite its more social tone, this trip also had political resonance. It demonstrated the Dutch Crown's attachment to the Caribbean part of its kingdom and the need to strengthen local democracy. This concern did not prevent widespread social unrest in the 1960s, the break-up of the federation and the ensuing constitutional reform; but it did contribute to preserving the appeal of liberal, pluralist democracy. Far from undermining it, local elites never ceased to call for its full enforcement in favour of all those whose Dutch citizenship still had a taste of wishful thinking (Oostindie Klinkers 2003).

With the Algerian war and African emancipations in full swing, General de Gaulle was the first French head of state to visit the French overseas territories. On 1 May 1960, he visited Martinique, where he was warmly greeted by a population eager to see an improvement in its living conditions. He strongly reasserted French sovereignty over the territory and its place in the Republic. He pledged to speed up the *départementalisation* process, which he saw as an unprecedented form of decolonisation in which the national community would bring one of its regions up to a level of development comparable to its own. However, the local economic and social situation, which continued to deteriorate, fuelled the nationalist tendencies of young anti-colonial activists. On 23 and 24 March 1964, General de Gaulle once again visited Fort-de-France to advocate the department's status and to articulate the territory's geopolitical role: "*This department's location, right in the middle of the ocean between North and Latin America and Greater Europe, means that Martinique is a beacon, a bridge, a base from which France must spread its influence across that ocean of which I speak. We must set that example right here and build on it to spread that influence, from here - which will be one of your tasks.*" A few hours later, Aimé Césaire, deputy mayor of Fort-de-France, welcomed him to the town hall before making a strong plea in support of local autonomy, to compensate for the shortcomings of the departmental status. The General flatly rejected this proposed status shift, likening it to a request for independence in disguise: "*Between Europe and America, there is nothing but dust, and you can't build states on dust.*" That same day, the island's first daily newspaper—"France-Antilles"—was published, with the purpose of relaying government communications and the "Policy of Grandeur" advocated by General de Gaulle. The media, tightly controlled by the State, invariably presented the *departmental* status as a binding horizon for the overseas territories, which acted as storefronts for the French republican model. France's effective sovereignty over its overseas territories, makes them relays of its diplomatic influence. Jacques Foccart, then Secretary General for African and Malagasy Affairs, worked very closely with the Head of State to ensure this (Turpin 2015).

The end of the Cold War altered the geopolitical assignments of overseas territories. Due to changes in the international arena, some were downgraded and others, (re)valued. In all cases, they continue to depend on their home countries' strategic priorities in response to the uncertainties of a less predictable world.

Conclusion

This chapter stressed how much overseas territories matter when it comes to strategy. More to the point, it pinpointed the many ways in which they served the geopolitical interests of their respective mainland. First and foremost, they proved to be very helpful military assets in dealing with the Cold War. At the same time, they experienced anti-communist policies that most often ignored democratic principles—especially freedom of opinion. Nevertheless, they were used to showcase and promote the merits of a liberal and pluralistic model of democracy while their "native" residents were denied the very rights and living conditions enjoyed by their compatriots in the mainland. With the end of a bipolar world and the rise of globalisation, a new period of fast changes propelled the world into new directions: how is it affecting the OT's geopolitical assignments?

PART II

Geopolitical Virtues in a Globalised World

"Far beyond their borders, geopolitical changes have altered the status and position of OTs, caught up in complicated, and sometimes dangerous, webs of international relations, involving their use for military and strategic purposes"
John Connell, Robert Aldrich (2020: 321)

In the last quarter of the twentieth century, the collapse of the Soviet empire along with the emergence of India and first and foremost the spectacular assertion of People's Republic of China as a global power, mark a third wave of globalisation shaped by *"the liberalisation of trade, investment and capital flows, and by the formidable contraction of time and space provided by new means of communication and the lowering of their costs"* (Boniface 2020: 45). Contrary to commonly held views, *"even in this age of globalisation, territory has not gone away"* (Immerwahr 2019: 18), including sometimes the very smaller ones which may retain or acquire strategic value, depending on—among other parameters—their geographical location. These international developments have gradually shifted the world's geopolitical epicentre towards the Indo-Pacific; coinciding with the rise of Sino-American strategic rivalry. My argument is that the overseas territories of the Indo-Pacific coastline have been attracting renewed interest while those of the Atlantic coastline have been relatively devalued. Of course, this trend comes with a few notable exceptions. In any case, the *"Pivot to Asia-Pacific"* (Doyle, Rumley, 2019: 68–84), ignited by President Obama and followed by most of the US' Western allies, has led to a reassessment of the OTs' geopolitical assignments worldwide. These changes take place gradually, at different paces. Everywhere the lines are moving at the intersection of national and international interests that inevitably bear subnational consequences. OT assignments adjust to the ways' metropolitan powers construe their national interests. In addition to or as a substitute for their traditional defence and security roles, the fight against climate change has turned some of them into biodiversity sanctuaries; while others have embraced sustainable and cultural tourism. In these fields too, overseas territories act as multipliers of influence and prestige, whatever it costs their inhabitants.

CHAPTER 5

Levers for Maritime Power and Sovereignty

Abstract Overseas territories are used by their administering countries as levers for maritime power and sovereignty around the globe, regardless of the practical consequences for their inhabitants. They play a twofold role here: on the one hand, they extend the maritime domains of the countries that administer them (for instance, 97% of France's EEZ is related to its overseas territories); on the other, they have the *potential* to turn some of the latter into *archipelagic* States (for instance, the Kingdom of Netherlands consists of the Netherlands, Aruba, Curacao and Sint Maarten). In so doing, they act as levers of sovereignty that provide strategic depth beyond the mainland segments of national territories. The growing number of disputes over the delimitation of EEZs is ample proof of this. The challenge is not just to stretch maritime lines. It is also a matter of displaying multiple regional affiliations and maintaining neighbourly relations with other continental and island countries. The political narratives used by these nations to define and present themselves on the international stage do not always reflect these mixed identities. Yet these countries, which view themselves as continental and vertical, are in reality *rhizomes with horizontal ramifications,* in Edouard Glissant's words (1990: 48) i.e., that their overseas segments, which might be out of sight—and too often out of mind—are actually integral parts of their national ensembles.

Keyword Globalisation · EEZ · Strategic assets · Maritime disputes · Sovereignty conflicts · International Court of Justice · Senkaku/Diaoyu · Paracel Islands/Xisha · Spratleys Islands/Nansha · Kuril Islands/Hoppo ryodo · Falkland/Malvinas

Offshore territories play a twofold role here: on the one hand, they extend the maritime domains of the countries that administer them; on the other, they have the *potential* to turn some of the latter into *archipelagic* States. In so doing, they act as levers of sovereignty that provide strategic depth beyond the mainland segments of national territories. The growing number of disputes over the delimitation of EEZs is ample proof of this. The challenge is not just to stretch maritime lines. It is also a matter of displaying multiple regional affiliations and maintaining neighbourly relations with other continental and island countries. The political narratives used by these nations to define and present themselves on the international stage do not always reflect these mixed identities. Yet these countries, which view themselves as continental and vertical, are in reality *rhizomes with horizontal ramifications*, in Edouard Glissant's words (1990: 48) i.e., that their overseas segments, which might be out of sight—and too often out of mind—are actually integral parts of their national ensembles.

Exclusive Economic Zone Multipliers

According to the United Nations Convention on the Law of the Sea (UNCLOS), EEZs are "maritime areas in which coastal States exercise sovereign and economic rights for the purpose of exploring and exploiting, conserving and managing the natural resources, whether living or non-living, of the waters subjacent to the seabed and of the seabed and its subsoil (...)" (article 56, 1982). The Montego Bay Convention—which came into force in 1994 and extends the sovereignty of coastal states to 200 and even 350 miles beyond territorial waters—sparked renewed interest in offshore territories, given their multiplier effect on EEZs. Here are a few striking examples. France, which boasts the world's second largest EEZ after the United States, owes it all to its overseas territories—which account for 97% of its surface area; i.e. 4,069,797 mi2 out of a total of 4,213,078 mi2. Without this considerable input, the

EEZ of mainland France would fall below 154,440 mi2. French Polynesia alone claims an EEZ of 1,842,127mi2—an area the size of Europe. Denmark, with the sixteenth largest EEZ in the world, is close on France's heels, with an almost identical multiplier. Its overseas territories account for 96.9% of its EEZ, i.e. 1,012,965 mi2 out of a total of 1,054,831 mi2. Without them, it would be just over 38,610 mi2. Greenland alone supplies 965,255 mi2, i.e. over two thirds. The Faroe Islands provide an additional 104,247 mi2.

Then comes the United Kingdom, in third global position. Its offshore territories represent 88% of its total surface area of 2,625,494 mi2. Without them, the UK's EEZ would total 298,843 mi2. South Georgia and the South Sandwich Islands cover 579,153 mi2, for a land area of about 1,544 mi2. The Pitcairn Islands bring in more than 308,881 mi2, despite a surface area of only 18.14 mi2. Portugal, whose EEZ is globally ranked twenty-first, ranks fourth in the world, according to that rationale. Its overseas territories account for 81% of the surface area of its EEZ. Out of a total of 503,630 mi2, the EEZ of mainland Portugal is just 95,338 mi2. The Azores provide nearly 291,554 mi2 while Madeira contributes about 145,776 mi2. New Zealand, which has the sixth largest EEZ in the world, takes the fifth place. Its offshore territories are worth 60% of its almost 2,040,874 mi2 EEZ—setting aside Ross' dependence on Antarctica. Without them, it would span about 1,020,436 mi2. The Cook Islands represent around 583,106 mi2 of a total 69,97 mi2—twice the size of Ethiopia. With 14,57 mi2 of land surface, the Kermadec Islands account for more than 145,776 mi2, which is similar to Zambia's surface area. The territories of Tokelau and Niue provide 87,466 mi2 each; the equivalent of the Commonwealth of the Bahamas. Including the Ross dependency, New Zealands EEZ would gain an additional 583,106 mi2.

These few examples provide tangible evidence of the exaggeration of some analyses claiming that globalisation had demonetized the very notion of territory. Not only do powerful countries continue to retain and maintain part of their past colonial empire; they also attempt to expand it by claiming what are sometimes but tiny dots on the world map. In some cases, this leads to bilateral political conflicts or legal disputes.

Sovereignty Conflicts and Maritime Disputes

The boundaries of these maritime areas are a source of conflict, which can sometimes threaten regional security. This is notably the case in the China Sea, where one of the most sensitive disputes pits the PRC against Japan over the *Senkaku* Islands (or *Diaoyu* in Mandarin) in its eastern sector. These uninhabited islets, barely 2.70mi2 in surface area and administered by Japan but also claimed by Taiwan, are crucial to the delimitation of each party's EEZ. Incorporated into the Japanese empire in 1895 during the Sino-Japanese war, the United States administered them for twenty years before handing them back to Japan in 1972. The PRC claimed sovereignty following the discovery of major hydrocarbon deposits, as well as considerable fishery resources. Its territorial claims became more pressing from the 2000s onwards, at a time when a significant proportion of the world's economic trade transited through the China Sea. In 2012, the city of Tokyo decided to acquire three of these previously privately-owned islands. The PRC, considering its rights infringed, extended its airspace over the *Senkaku*, where the Chinese coast guard had also been increasingly present. The United States supported its Japanese ally, while the PRC took counter-measures aimed at Japanese firms. Nationalist sentiments, on the rise on both sides, have led to a steady militarisation of this sovereignty issue. The PRC has officially listed the *Senkaku* as a strategic interest (along with Taiwan and Tibet) over which it is willing to use force. This determination on the part of China, which relies on the superiority of its navy, is equally relentless in disputes over the Paracel Islands (*Xisha* in Mandarin, *Hoang Sa* in Vietnamese) and the Spratly Islands (*Nansha* in Mandarin, *Truong Sa* in Vietnamese). These two archipelagos, which are no larger than 5.79 mi2 (in land area), comprise dozens of tiny islands and over two hundred islets and reefs covering 6,177.63 mi2 and 158,302 mi2 respectively. Like the *Senkaku*, they are located in an area that is ideal for fishing and where there is documented evidence of oil deposits. Under Chinese and then French sovereignty, occupied by Japan during World War II and then administered by the PRC until 1952; the Paracel Islands subsequently fell under South Vietnamese jurisdiction with the Chinese People's Army taking over in 1974. In 1976, the Republic of Vietnam vainly protested against this *coup de force*, but the United States preferred to pursue a policy of *rapprochement* with the PRC in order to contain Soviet influence. As a result, the Paracels remained in China's hands—unlike the

Spratly archipelago, which was divided between all the countries claiming sovereignty over them. The Philippines took possession of eight islands in the north of the archipelago, while three were transferred to Malaysia. Vietnam followed suit in stages until it controlled around twenty of them. The PRC occupied nine in the west and south-west before asserting its hold on the entire Spratly archipelago. Its displays of force (ranging from acts of intimidation to outright aggression) earned the disapproval of ASEAN, which repeatedly spoke out against the militarisation of the Spratly's. Bolstered by its military supremacy, the PRC is *illegally* building a "great wall of sand" in the archipelago, consisting of a network of seven military bases built on artificial islets reclaimed from the sea and fitted with modern airport infrastructure. In 2016, the Permanent Court of Arbitration (PCA), which the Philippines had appealed to, rejected China's requests to extend its EEZ. Nevertheless, the militarisation of the China Sea continues at a sustained pace. Other riparian countries are strengthening their arsenals and turning to the United States to help ensure freedom of navigation.

Another dispute, iconic both in terms of duration and stakes, opposes Russia and Japan. This long-standing quarrel revolves around the Kuril Islands (*Hoppo Ryodo* in Japanese), which stretch from the south of the Kamchatka peninsula to the north of Hokkaido Island, along a line that separates the Sea of Okhotsk from the Pacific Ocean. After sharing colonial control of the area in the eighteenth century, the two neighbouring countries battled for total sovereignty until the end of World War II, when the USSR occupied and annexed all four islands (*Habomaï, Shikotan, Kunashiri* and *Iturup*) which were then under Japanese jurisdiction. The bilateral dispute only involves these "northern territories", as they are known in Japan, which have since been administered by Russia under the name of "Southern Kurils". Japan does not challenge the fact that the other islands in this archipelago belong to Russia, but as a matter of principle it claims sovereignty over the islands to the north of its national territory, which were an integral part of its empire (along with half the island of Sakhalin) before its defeat in 1945. If both sides are showing such remarkable persistence in this territorial dispute, which holds no vital significance to either of them, it is because they regard it as a political, strategic and symbolic issue of far greater magnitude than the size of the territories (around 1,930 mi2) and populations involved (about 12,500). For Russia, it is primarily a matter of principle. Any compromise with Japan would set a precedent that could encourage other countries to follow suit. For Japan, it is a case of national pride. Restoring its territorial integrity would help to repair a historic "injustice" and atone for the "dishonour" of those of its nationals who were expelled at the time of Russian annexation. In both countries, the revival of nationalism is feeding an equal determination to reject any form of compromise. In a statement released on 17 October 2009, the Japanese authorities used the expression "illegal occupation" for the first time and firmly condemned it. On 1 November 2010, President Medvedev visited the Southern Kurils to reassert Russian sovereignty. This was followed by a phase marked by a large deployment of Russian military forces and the modernisation of the island's infrastructure. Japan raised the alert status of its "self-defence forces" positioned on the island of Hokkaido, and increased its naval resources. From Russia's perspective, the Kuril Archipelago is a major defence asset. It provides its ships and submarines based in Vladivostok with continuous access to the Pacific, as well as numerous locations to pre-position forces and equipment. Returning the disputed islands to a United States ally would undermine its national security. From Japan's angle, the presence of a Russian military arsenal to the north of its territory poses an open threat to its security, even if the possibility of Russian aggression seems unlikely. It is also a sensitive issue in domestic affairs, as Japanese public opinion is keen to see the islands return in the national fold. For the time being, the bilateral talks that are routinely held to discuss the subject have failed to yield any tangible solutions. As a result, the dispute continues to plague relations between the two countries (Lafrance 2021).

The same applies to the sovereignty conflict between the United Kingdom and Argentina over the Falklands, which has been going on for 150 years. Of all the disputes over offshore land, this is the only one to have caused a conventional war between two Western countries in the twentieth century. At first sight, such escalation of violence is puzzling: there are no strategic interests at stake for either of the parties involved in this long-running rift. Neither has a critical use for this archipelago of 5,019 mi2, made up of two main islands and countless islets, located in the South Atlantic some 250 mi from *Tierra del Fuego* and home to just three thousand people. With his usual flair, Jorge Borges once compared this rivalry to *"two bald men fighting over a comb"*. Nevertheless, this territorial row has deep historical roots. Argentina inherited the Falklands from Spain upon achieving independence in 1816, and administered them until 1833—at which point they were forcibly seized by the British navy. Since then, the United Kingdom has been exerting sovereignty over the Falklands; emphasising that most of the island's population is of British origin, with English as the primary language. The principle of *utis possidetis juris* (inviolability of borders) has been its ongoing diplomatic position. But Argentina has never given in to what it views as a "*fait accompli*", based on arguments that are both geographical and historical. The Falklands are part of a geological continuum with Patagonia, of which they are an extension. What is more, they were conquered by violence. For the British, it is up to the people of the Falklands to decide freely. For the Argentinians, it is a matter of decolonising an archipelago arbitrarily torn from the nation it has been historically attached to. The dispute came to a head in 1982 when General Galtieri decided to reclaim the archipelago by force in order to divert attention from his own political debacles at home. The Argentinian army invaded South Georgia and then the capital Port Stanley; war had been declared on the United Kingdom. In England, Margaret Thatcher's Conservative government was going through a difficult time. Her controversial economic reforms had made her very unpopular. With one year to go before the general election, the British Prime Minister made it a national cause. Public opinion approved of her decision to intervene militarily. The United Nations Security Council adopted an unsuccessful resolution demanding the withdrawal of Argentina's troops. Confrontation was inevitable. In two and a half months, the Royal Forces re-established the United Kingdom's sovereignty over the Falklands, at the cost of a thousand deaths. This British victory led to the Iron Lady's resounding re-election in 1983, while it triggered Argentina's transition to democracy with the election of Raúl Alfonsin. In addition, the Falklands granted the victor access to a major offshore oil field as well as a gateway to Antarctica. In 2010, drilling operations confirmed the extent of these oilfields and led to fresh tensions between the two protagonists. In 2013, the United Kingdom held a referendum on self-determination. Voters in the Falklands voted in favour of British citizenship. Argentina, which contested the legal validity of the referendum, continues its battle. More than forty years on, the Falklands War is hardly over (Lisinka 2019).

The Proliferation of Regional Affiliations

Overseas territories enable their administering countries to maintain cross-border relations with countries far away from their "mainland" base. This multiplier effect varies according to the number of offshore territories, their geographical location but also the narrative identity they intend to project on the international scene. This narrative serves to assert geopolitical interests, justify strategic partnerships and claim regional affiliations. Usually perceived as a European country, France as a state is actually much larger and more branched than it seems—because its overseas territories embed it in multiple regional geographies. French Guiana gives it a foothold in South America; the French Antilles make it a Caribbean Island State; and Saint-Pierre-et-Miquelon, a direct neighbour of Canada. The Scattered Islands embody its presence in the Mozambique Channel; while Reunion Island, Mayotte and the TAAF allow it to share an Indian Oceanic identity with Madagascar, Mauritius and Seychelles. While New Caledonia and the Kerguelen Islands offer a maritime border with Australia; French Polynesia and Wallis and Futuna make it a neighbour of New Zealand. The French strategy in the Indo-Pacific relies to unprecedented extents on this archipelagic scope. For a simple reason: "*It is its island territories in the Indian Ocean and the Pacific that make France an Indo-Pacific State and power. France is an island that basically maintains relations with other island States and territories.*" (Lechervy, 2019: 18). In contrast with its longtime preference for continental countries, France has been increasingly nurturing relations between Reunion Island and India, New Caledonia and Indonesia, Polynesia and Japan; as well as exchanges with small island States such as Mauritius or Vanuatu. In the Pacific; New Caledonia, Polynesia and Wallis and Futuna make it a Melanesian and Polynesian State, which strengthens its legitimacy in regional arenas—especially when it co-opts locally elected officials through its official delegations.

Like its French ally, the United Kingdom benefits from the multiplication of regional affiliations enabled by its fourteen offshore territories. Admittedly, their geographical locations show less diversity than their French counterparts, but they still provide the UK with a worldwide base. Far from limited to its European segment, the United Kingdom boasts land and sea borders that multiply its "mainland" sevenfold. It is established in the North Atlantic through Bermuda, with the United States as a neighbour; and in the South Atlantic where it borders Argentina via the Falkland Islands as well as South Georgia and the South Sandwich Islands. In the Caribbean, it holds border relations with a dozen independent States—including France, the Netherlands and a host of small island states—thanks to seven overseas territories. It is also present in the Indian Ocean where it controls the Chagos Archipelago, which shares a common border with the Maldives. In the Pacific, the UK's only base lies in the Pitcairn Islands, about 1,200 mi away from French Polynesia. Unlike France, the United Kingdom does not seem to emphasise its overseas territories in the political narrative that supports its self-representation onto the international stage. The exception being the Falklands War, which mirrored political issues that prevailed on a domestic level. This lack of emphasis results from the UK's rather loose ties with its offshore territories, which are not represented in the British Parliament while they continue to be subjected to the sovereign powers of Her Majesty's Government. It probably also reflects the overseas' marginal place within the Commonwealth, which spreads the UK's politics of influence across the world.

The United States does not value its overseas territories either, in the way it represents itself globally. Most US citizens are unaware of their existence or view them as foreign territories. And yet, they allow the US to share additional borders with several countries. In the Atlantic, the Gulf of Mexico and the Caribbean Sea, the world's leading power maintains neighbourly relations with several states such as Jamaica, the Dominican Republic and Cuba. Little known to the general public: the United States also shares a maritime border with Russia; in the Bering Strait that separates Siberia from Alaska. Big Diomede, which is administered by Russia, lies barely 2.5 miles away from Little Diomede, which is under US sovereignty. In the Pacific, the United States shares borders with Japan, the Federation of Micronesia and the Republic of Kiribati. However, the political narrative that supports its strategic shift towards the Pacific tends to highlight continental regions at the expense of small island states. From the United States' perspective, the main task at hand is to contain the rise of PRC. Against this geopolitical backdrop, the US administration has been seeking to consolidate its long-standing alliance with Japan and South Korea, while also trying to co-opt India and Indonesia.

Russia's position resembles that of the United States. It refuses to yield an inch based on the principle of territorial integrity—which its nationalist impulses can sometimes translate very creatively. Its self-image and representation onto the international scene, relies on Russia's imperial matrix.

With over 6 950 000 mi2, it is the world's largest state: doubly continental (Europe and Asia); bordered by the Arctic Ocean to the north; by Kazakhstan, Mongolia, China as well as North Korea to the south; and to the west, by several countries ranging from Norway to Azerbaijan. With extensive Arctic and Pacific coastlines, Russia is also a multi-archipelagic state that comprises several sets of islands distributed between these two oceans and the Baltic Sea. Novaya Zemlya, is as widespread as French Guiana and located between the Barents and Kara seas. New Siberia, which lies between the Laptev and East Siberian seas, is for the most part covered in ice. Sakhalin is the largest Russian island—while the Kurils extend to the north of the Japanese Empire. The reason this archipelagic scale is excluded from the political narrative, is probably that Russia views itself and continues to be widely viewed as a Eurasian continent. Nevertheless, it uses these offshore assets freely for military or economic purposes, depending on the circumstances and its national interests.

The PRC offers another full-fledged example of a nation that politically emphasises its mainland geography. With over three million eight hundred and sixty mi2, it counts fourteen land borders and a seafront of nearly 9,300 mi. To the north, it borders Mongolia and Russia. To the northeast, it shares boundaries with Russia and North Korea. To the east, it fronts the Yellow Sea and the East China Sea. In the south, it opens onto the South China Sea and shares borders with Laos, Vietnam, Burma, India, Bhutan and Nepal. To the west, it is bordered by Pakistan, Afghanistan and Tajikistan. Finally, in the north-west, its neighbours are Kyrgyzstan and Kazakhstan. It is also a multi-archipelagic state made up of nearly 160 island groups mainly located in the South China Sea - which the Asian giant sees as a matter of national security. Primarily for this reason, it has been monitoring them closely: from Wanshan which includes over a hundred islands, to Hainan, which is the largest (13,707 mi2) and most populated (nine million residents); from Sang Shuan and Xiachuan which are attached to the province of Guangdong, to Heng King, located in the delta of the Pearl River—not to mention Weizhou in the Gulf of Tonkin or Hong Kong and Macau, which have been reincorporated to the national territory. It leverages these island outposts to assert its regional supremacy and justify its territorial claims. The standoff with Taiwan, which it views as a rebellious province, is a measure of the PRC's determination to establish its pre-eminence in the South China Sea. From its standpoint, reunification matters in two particular respects: in domestic affairs, it would epitomise the PRC's renewed unity; in global affairs, it would symbolise a victory over the United States. For now, it is an island of 13,513 mi2 that has come to crystallise Sino-American tensions in Asia (Niquet, 2022).

Conclusion

This chapter further illustrates the contrast between the OTs' contributions to their administering countries' international standing, and their invisibility in the official representation of the latter. It showed the extent to which they provide assets in terms of EEZ to the point of inducing sovereignty conflicts between states seeking to retain or expand such domains. In the same line, it examined the ways in which OTs enable their metropolitan powers to maintain bilateral relations with countries far away from their mainland base. Finally, it calls for a reconsideration of the morphology of these postcolonial states, whose territories are sometimes so ramified and reticulated that they embody Immerwahr's concept of a "pointillist empire" (2019: 18).

CHAPTER 6

Security/Defence Assets

Abstract From the beginning to the present day, the overseas territories have had an unwavering military assignment. That assignment finds new impetus in contemporary geopolitical shifts that are redefining its terms. From the Sino-American competition for global leadership to Russia's manoeuvres to get the lead; from NATO's uncertain future to the US strategic Pivot to the Indo-Pacific; these shifts—coupled with the metamorphosis of transnational threats (including cybercrime and asymmetric wars)—have led nations to adjust the overseas' roles in national defence and security strategies. Depending on their geographical location and the goals targeted, their assignments fall into four main sectors: the pre-positioning and dispatch of conventional forces; nuclear deterrence; space defence and cyber defence. In all critical regions of the world, overseas territories are home to power display platforms. The strategic transformations underway in the Indo-Pacific are pushing the countries in charge of their administration to strengthen their military capabilities in order to prevent the risk of a potential rift in regional balances. For instance, the US Naval Air Bases at Guam and Diego Garcia are being upgraded while the military facilities in Puerto Rico and Vieques are being dismantled. Due to this strategic shift to the Indo-Pacific zone, some overseas territories are gaining value while others in the Atlantic and the Caribbean are losing some.

© The Author(s), under exclusive license to Springer Nature Switzerland AG 2024
F. Constant, *Overseas Territories in World Affairs*,
https://doi.org/10.1007/978-3-031-64233-3_6

Keywords Security and defence assets · Offshore military platforms · Asia Rebalance · Strategic revaluation and devaluation of overseas territories · Pacific Deterrence Initiative · Space Defense and Cyber Defense · Guam · Diego Garcia · Novara Zemlya · Mururoa and Fangataufa · Hawaii · Guiana Space Center · Wenchang Space Center

From the beginning to the present day, the overseas territories have had an unwavering military assignment. That assignment finds new impetus in contemporary geopolitical shifts that are redefining its terms. From the Sino-American competition for global leadership to Russia's manoeuvres to get the lead; from NATO's uncertain future to the US strategic Pivot to the Indo-Pacific; these shifts—coupled with the metamorphosis of transnational threats (including cybercrime and asymmetric wars)—have led nations to adjust the overseas' roles in national defence and security strategies. Depending on their geographical location and the goals targeted, their assignments fall into four main sectors: the pre-positioning and dispatch of conventional forces; nuclear deterrence; space defence and cyber defence.

PRE-POSITIONING AND DISPLAY OF CONVENTIONAL FORCES

In all critical regions of the world, overseas territories are home to power display platforms. Their effectiveness relies on their prepositioning as close as possible to the tensions navigating them. The strategic transformations underway in the Indo-Pacific are pushing the countries in charge of their administration to strengthen their military capabilities in order to prevent the risk of a potential rift in regional balances. The strategic rebalance strategy (*Asia Rebalance*) endorsed by President Obama's successors in the White House, involves a relative reclassification of the US overseas territories: the Indo-Pacific ones have been gaining value while those in the Atlantic and the Caribbean have been losing some. The military facilities in Puerto Rico and Vieques were gradually dismantled as part of a downgrading of the United States Southern Command's capabilities. Conversely, the Naval Air Bases at Guam and Diego Garcia were upgraded due to the rise of the United States Indo-Pacific Command. Because it hosts all three-army corps (air, sea and land) as well as intelligence, special operations and cyber defence, this command—headquartered in Hawaii is now the largest in the United States. With a jurisdiction of some forty countries including China, India and Indonesia, it manages 375,000 military and civilian personnel stationed in allied countries and US overseas territories. Guam and Diego Garcia are its primary hubs, given their geographical location and offshore status. They both allow US and British authorities to operate freely. Designated as *"tip of the Spear"* by the Department of Defense, Guam is home to a joint base that combines naval air forces with a logistics hub in support of regional operations. It boasts considerable storage capacity (for ammunition and fuel) and a sophisticated intelligence, surveillance and reconnaissance system. It is also the home port of several units such as Submarine Squadron 15, the Pacific fleet, a squadron of F.22 stealth fighter jets, or the Navy's special forces. It also has a very sophisticated communication system (Advanced Battle Management System) that optimises the deployment of available resources by instantaneously processing the movement of enemy forces. In 2018, Guam was for the first time the cornerstone of a joint exercise (air, sea, land) involving Japanese and Indian forces with the aim of increasing their interoperability; i.e. their ability to conduct joint operations. The Biden administration's Pacific Deterrence Initiative plans to increase its capacity by 2025. The island's military complex will be equipped with new cruise missiles, short-range ballistic missiles and glide bombs. Its personnel will double with the repatriation of 5,000 Marines stationed in Okinawa (Japan), to be accommodated in new facilities (Camp Blatz) adjacent to the main base of Andersen. In many ways, Diego Garcia is technically equivalent, in the Indian Ocean, to Guam in the Pacific Ocean. The United States' main strategic and logistical support base, this atoll under British sovereignty—leased by the United Kingdom to its US ally—enjoys a prime location within striking distance of all vital lines of communication (primarily the maritime routes of world trade), all maritime choke points (including the Straits of Hormuz, Malacca and Bab el-Mandeb), as well as Chinese military bases in the area (in particular, Djibouti, Pakistan, Sri Lanka and Myanmar). It hosts extensive logistical support infrastructure for the US and British military commands that operate it jointly. Its operational relevance was successfully tested in several regional arenas: during the Iranian (or Islamic) Revolution in 1979, the Gulf War in 1990 and the War in Afghanistan, in 2001. With China's incremental presence in the Indo-Pacific and rising tensions on the Sino-Indian frontier, its strategic value continues to be appreciated.

In the Indian Ocean, where it has no overseas territory, the PRC has been relying on a military base built in Djibouti in 2016, near the Bab el-Mandeb Strait that connects the Red Sea to the Gulf of Aden. It is supposedly building another one in Pakistan as an extension of the port of Gwadar, near the border with Iran. Its massive investments in communication infrastructure in several bordering countries grant it additional support to ensure close monitoring of a maritime space used to ship its supplies of raw materials (oil and mineral resources) and exports of consumer goods to Europe. For the time being, it allegedly does not want to turn them into military outposts but the possibility cannot be ruled out, given its financial grip on some of them and its strategic rivalry with the US powerhouse. The Chinese navy has been increasingly venturing into the western part of the Indian Ocean, just to prevent the US from monopolising the protection of sea lines of communication. Its top priority, however, remains the Western Pacific and the South China Sea. The construction of a "Great Wall of Sand" on artificial islets, is intended to protect the southern part of its mainland geography. In the Paracels archipelago, four airport bases were built on rights-of-way reclaimed from the sea. In the Spratly Islands, four more have emerged from the backfill of usually submerged reefs. This defence system locks all sea access to the underground base of *Yulin*, on the island of *Hainan*; home port of about twenty nuclear submarines. It allows the PRC to display the almightiness of its naval and air forces and thereby to deter riparian countries from disputing its supremacy across the China Sea. Paradoxically, the credibility of these forces rests on their prepositioning on tiny land-based support facilities, partly reclaimed from the sea. Once again, the determination of the Chinese authorities to keep or even expand the surface area of these micro-territories underlines all their political and military added value.

The only member state of the European Union to enjoy permanent presence in the region, France relies on its overseas territories in the Indo-Pacific to position itself as a riparian power. These OTs are home to over a million and a half of its citizens, and three-quarters of its EEZ. It keeps a permanent military presence to fulfil its duties as an administering power; and contributes to regional security along with its allies. The defence strategy it adopted in 2019 pursues four objectives that take stock of the evolution of ongoing geopolitical dynamics: the protection of its peoples, island territories and economic interests; the development of military cooperation to secure regional arenas; maintaining free access to shared maritime spaces and preserving political stability through the promotion of multilateralism. Their implementation relies mainly on those of its offshore territories which are distributed in the two oceans, and multiply its operational capacities. France counts five military commands: the armed forces of the Southern Indian Ocean Zone (FAZSOI) which are based in Reunion Island and Mayotte; the armed forces of New Caledonia (FANC) stationed in Nouméa and the armed forces in French Polynesia (FAPF) located in Papeete. These joint regional commands, which total seven thousand personnel distributed in various regiments and operational units, are equipped with land, naval and air assets. These dedicated resources are provided by French Forces in the UAE (FFEAU) as well as those stationed in Djibouti (FFDj)—but there is a discrepancy with the missions assigned, that could jeopardise the State's actual capacity to properly fulfil its sovereign duties. To remedy this situation, the military programming law (2019–2025) plans to strengthen the facilities and manpower of those sovereignty forces, with the commissioning of six additional patrol boats in New Caledonia, Polynesia and Reunion Island, added to the dispatch of new human resources by 2024. This capacity upgrade responds to pressing domestic policy issues (protection of the populations and the fight against illegal trafficking; monitoring of the EEZ) and to the exponential growth—and associated requirements—of bilateral cooperation with India, Japan, New Zealand and Australia, as well as with Mauritius or Seychelles. Similarly, the overseas territories are irreplaceable as logistical bases to be used for the implementation of the joint exercises scheduled each year.

AT THE FOREFRONT OF NUCLEAR DETERRENCE

Since the advent of the nuclear age, overseas territories have been deeply involved with atomic weapons. With the exception of the PRC, which conducts all testing from its mainland base at Lob Nor, all permanent members of the United Nations Security Council have been using their overseas territories to build, test and preposition their nuclear arsenals. Sites that, on paper, seemed unlikely for such tests—given their small size or geographical location—thus became places where a technology of mass destruction, unprecedented in the history of mankind, would take shape and develop at full scale. In the eyes of nuclear-weapon states, these offshore territories provide ideal conditions to lead the experiments required to develop atomic bombs, and to prove their effectiveness. Perfectly isolated in the vast ocean, far from the most densely populated areas; these enclaves ruled by special statutes offer greater flexibility to lead such experiments. In the aftermath of World War II, the United States, the USSR, the United Kingdom and France all conducted hundreds of nuclear tests outside their mainland territories. Each of these powers carried out atmospheric, underwater, extra-atmospheric or underground testing. They had no restriction to test either type of bomb—A (atomic fission) and H (hydrogen fusion)—or a variety of explosion methods—thereby dropping bombs from aircrafts, boats or using balloons. The United States initiated this test cycle with a bang; with more than a hundred tests conducted on dozens of South Pacific atolls turned into shooting ranges—after their residents had been transferred to other atolls. From 1946 to 1958, the Marshall Islands, then placed under its administration by the United Nations, was the stage of sixty-seven US launches. The first post-war nuclear test took place on Bikini Atoll on 1st July 1946, releasing significantly more energy than the atomic bombs dropped on Hiroshima and Nagasaki in August 1944. Its purpose was to assess the effects of the explosion on a hundred "guinea pig" ships, and to show the USSR clear evidence of the US' supremacy in terms of nuclear capabilities. In 1952, it was the Enewetak Atoll's turn to stand in the spotlight of international news. It hosted two world premieres within a fortnight, consisting of the successful testing of both the hydrogen bomb and the most powerful atomic bomb of the time. In 1954, Bikini Atoll returned to the main stage with the launch of the most powerful thermonuclear bomb the United States had ever tested; producing an unprecedented yield of fifteen megatons. In the North Pacific, dozens more bombs were launched from the Johnston and Kiritimati atolls before technological progress led U.S. administrations to focus on the Nevada nuclear test site—until the end of all nuclear testing in 1992. However, the real front line of nuclear confrontation lies in overseas territories and naval bases. They are home to hundreds of nuclear weapons, pre-positioned as close as possible to potential conflict zones in order to leverage the tactical capabilities of US forces. Their spread goes to deter any and all attacks on the contiguous United States because of the many "second strike" opportunities they offer—i.e., retaliation from its offshore bases. The safeguarding of the US mainland, however, comes at a high cost for some overseas territories that have become designated targets for their Communist foe's missiles; while others face irreversible health and environmental scandals induced by radioactive fallout and the storage of nuclear waste.

Between 1949 and 1990, the USSR—the United States' main rival at the time—carried out nearly seven hundred tests between its mainland station of Semipalatinsk in Kazakhstan, and its offshore platform of Novaya Zemlya in the Arctic Ocean. The Soviet authorities launched ninety missiles on this two-island overseas territory, from three sites built on rights-of-way vacated by their former residents. According to a report by the French parliament that was published in 2001, these tests total a 240-megaton load, accounting for 97% of the energy released by the Soviets' atmospheric testing. They strove to achieve a technological advance on the United States that would upset the balance of terror. To this end, Nikita Khrushchev launched a vast program of research in nuclear physics that led to the birth of the Tsar Bomba, tested on 30 October 1961 in Novaya Zemlya. With this test of unprecedented power, began a period of peaceful coexistence with the United States until the Soviet invasion of Afghanistan, which revived the arms race. Novaya Zemlya was once again the stage of atmospheric nuclear testing, until Mikhail Gorbachev's rise to power. In line with the *Glasnost* policy, he then favoured underground testing until those came to a permanent stop in October 1990. As a result, the firing range in Novaya Zemlya was partially decommissioned. Radioactive contamination and storage of nuclear waste remained unresolved issues as the Russian Federation gradually emerged from the late Soviet empire. To this day, Novaya Zemlya continues to be a critical link in Russia's military structure. As part of a network that includes the Murmansk naval bases and the ones located in the Franz Josef Archipelago, it ranks among the home ports of the Northern Fleet—which includes surface ships, nuclear submarines and strategic bombers.

The British also leveraged some of their offshore territories to fine-tune their atomic weapon. Atmospheric testing took place in Oceania; in the Montebello archipelago and then atolls of the Kiribati Islands, then under British administration. In 1957, the Kiritimati Atoll, shared with the United States and also known as Christmas Island, hosted the very first test-launch of an English-made thermonuclear bomb. About thirty other launches would take place as well on Malden Island, until 1962. From then on, the British government chose to focus on underground tests that were carried out at the Nevada site, thanks to a cooperation agreement with the United States. Again, the end of that testing cycle failed to give way to the adequate sanitation of launch sites and proper care for local employees suffering from radiation-induced diseases. After the independence of Kiribati in 1979, veterans' associations filed unsuccessful lawsuits against the UK government.

France, in turn, became a nuclear-weapon state in 1960 after successfully firing its first atomic bomb in the Algerian Sahara. The credibility of its deterrence doctrine owes much to French Polynesia, where it built its nuclear experimentation centre (i.e. the Pacific Test Centre—CEP) *ex nihilo*. Its headquarters are located in Papeete. The two firing ranges were established on the atolls of Mururoa and Fangataufa in the Tuamotu archipelago, more than six hundred miles from Papeete. An airbase was also built on Hao Atoll, upstream of Mururoa. But the CEP literally turned local communities upside down. It created a shock with both positive and negative effects. Hundreds of soldiers, engineers, technicians and their families flew from France to Papeete—where thousands of Polynesians also flocked in search of jobs. But little information transpired about CEP activities—even among locally elected officials. Between 1966 and 1974, forty-six atmospheric tests were carried out from the two launch sites of Mururoa and Fangataufa. The measures taken to protect the population were notoriously lacking. The first test involved an A-bomb that detonated over the Mururoa atoll. The most spectacular one was an H-bomb, tested for the first time on the Fangataufa atoll. And the last ion the list consisted of the airdrop of a tactical nuclear bomb. These highly toxic aerial tests raised local and national protests as well as international disapproval from Australia, New Zealand and Japan. During Valéry Giscard d'Estaing's term as President, the testing continued underground to avoid atmospheric fallout. On one hundred and forty-seven occasions, bombs exploded in wells dug under the atolls of Mururoa and Fangataufa. While these bombs were indeed less powerful energy-wise, radioactive gases continued to contaminate the lagoon. Along with the aforementioned Pacific countries, NGOs like *Greenpeace*, among others, stood up against the continuation of nuclear testing. An international treaty was signed by a dozen riparian states in 1985 in Rarotonga, to establish the South Pacific as a nuclear-free zone. The testing went on, however, until 1992 when François Mitterrand declared a three-year moratorium. His successor, Jacques Chirac, put an end to it in 1995 and launched a final testing campaign that sparked a worldwide outcry. In 1998, the French parliament ratified the Comprehensive Nuclear-Test-Ban Treaty (CTBT) and the CEP was gradually dismantled. Presidents Sarkozy and

Hollande quantitatively reduced the nation's nuclear deterrent, but reinforced its two strategic components: air and submarine forces. Motivated by budgetary considerations, this downgrading of operational vectors has eroded the capabilities of sovereignty forces pre-positioned overseas. The French military programming law (2019–2025) is supposed to remedy this—as in other sectors where the French defence has yet to rise up to the level of new potential threats.

Space and Cyber Defence

Overseas territories are involved, to varying extents, in the space and cyber defence of the countries that administer them. From surveillance to safeguarding military satellites, from the prevention of cyber-attacks to the protection of information systems deemed essential; some of them are used to ensure stability and security in outer and cyber space. There is a sharp contrast between the situations of those boasting world-class critical infrastructure, and those of others; mere cogs in national defence mechanisms. France stands out in this regard: the French Guiana Space Centre (CSG) went from serving as a national launch base, to becoming Europe's spaceport and a renowned platform for launching international satellites into orbit. In this sector characterised by very high added value and major geopolitical stakes, it is an overseas territory that epitomises French and European strategic autonomy. In fact, the Kourou site features several comparative advantages. Due to its latitude, which is very close to the equator, launches enjoy additional speed thanks to the Earth's rotation. This is a physical factor that makes it possible to increase the launchers' payload and to proportionally lower fuel costs. The Kourou firing base yields 27% more than Cape Canaveral's (USA) and 55% higher than Baikonur's (Russia). Its coastal location enables launches to the Atlantic Ocean without overflight of inhabited areas; in addition to the stationing of satellites in geostationary orbits (i.e. eastward launch) and polar orbits (northward launch). As well, French Guiana displays very favourable geological and weather conditions. Sheltered from cyclone trajectories in an area with a low seismic risk, it benefits from a favourable topography and natural hills that facilitate the required post-launch surveys. Since Ariane 1's maiden flight in 1979, the CSG has launched hundreds of civilian and military satellites into orbit. No other power depends this much on an offshore territory for both its space and cyber defence—given the close relationship between digital and satellite technologies.

PRC, which took the lead in space launches in 2021 with a total count 55 shots higher than the United States', has four launch bases located on its mainland—with the exception of Wenchang, on the island of Hainan. This location—best known in China for its tropical climate and the seaside resorts favoured by the jewels of national middle classes—was chosen because of its proximity to the equator, which optimises the loads placed in geostationary orbit. Officially, it is the home port of the Chinese launchers of the "Long March" series, whose purpose is twofold: ultimately taking over from the other space ports used to launch telecommunications satellites; and routing the modules of the manned space program. Each year, at the rate of three to four launches, it places a dozen satellites in orbit for supposedly civilian applications. In fact, launchers also carry satellites that are used to monitor and intercept communications. The Wenchang spaceport is connected to two tracking and control stations located at the tip of Hainan Island, and in the Paracel archipelago. Their mission is to continuously compute the spatial coordinates of satellites and to orient the terrestrial antennas in charge of picking up sensitive signals. The data collected is then used by the Ministry of State Security (MSE) in liaison with the intelligence services of the People's Army, which hold a branch in this offshore territory. Clearly, that branch monitors the activities of riparian countries in the South China Sea that have been challenging the regional hegemony of the People's Republic of China—in particular its control over several reefs and islets turned into military bases. To fulfil this mission, it leads cyber-espionage operations aimed at collecting intelligence on their neighbours' intentions, thwarting their initiatives and launching counter-offensives in cyberspace if necessary. In July 2021, the Japanese authorities condemned cyber-attacks against several of their military entities, carried out by an organisation called APT 40 and operating on behalf of the PRC. Likewise, the Wenchang launch base is involved in the satellite warfare that has been escalating in space since the 2000s. The Chinese military has acquired the ability to send programmed satellites into orbit from the ground in order to approach other satellites for intelligence and surveillance purposes. Some of these programmed satellites can scramble others' signals or make them inoperative.

To deal with these threats, President Donald Trump created a "Space Force" in 2018, to ensure US supremacy on this new battlefield. To this end, two commands were respectively put in charge of satellite surveillance, cyberspace protection and offensive digital operations. Their headquarters are located in mainland states, but they rely on a web of offshore bases. The Space Command holds two in Hawaii and one in Greenland, for the remote monitoring and control of satellites in orbit. During his visit to Colorado in November 2021, the POTUS' Chief of Staff stressed the need to adjust the United States' space defence strategy, considering the proliferation of threats to national and NATO military satellites. When it comes to cyber defence, military bases overseas are home to branches responsible for monitoring computer networks and preventing cyber-attacks. These branches are linked to the national command, which can dispatch expert teams on site if need be. For instance, the Guam military facilities host several digital switches using various technologies, to secure the routing of communications between the several U.S. military bases in the Indo-Pacific and towards mainland command centres. In spite of this fleshed out device, US spatial and digital sovereignty is quite relative. Russia, which is among the five most active powers in this sector of defence, is capable of sending anti-satellite weapons into orbit that have the capacity to paralyse or destroy other satellites. Its space force includes several mainland-based units, which interact with the country's four space ports. Two can be found in Russia and the other two in Kazakhstan—including the most famous one in Baikonur. However, several offshore military bases are home to branches of these space forces—especially in the Arctic where they are established in former Soviet rights-of-way in Novaya Zemlya, New Siberia and the Franz Josef archipelago. Since its beginning in 2022, Russia's economy has grown ever more structured around the war in Ukraine. Despite international sanctions, the nation's budget has proven resilient enough to invest massively into its military apparatus, including Cyber defence where it already holds a strong position.

Conclusion

This chapter has outlined the many ways in which the administering countries use their OTs as military outposts, according to their respective strategic doctrine. It showed that the metropolitan powers, especially the permanent members of the UNSC, would not have had the same surveillance and response capacity if they did not exercise their sovereignty over these jurisdictions scattered all over the planet. When it comes to security and defence, these out-of-sight dots on the map suddenly take on prime importance. Some even find themselves at the forefront of the Sino-American competition for global leadership. Others are becoming new vehicles in the wars of influence waged by nations in the international arena.

CHAPTER 7

Vectors of Influence and Prestige

Abstract Levers of maritime power and sovereignty, assets to security/defence systems; the overseas territories are also vectors of influence and prestige in three main areas: economy, ecology and culture. In this age of globalisation, economic competition—which is inherent in geopolitical rivalries—is becoming ever more salient; while environmental and sustainable development themes are gradually taking their seat at the table of international relations. For instance, the Russian Island of Sakhalin is home to one of the world's largest offshore deposits of combined hydrocarbons (gas and oil). So is potentially Greenland/Kalaallit Nunaat to Denmark's oil and gas industry. Hong Kong is one the leading global players in offshore banking. Other overseas territories have exceptional geoenvironmental resources such as Madeira's primary forest of the Laurisilva, French Guiana's national park or the archipelago of New Siberia. At the same time, culture has grown into both an instrument and one of the stakes involved in the symbolic struggles opposing nations in the field of soft power. Ironically, it was the political struggles they provoked in some overseas territories that forced public protection policies onto the agenda—sometimes leading to international consecrations; such as the Easter Island National Park. Here again, the overseas territories stand at the forefront in each of these areas.

Keywords Geoeconomic resources · Sakhalin · Greenland/Kalaallit Nunaat · Hong Kong · Cayman Islands · Geoenvironmental resources ·

© The Author(s), under exclusive license to Springer Nature Switzerland AG 2024
F. Constant, *Overseas Territories in World Affairs*,
https://doi.org/10.1007/978-3-031-64233-3_7

Green diplomacy · Madeira · French Guiana · New Siberia · Geocultural resources · Cultural diplomacy · Identity politics · Easter Island · Canary Islands · Curaçao

Levers of maritime power and sovereignty, assets to security/defence systems; the overseas territories are also vectors of influence and prestige in three main areas: economy, ecology and culture. In this age of globalisation, economic competition—which is inherent in geopolitical rivalries—is becoming ever more salient; while environmental and sustainable development themes are gradually taking their seat at the table of international relations. At the same time, culture has grown into both an instrument and one of the stakes involved in the symbolic struggles opposing nations in the field of soft power. Again, the overseas territories stand at the forefront in each of these areas.

SIGNIFICANT GEO-ECONOMIC RESOURCES

While many overseas territories depend on the financial support of the states to which they are attached, others provide them with extremely attractive returns on investment. The Russian Island of Sakhalin is one emblematic example. This wide and inhospitable territory along the Siberian coast is home to one of the world's largest offshore deposits of combined hydrocarbons (gas and oil). It is exploited by several consortia of international operators that have invested, as a whole, a total of some forty billion US dollars. Reserves are estimated at forty-five billion in oil equivalent—which is equal to those in the North Sea. The Sakhalin I project began in 1996 with the creation of a consortium of US, Russian and Japanese energy groups (Exxon Mobil Corp., Sodeko, RGC). Despite very restrictive operating conditions, the conglomerate produces oil and gas in three fields (Chayvo, Odoptu and Arkutun-Dagi) located in the northwest of the island. An underwater pipeline connects the platforms to the mainland where the gas is then transported towards Asian markets. In 1998, Sakhalin II was inaugurated by the Russian authorities who forced their national champion Gazprom onto Anglo-Saxon and Japanese majors (Shell, Mitsui, Mitsubishi). This second project was broader in scope. The deposit is colossal: more than a thousand million barrels of crude oil and five hundred million cubic metres of natural gas. In 2009, Sakhalin III further expanded the exploitation of these gigantic hydrocarbon reserves sheltered by the jewel of all Russian overseas territories. Vladimir Putin arbitrated the round table between domestic investors (Rosneft) as well as Chinese (Sinopec) and Anglo-Saxon (Chevron, Exxon, Shell) stakeholders. Since then, Russian authorities have periodically released new blocks on the international market, and have been granting exploration and exploitation licences to international operators. Sakhalin IV and Sakhalin V are on track but the war in Ukraine has temporarily deprived their promoters of funding from Western companies. In addition, Exxon Mobil Corp. issued force majeure in Mid-2022 and abandoned the Sakhalin I offshore project due to Western sanctions. The Russian authorities retaliated by blocking and sometimes seizing foreign investors' assets, but the oil production collapsed. A new entity was established, rallying an Indian operator (ONGC Videsh) and a consortium of Japanese firms under the stewardship of Russian champion Rosneft. About one year after Exxon Mobil Corp.'s withdrawal, the oil output of the Sakhalin-1 project had recovered about 65% of its capacity and has since returned to full production levels (Tan, Valle 2022). Given the strong global demand for hydrocarbons, this Sakhalin project remains pivotal for the flagship industry of the Russian economy.

Mutatis mutandis, Greenland/*Kalaallit Nunaat* could become one day to Denmark's oil and gas industry what Sakhalin is already to the Russian one. Though at this stage, its mineral and energy resources are but a promise on the horizon, global warming will soon allow for their full exploitation. They show outstanding diversity. In addition to 15% of the world's oil and 30% of its gas, they comprise iron, lead, zinc, nickel, uranium, gold, platinum, diamonds and rubies. In the south of the island, an exceptional deposit of rare earths has also been discovered, which is estimated to contain up to a quarter of the world's reserves. Paradoxically, the ice melt is a source of opportunity for this widespread territory, both underpopulated and heavily dependent financially on Denmark and the European Union. At that pace, it will also open a new sea route across the Arctic that will connect the Atlantic to the Pacific. These prospects, which further enhance its geopolitical value, have not failed to attract the attention of global powers. During his term in office, President Trump repeatedly mentioned his interest in this Danish overseas territory, and even offered to buy it as if it were a simple real estate transaction. He had two motives to do so: terminating China's global supremacy over rare earths and discouraging Russia from overtaking Greenland's precious minerals. So far, dozens of exploration and exploitation licences granted by the Greenlandic authorities have yet to transform a territory that remains largely dependent on the fishing industry. On the other hand, they have irrevocably forced it into a global economy hungry for hydrocarbons and raw materials—exposing it to the instability of their pricing and subjecting it to complex equations, at the crossroads of environmental preservation and local development. In 2021, the Greenlandic government decided to suspend a strategy of searching for oil and stopped granting exploration licences. According to Naaja Nathanielsen, Minister for natural resources, *"it is a decision where climate considerations, environmental considerations and economic common sense go hand in hand."*[1]

Nevertheless, there are four active exploration and exploitation licences left up to 2027 and 2028: three onshore in Jameson Land, on the east coast; and one offshore in the southwest part of the island.

These aspirations, which are hard to reconcile, also apply to New Caledonia where "King Nickel" is still the epicentre of an industry that put it on the map. With 25% of the world's resources (estimated from an extrapolation of geological data) and 12% of global reserves (based on known and probed deposits); it is the fifth largest producer on the planet—after Indonesia, the Philippines, Russia and Canada. Flagship of the island, the Doniambo polymetallic plant operated by *Société Le Nickel* (SNL)—a subsidiary of the Eramet group—owns 75% of all local mining reserves. In the wake of the Matignon agreements followed by the Nouméa Accord which put an end to the socio-political unrest of the eighties, the French authorities strove to promote the economic growth of those provinces still on the margins of development. Two other world-class factories were established: *Société Minière du Sud Pacifique* (SMSP) in 2010 and Koniambo Nickel SAS in 2014. SMSP joined forces with the Korean group POSCO, a world leader in stainless steel. This investment ensures not only a commercial outlet for the New Caledonian green ore, but also its transformation into ferronickel for the Asia-Pacific market. However, volatile nickel prices and competition from lower-cost Asian producers, have been pushing New Caledonias mining sector to constantly adapt. In 2022, the war in Ukraine—which caused a dramatic rise in the price of a ton of metal—challenged its capacity to increase production in order to meet an

---

[1] Quotation in "Greenland Ends Unsuccessful 50 years-bid to Produce Oil", *Reuters*, July 16, 2021.

exponential global demand. From that perspective, new investments are needed that will require fundraising efforts on international markets. To date, these efforts have been unsuccessful. The on-going deterioration of the economic performances of the three existing plants and the risks of a further deterioration in the social climate, prompted the French government to coordinate a rescue plan for the nickel sector. This ten-year plan (2024–2034), rising against a tense political backdrop,[2] involves the State, industry operators and the local public authorities. Given the significance of the nickel sector in the island economy, the stakes are high politically and socially as it permeates the daily lives of thousands of Caledonians.

Another economic pillar is the very lucrative offshore finance sector, in which several overseas territories stand out. Hong Kong is the leader of that very selective club. Controlled by the Chinese Communist Party which quickly took stock of its pivotal importance, the former British colony continues to stockpile record-breaking stats. As of 2020, it was the world's fifth-largest market capitalisation and the third-largest financial centre in Asia, after Shanghai and Tokyo. In eleven years, it has ranked seven times as the world's number one for initial stock market introductions. In 2019, it rose to the third place in the global market for interest rate derivatives—after the United States and the United Kingdom, but ahead of Japan, Canada and France. In 2020, it was on Switzerland's tail in the management of private fortunes and patrimonies. The only centre in charge of managing stock market connections with Shanghai and Shenzhen, it remains Asia's undisputed leader in asset management. The world's largest Chinese companies have headquarters, investments and stock market quotes in Hong Kong. The communist government uses holding companies as outlets for its massive liquidity. Chinese billionaires recycle their profits and corporate shell companies invest huge sums of money to escape taxation. Like Hong Kong, other overseas countries have gained international recognition in offshore finance. The best-known are British. They can be found in the English Channel—Jersey, Guernsey— and in the Caribbean—Bermuda, the Cayman Islands, the Virgin Islands. Their economies are officially based on tax optimisation but they feed into tax evasion and/or money laundering schemes. These tax havens thus channel billions of dollars entrusted to them by international companies and large fortunes, in exchange for guaranteed tax exemption, the

[2] See more in Chapter 8.

anonymity of transactions and high returns. Since its creation in 2013, the International Consortium of Investigative Journalists (ICIJ) has exposed their mechanisms thanks to the leak of confidential documents. The China Leaks in 2014, the Panama Papers in 2016, the Paradise Papers in 2017 thoroughly document the worldwide spread of these illegal tax evasion practices. Queen Elizabeth II and her successor King Charles III hold assets in Bermuda and the Cayman Islands while Chinese Communist Party dignitaries and relatives of President Xi Jinping hold capital in the British Virgin Islands. According to economist Gabriel Zucman, tax optimization of large corporations and global fortunes is causing the world's nations to lose three hundred and fifty billion euros a year—which is equivalent to the Philippines' GDP. In *The Hidden Wealth of Nations* (2015), he unravels the mechanism of tax secrecy and evasion over the past century—as an illegal activity that has never been as lucrative as it is today—and suggests sound measures to put an end to it. Paradoxically, nations seem comfortable with that state of affairs—just like the administering countries that have endowed these offshore jurisdictions with ad hoc legislation that makes tax optimisation perfectly legal.

Part of this large-scale evasion of taxes permeates the tourism industry, which is another vector of international influence offered by overseas territories. All models are represented in that field: from mass tourism in the Canary or Balearic Islands; to the more exclusive approach embraced in French Polynesia or Hawaiinot to mention the halfway models found in Madeira, Curacao or Macau. The third largest tourist destination in the world, Spain receives an average of seventy-five million visitors each year. The Balearic and the Canary Islands alone host nearly 30 million of those—which is more than Catalonia. In the Balearic Islands, tourism accounts for 80% of the local GDP. It generates about eighteen billion euros a year. Over half of the population depends on it—directly or indirectly. The archipelago ranks second among Spain's tourism regions, followed by the Canary Islands where the sector is also the mainstay of the economy. Though its spectacular rise has transformed the lives of islanders, it has also sparked some backlash due to excessive tourist flows. French Polynesia and the Hawaiian Islands, which favour luxury tourism, attract a smaller clientele—but one with high purchasing power. Firmly committed to protecting the environment, their hotels occupy the market's top segment, with a product that promotes local cultures. In both archipelagos, tourism accounts for a predominant share of GDP— but it generates four times more income in Hawaii than in French

Polynesia, which is hampered by a less competitive offering. Far from affecting its economic performance, Macau's return to the PRC has, on the contrary, bolstered it. The gambling industry is doing well—with the blessings of the Chinese authorities who intend to make it a world capital of entertainment. The island counts some forty casinos on a surface area of just twelve square miles, and welcomes around six million visitors each year. Most are gambling enthusiasts coming from all over the planet but also from mainland China, where it is prohibited. Gambling activities generate an annual windfall of two billion US dollars, which represents nearly 70% of Macau's revenue. The Chinese authorities' control over this "gambling paradise" is two-fold; as it is both a stakeholder in local casinos and the overseer of island politics. Alongside industry professionals, they promote the diversification of the tourism offering in view of attracting a clientele less interested in gambling than in natural and cultural sites. With the advent of the Anthropocene, sustainable tourism has gradually established its standards at an international scale.

Exceptional Geoenvironmental Resources

From the Netherlands Antilles to the Spanish Balearics, from the US Virgin Islands to Portugal's offshore lands; many overseas territories shelter nature reserves or national parks like the famous primary forest of the Laurisilva of Madeira, listed as a UNESCO World Heritage Site. To boost their international reputation and at the same time respond to the pressure of public opinion, their administering countries have ramped up their initiatives. With 80% of its biodiversity located overseas, France stands out as one of the most enterprising. A quarter of its national parks are offshore. The one in French Guiana, created in 2007, covers nearly 25,000 square miles of Amazon rainforest, and is the largest in the European Union. It is home to one of the most remarkable biodiversity hotspots with 6,000 plant species in addition to the unique lifestyles of the river and forest populations. The one in Reunion Island includes the *calderas* of Mafate, Cilaos and Salazie which surround the Piton des Neiges that lies at its core and has been among UNESCO's World Heritage Sites since 2010. Guadeloupe's national park, which spreads around the Soufrière massif with its very own rainforest and biodiversity, is a national biosphere reserve. New Caledonia's lagoon, which is the largest in the world—with a coral reef ranked right after Australia's in length—has also been part of the UNESCO World Heritage List since 2008.

Likewise, the United States and the United Kingdom have upgraded their overseas territories; sometimes by transforming former military facilities into natural sanctuaries—such as Midway Atoll—or, on the British side, by creating a "blue belt" that includes the Chagos Archipelago, the Ascension Islands, St. Helena, Tristan da Cunha, South Georgia and South Sandwich, Pitcairn and the British Antarctic Territoryand is home to 90% of the United Kingdom's biodiversity. In Antarctica, the United Kingdom has been very busy in terms of environmental diplomacy, striving to make its mark on an overseas territory that is also claimed by Argentina and Chile. Investments made in the name of the greater good of humanity, are always rooted in politics of influence. In the Arctic, however, Russia has proven heavily dependent on its fossil energy exports, structurally reluctant to embrace a greener economy, and therefore compelled to give in under the joint pressure of riparian countries and the effects of climate change. The archipelago of New Siberia was thus labelled a terrestrial ecoregion, and a national park was created in the Arctic. Composed of a segment Novaya Zemlya in addition to Franz Josef Land, it covers nearly 34,750 square miles, making it the largest in the Russian Federation. In cooperation with Norway, which has protected two-thirds of the Svalbard's, the Russian authorities have been promoting the development of ecotourism while preserving the activities of their Nagurskoye military base. Unlike Russia, Denmark is a pioneering state when it comes to environmental policy. In 1974, it opened the world's largest national park in Greenland, with a surface area of over 386,102 mi2. Admittedly, the Greenland ice sheet forms its core, but it also counts with some ice-free areas. This huge sanctuary is not only a natural air conditioner for the planet, but it is home to remarkable biodiversity. In 1977, the park was granted the status of Biosphere Reserve by UNESCO, and became a showcase for Denmarks green diplomacy. Nevertheless, it is a vulnerable ecosystem—just like the overseas islands in the Mediterranean or the Caribbean, which face strong demographic pressure in addition.

Remarkable Geocultural Resources

Offshore territories are also places of great cultural diversity and vitality that enjoy growing national and international recognition. Like the natural environments they belong to and give symbolic significance to, these cultures are subject to many external influences: first and foremost, those of their administering country; as well as those inherent in globalisation. Ironically, it was the political struggles they provoked in some overseas territories that forced public protection policies onto the agenda—sometimes leading to international consecrations; such as the Easter Island National Park. After decades of grassroots advocacy, the descendants of the indigenous population persuaded the Chilean state, then in democratic transition, to help preserve their ancestral roots and reinvent an identity that colonial history had partially erased. In the span of a few years, they reappropriated an original memory materialised by a one-of-a-kind sculptural and architectural tradition. These monuments, which represent distinctive figures carved in stone and are called *moai* in the *Rapa Nui* language, form an outstanding statuary landscape that has fuelled worldwide fascination. Listed as a UNESCO World Heritage Site in 1995, this cultural site, which bears witness to a remarkable artistic and spiritual legacy, covers forty percent of the territory. Along with the restored memory and pride of a community facing dissolution within the national ensemble, this international recognition fostered a spectacular boom in tourism. Visitors and investors from both Chile and abroad flocked to the island. Some of them settled to the point that the indigenous population no longer was the majority group. Faced with the mobilisation of the Pascuan people, who vigorously rejected the transformations underway in their territory, the public authorities could not let this happen. In 2018, the President of Chile, Sebastian Pinera, decided to limit the number of tourists allowed each year, as well as the duration of their stay. He also signed a bill to formally restore the island's original name, *Rapa Nui* which means "navel of the world"— so as to pass on to future generations that Polynesian part of Chile's cultural diversity.

The symbolic relationship between a former colonial power and a former colony always shows in the public management of territorial identities. Especially when the latter continues to depend politically on the former. Known for its considerable mineral resources as well as for its exceptional and fragile natural areas, Greenland/*Kalaallit Nunaat* is no exception to that rule. The defence of Inuit identity is the cornerstone of its tormented relationship with the central government of Denmark. *Kalaalisut* replaced Danish as the official language in 1979. A policy of "greenlandisation" of jobs was implemented in 2009 but it ran out of a sufficient pool of indigenous executives. Other heritage aspects have also come to the forefront of political mobilisation. After a decade of efforts, Greenland was doubly acknowledged by UNESCO. In 2017, an Inuit farming landscape on the edge of the ice sheet, the *Kujataa*, was thus listed as a UNESCO World Heritage Centre. In 2018, Inuit hunting grounds between sea and ice, located in the central part of western Greenland, gained similar international recognition. With this track record, Greenland has become the leader in the promotion of Inuit culture in the Arctic; thereby granting the Kingdom of Denmark a two-pronged advantage: in domestic affairs, as a way to ease tensions without yielding to pressures from Greenland/*Kalaallit Nunaat*; and in foreign affairs, to assert the image of a nation respectful of cultural diversity. Obviously, all parties are also keen to benefit from tourism incomes—even as they confront the Inuit population, who gets additional revenues in the process, to the Cornelian dilemma of either increasing their economic autonomy, or preserving their way of life.

Other overseas countries face the same dilemma. From Macau to Willemstad, from Hong Kong to Risco Caido in Gran Canaria, from the Puerto Rico to Curaçao; cultural policies are at the centre of power issues. Some want to revitalise traditional local cultural practices—mostly in music, dance or crafts—which are currently being marginalised, while others seek to leverage them mainly for tourism. On the one hand, activists are seizing elements of intangible heritage to turn them into banners of struggle against national authorities. On the other hand, tourism professionals are seizing on it to promote their economic activities. While it contributes to the patrimonialisation of territorial identities, it should not be misinterpreted. Far from translating a dynamic compromise, it crystallises the recurring tensions between local elites who intend to control the public management of internal affairs, and national authorities who wish to keep ruling for the sake of their own geopolitical interests.

Conclusion

This chapter shed some light on the—sometimes—under-estimated potentialities of OTs. Contrary to common views, some have considerable economic potential, even if they are not always beneficial to their inhabitants. Unsurprisingly, local development often involves competing interests at the subnational, national and international levels. The same applies to environmental matters, where tensions exist between those who want to preserve their territory and those who favour development despite inherent ecological hazards. The divides are not only vertical—i.e. mainland/island relations—but are also often horizontal—i.e., inside the island jurisdictions. The cultural sector, which is particularly vibrant, is no exception. Some promote a territorial identity focused on the protection of popular arts and traditions. Others project a distinct cultural banner designed to seduce the global tourism industry. Each of these sectors reflect in its own way the political vitality of these subnational jurisdictions, which we will now study in more depth.

PART III

Local Checks on Geopolitical Assignments

"(..) non-sovereignty continues to create ambiguities, debates, and controversies. Lack of full autonomy, metropolitan domination and control, contentious colonial history, and cultural tensions create a situation in which citizens of these territories perceive non-sovereignty as a rationally pragmatic, but ideologically, culturally, and possibly even psychologically deeply unsatisfactory political outcome."
Gert Oostindie and alii. (2019: 44)

Mainland-island political relations are an integral part of geopolitics. Despite their heteronomy—as in, dependence on their administering countries—the overseas territories do have resources to oppose, influence or benefit from it. This peripheral resistance is mirrored by electoral behaviours; recurring and symptomatic statutory debates; social mobilisations that circumvent vertical coalitions between local and national elites; or the use of violence. Certainly, independence is not a credible political alternative in most cases; but current statuses are far from unanimous. Decolonisation without sovereignty may appear as an optimal political option (Rezvani 2014, Prinsen 2018) but its aftermath engenders a lot of dissatisfaction. Whatever its institutional form, it generates its share of ambiguities, frustrations and discontent which lead to conflicts with the central power. These socio-political antagonisms are not only a source of surprise, incomprehension, disarray or indifference in mainland areas; they also invariably express *structural issues* relating to the partition of power, the redistribution of resources, the sense of belonging to the national community or historical disputes pertaining to postcolonial identities. Their convergence underlines shared representations, as it draws a *symbolic* frontier between the nation's *imagined* and *legal* bodies. The former is invariably associated with its *mainland* while the latter is inseparable from its overseas dimension. This split between the *actual* and the *legal* country is experienced all the more acutely by the overseas populations—including those based in the *motherland* and exposed to the microaggressions of a devastatingly ordinary form of racism. This is why the political dynamics at work in these offshore territories have been nurturing two seemingly contradictory goals: a demand for *true* equality with "mainland" citizens; and a fierce desire to be recognised in their *uniqueness*. These seemingly contradictory aspirations also transpire from the overseas territories' commitment to environmental protection, and from their inclusion in national narratives.

CHAPTER 8

From Citizenship Deficits to Demands for Real Equality

Abstract Despite their heteronomy, the overseas territories do have resources to oppose, influence or benefit from it. This peripheral resistance is mirrored by electoral behaviours; recurring and symptomatic statutory debates; social mobilisations or the use of violence. Certainly, independence is not a credible political alternative in most cases; but current statuses are far from unanimous. They may appear as an optimal political option (Rezvani 2014, Prinsen 2018) but its aftermath engenders a lot of dissatisfaction. Whatever its institutional form, it generates its share of ambiguities, frustrations and discontent which lead to conflicts with the central power. Clearly, the natives are neither in *law* nor in *practice* citizens like any others—not only because of the gaps between their *standards of living* and those of their mainland compatriots; but also and above all because of the discriminations they face both overseas and in the mainland. The resulting anger, emotions and expectations express a compelling need for *recognition, consideration* and *respect*—which cannot be met with financial compensation alone. These "pathologies of equality" raise a central question: What type of relationship can exist between continental states and geographically remote territories, usually endowed with complex legacies stemming from slavery and colonisation—not to mention unique histories and cultures—but which aspire to be part of a greater political ensemble, provided their acceptance and recognition as fully-fledged components of the latter?

© The Author(s), under exclusive license to Springer Nature Switzerland AG 2024
F. Constant, *Overseas Territories in World Affairs*,
https://doi.org/10.1007/978-3-031-64233-3_8

Keywords Island/Mainland's political conundrum · Citizenship shortcomings · Peripheral resistance · Politics of identity · Flag-territory · Puerto Rico's mobilisation after hurricane Maria · 2009 French overseas départements general strike · Greenland/Kalaallit Nunaat's political frustrations · Hong Kong's pro-democracy movement

George Orwell sums it up wonderfully in *Animal Farm*: "All animals are equal but some are more equal than others." Clearly, the natives of offshore territories are neither in *law* nor in *practice* citizens like any others—not only because of the gaps between their *standards of living* and those of their mainland compatriots; but also and above all because of the discriminations they face both overseas and in the mainland. The resulting anger, emotions and expectations express a compelling need for *recognition, consideration* and *respect*—which cannot be met with financial compensation alone. These "pathologies of equality," in the words of Pierre Rosanvallon, fuel a political debate that has always stumbled on a central question: What type of relationship can exist between continental states and geographically remote territories, usually endowed with complex legacies stemming from slavery and colonization—not to mention unique histories and cultures—but which aspire to be part of a greater political ensemble, provided their acceptance and recognition as fully-fledged components of the latter? (Constant et al. 2009). Below are some examples of how overseas populations have tackled this nagging dilemma in the face of the many challenges raised before them.

PUERTO RICO, HURRICANE MARIA AND A FAINT-HEARTED FEDERAL ADMINISTRATION

On 20 September 2017, Hurricane Maria wrecked Puerto Rico. It was the most violent to cross the island in nearly a century. In a few hours, the population—nearly half of which lives below the poverty line—ended up in a catastrophic humanitarian situation. Nearly three thousand had perished, while tens of thousands of people were injured and hundreds of thousands, homeless. The estimated damage amounted to over a billion US dollars; exacerbated by the dire fiscal and budgetary crisis the territory had been facing since 2008. More than three hundred thousand Puerto Ricans joined the mainland to try to get by on their own given the abysmal lack of financial aid released by the federal state. Two weeks after the disaster, President Trump visited Puerto Rico where he praised the work of national agencies and minimised the damage caused by the hurricane in comparison to Katrina's rampage in New Orleans. His visit, punctuated by insinuations about the failures of local governance, sparked an outcry in the island's media, which condemned the indifference and even contempt of the federal administration towards a territory in distress. Thousands of protestors marched in Washington DC to demand emergency relief for disaster victims and the rehabilitation of local infrastructure (electricity, water, roads); vilifying the federal administration and Puerto Rico's governor in solidarity. This collective trial, which brought the island's vulnerability to the forefront of mainstream awareness, revived the statutory debate. On 3 November 2020, for the third time in a row, annexationist ideas, hitherto unpopular, won a narrow majority of the electoral vote. The vote in favour of integrating the island into the United States' federal ensemble has registered a steady growth. For the record, Puerto Rico has held six referendums about its political status since the 1960s. Most voters rejected a status change in 1967, 1993, and 1998. According to Jorge Duarny, one of the leading scholars on Puerto Rican affairs, *"The 2012 results were not clear because many voters did not answer both parts of a two-parts status question. In 2017, statehood won decisively – over 97% of those who participated – but the turnout was very low at 23%. In the most recent 2020 vote, almost 53% of the voters supported becoming the 51st state of the American union. But nearly half of the electorate rejected this option, underscoring the split among Puerto Rican voters."* (2023).

In December 2022, the House of Representatives passed the Puerto Rico Status Act which aimed at solving its territorial status and relationship with the US through a federally binding plebiscite. For the first time, Congress would have been compelled to implement the outcomes. But the Senate failed to consider the bill. As it is now stated in the law, only Congress can decide to incorporate a new state into the Union, through an Admission Act or a House Resolution that requires approval by a simple majority in the House and Senate. In May 2023, the Puerto Rico Status Act was reintroduced to the House thanks to a joint initiative led by advocates of a pro-statehood bill and proponents of a Puerto Rico Self-Determination Act. To date, it seems unlikely to secure enough Republican votes in the Senate, given the lack of congressional bipartisanship. In any case, the leap forward of the annexationist current reflected the Puerto Ricans' wish to be treated like other US citizens and to participate fully in national democratic life. It mirrors a tangible request for *protection* from the federal state and a particular eagerness for *recognition* among their mainland compatriots. Last but not least, it forcefully expresses the rejection of the current status of "in-betweenity" (Baldacchino 2010), which Jorge Duarny describes as "a colony except in name" (2023). But the United States Congress stood its ground. It stubbornly refused to change a status that would generate additional public spending for a territory that in its view no longer held the same strategic value as it did during the Cold War. This stance was reinforced by the steady deterioration of the island's public finances, the underperformance of its economy, the poverty of its population and its strong Latin American cultural ties. In June 2015, Governor Alejandro Garcia Padilla stated publicly that Puerto Rico's huge public debt—over 72 billion USD—was "not payable". As the jurisdiction is not a state, it was not eligible for federal bankruptcy. In order to curb the debt, Congress voted a special bill—the Puerto Rico Oversight, Management, and Economic Stability Act—in June 2016, which gave federal authorities full control over the island's fiscal affairs. President Obama appointed an ad hoc board composed of 7 members including four Puerto Ricans, which is supposed to remain in office until the budget is balanced.

In many ways, Puerto Rico is a prime example of a flag-territory where the United States' star-spangled banner adorns official buildings but the local population does not enjoy the same prerogatives as mainland citizens (Ramos, 2021: 515). Its current status underlines the ambiguities and shortcomings of being, technically, *"an "unincorporated territory" that legally belongs to but is not part of the United States"*—that is to say *"foreign to the United States in a domestic sense"* as per the US Supreme Court's wording. This paradoxical situation contrasts sharply with its translation in Spanish as *Estado Libre Asociado* while actually it has never been a state, nor free. Retrospectively, it is almost unthinkable that Puerto Rico could find itself in such a political limbo after more than 125 years of attachment to the US, whose self-image is that of a champion of freedom and democracy around the world. More to the point, Puerto Rico's geographical proximity to the American continent—2.5 hours by air from New York and 3.5 hours from the federal capital, does not change the picture at all. Despite an estimated 5,8 million Puerto Ricans residing in the mainland (Moslimani, Noe-Bustamante, Shah 2023), the vast majority of US citizens keep on viewing their country as a continental space bordered by Canada and Mexico, the Atlantic and the Pacific—sometimes adding Alaska or Hawaii but always excluding the overseas (Immerwahr, 2019:). However, the demand for material equality with mainland citizens and the active preservation of an irreducible island identity will certainly continue to structure Puerto Rico's political interactions with federal authorities in the foreseeable future. The same is true in other overseas locations (including Curaçao, Greenland, Sint Maarten or Guam to name few) which periodically display social movements of high magnitude to oppose adverse decisions made by central government. In their own ways, these popular mobilisations invariably carry egalitarian demands coupled with a claim for greater local autonomy.

GUADELOUPE, FRENCH GUIANA, MARTINIQUE, REUNION ISLAND: FROM POPULAR MOBILISATION AGAINST "PWOFITASYON" TO THE DESIRE FOR IDIOSYNCRATIC RECOGNITION

On 24 November 2008, the sudden increase in fuel prices triggered a general strike against high prices in French Guiana, which then spread to Guadeloupe and Martinique, followed by Reunion Island. Prices overseas were on average 34–49% higher than in mainland France, while the median income per household was 38% lower in the overseas compared to the mainland. Protestors called for price reductions prioritising basic necessities (in particular, food and gasoline) as well as a raise of the lowest wages. Roadblocks bloomed on major traffic arteries. All economic sectors were impacted and social life was severely disrupted as a result. In terms of scale, duration and radicality, this mobilisation was unprecedented in all of the SNIJs involved. Often described as fundamentally individualistic and shackled by endemic clientelism, their populations had been able to rally around the joint denunciation of *Pwofitasyon*, which could be translated from Creole as an outrageous form of capitalistic and colonial exploitation, which reactivated efficiently the *mythe du Peuple et des Gros*[1] (the "Big Guys versus Good People" myth). Sociologist Pierre Odin, who authored the first in-depth analysis of this pan-insular and

---

[1] It describes a handful of "big guys", holders of economic and political power, who crush the good people, encompassing all social groups (workers, peasants, employees, shopkeepers, small bosses). See more in Pierre Birnbaum (1979).

trans-oceanic social phenomenon, highlighted one particular characteristic of its popular success i.e., the concept of *Pwofitasyon* which acted as a rallying cry for people who did not necessarily have much in common otherwise. According to him, "*In itself, the word Pwofitasyon carries strong semantic and symbolic weight, making it possible to encompass issues that span Guadeloupean and Martinican societies and affect their populations. This attitude of denunciation came along with a connection between the economy of the colonial period and that of the present period*" (2019: 19). Violence broke out in urban centres but the population maintained its support to the *Liyannaj Kont Pwofitasyon* (L.K.P)—a collective of about 50 Guadeloupean unions rising against capitalistic and colonial exploitation—and to the *Collectif du 5 février 2009 contre la vie chère et pour l'emploi* (K5F)—a collective of 20 unions and ad hoc associations against the expensive cost of living and in favour of job creation. In both islands, the carnival's cultural extravaganza was cancelled for security reasons but even more so because L.K.P and K.F.5 had decided to organise instead an impressive silent march which took thousands of demonstrators to the streets—including children and the elderly—in all major cities. Breaking away from conventional observations and analysis, this social mobilisation which coordinated two island populations often portrayed as rivals and competitors brought turmoil and uncertainty all the way to the top of the French state.

President Sarkozy and his government were urged to engage in discussions with the collectives of unions. Relayed by local elected representatives, the first negotiations with the Prefect—i.e. local representatives of the central authorities—failed while the protests gained in intensity. Three months after the conflict began, Yves Jégo, the French Minister for the Overseas flew to Guadeloupe but was unable to finalise the ongoing negotiations or restore social harmony. The movement hardened and activists began to use force to compel some merchants to keep their establishments closed. In Paris, Prime Minister François Fillon conditioned the pursuit of negotiations on the return of public order. Several squadrons of *gendarmes* were expedited to the French Antilles, where their arrival only exacerbated tensions with the strikers. Nights of violence followed in chain reaction. Shops were looted. Clashes with the police, broadcast by the media, triggered responses of outrage and indignation. A Guadeloupean trade unionist was shot dead on his way home. President Sarkozy finally came out of his silent stance. He forecast additional budgetary resources, the launch of the Overseas States General and his agreement to reopen the debate on institutional reform. The minister for OTs was compelled to resign even if he did plead not guilty. In Paris, the ultramarine diaspora mobilised in solidarity with the local populations who continued to demonstrate under a single slogan adapted to each territory, in Creole: *la Gwadloup sé ta nou, a pa ta yo* ("Guadeloupe is ours, not theirs"). This slogan pinpoints the actual scope of a social movement that has often been wrongly reduced to its focus on consumerism. In fact, it also translates the need for a new partition of responsibilities to be shared with the State, which would allow citizens to participate further in the public management of local affairs and implement a more sustainable and inclusive development approach. After several political twists and turns, agreements to end the strike were finally signed. A list of basic commodities was to enjoy lower prices while the lowest wages would be raised by an average of 200 euros.

On 6 November 2009, President Sarkozy chaired for the first time ever under the Fifth Republic, an Inter-Ministerial Council devoted to the Overseas Territories (CIOM). Based on a report resulting from a nine-month consultation of the OTs involved, the CIOM approved a package of 137 measures. One third of those measures were implemented by the end of his five-year term. Another third remained in the pipelines and the last third never made it past wishful thinking. For the government, the main goal was clearly to terminate the on-going social conflicts, not to eradicate their roots. More to the point, it was to restore social peace for islanders to resume their daily activities. It was not intended to initiate—badly needed—structural reforms aimed at mitigating the risk of recidivism, given the considerable economic costs of the strike in these SNIJs highly dependent on public funding. In his personal memoir, Yves Jégo, former minister for the French OTs, unveils the "behind-the-scene manoeuvres" of all sorts of lobbies whose combined and pernicious actions rose all the way to the top to undermine the French State's initiatives. He went further to denounce: "(..) the local Guadeloupean employers, supported by relays and solid networks in mainland France, which played a murky game throughout the crisis. Some senior civil servants, who preferred *status quo* to action and reform. Especially the Prime Minister, François Fillon, who, except for a single stunt, was as if absent from the government he led" (2009: 43). Very often, in politics, what is not handled by a President, is bound to fall into the legacy of his successor. As a result, François Hollande was to deal with the discontent engendered by his predecessor's half-hearted policies. In turn, he charged

Prime minister Ayrault to take urgently action to avoid any setting back. The latter adopted various measures aimed at stimulating local production, controlling pricing and promoting *real* equality with citizens living in mainland France. A law was passed *in extremis* in Parliament in 2017 a couple of months before the end of François Hollande's first and last term. Here again, it has contributed to occasionally sooth local tensions but it has obviously failed to carry any sort of structural reform; nor did it normalise the symbolic belonging of OTs to the French Republic. An example of this is the City of the Overseas Territories that in 2002 Jacques Chirac promised to erect in Paris, taken over by Nicolas Sarkozy in 2007 and then by François Hollande in 2012—without ever seeing daylight at either end of their respective terms. Coupled with the nagging matter of purchasing power, the desire for idiosyncratic recognition brews in many other French overseas (for example, Mayotte) and foreign offshore territories (in particular, the Cook Islands, Samoa or Aruba).

Greenland/Kalaallit Nunaat and Faroe: Dual Power, Frustrations and Resentment

Unlike their US and French counterparts,[2] Danish overseas territories are characterised by the coexistence of egalitarian claims with the omnipresent question of independence. In fact, their differences outweigh their similarities by far (Koci and Baar 2021). And yet, both SNIJs harbour a fierce spirit of independence that is deeply ingrained in their respective colonial history (Ackren 2006). In order to avoid lengthy comparisons, I will focus on the case of Greenland/Kalaallit Nunaat to flesh out the power of frustration that lies at the heart of its nationalism. Since home rule was established in 1979, the pro-independence political party *Siumut* has dominated Greenlandic politics. The general elections in 2018[3] and 2020[4] have confirmed its prevalence, despite internal dissensions among its members over leadership matters. In the 2018 elections, *Siumut* secured 27% of votes and 9 seats in *Inatsisartut* (Greenland's Parliament). The party lost 2 seats but its leader Kim Kielsen stayed in office as Prime Minister. During the 2021 elections, *Siumut* garnered

---

[2] With the notable exception of New Caledonia and to a lesser extent French Polynesia.

[3] For an in-depth analysis, refer to Zhang et al. (2021).

[4] More in Colm Quinn (2021).

30% of the votes and 10 seats, but was defeated by the opposition—as pro-independence party *Inuit Ataqatigiit* got 37% of votes and 12 seats. The elections revolved around one major issue: should Greenland allow multinational firms to exploit the rare-earth deposits found in its soil, or should environmental protection prevail? *Siumut* campaigned for exploitation on economic grounds, while *Inuit Ataqatigiit* opposed it for environmental reasons. The leader of the latter and current Prime Minister, Müde B. Egeden, does believe that an independent Greenland/ Kalaallit Nunaat should be competitive while preserving its natural environment as much as possible. Erik Jensen,[5] the new leader of *Siumut*, declared his intention to push for independence more energetically than his predecessor: "*(..) We are on the path towards independence. That is what provides warmth in any heart in Greenland. We aim to take over more areas of responsibility from Denmark*".[6]

Still: Faroese and Greenlandic populations and elites are aware that their territories do not currently boast the economic means and sufficient skilled human resources to achieve their political goals. They know that financial transfers from the central government, which represent an average of 30% (Faroe Islands) and 50% (Greenland/Kalaallit Nunaat) of their respective budgets, are essential to ensure living conditions comparable to those prevailing in the Danish mainland. Separatist sentiments remain strong nonetheless, in spite of those territories having a very high level of internal autonomy. How can one make sense of this apparent paradox? Regardless of their small population sizes, the central authorities of Denmark have endowed them with a multilevel governance system as sophisticated as the mainland model—though not adapted to local contexts. In Greenland/ Kalaallit Nunaat, in addition to the Primature, there is no less than one ministry for every five thousand residents—i.e., for every 2.8 deputies or 1.5 members of the ruling coalition. Each of them requires a dedicated body of officials. The territory also counts four city districts that comprise, on average, eight commissions that assist the city council. The quality of their work also relies on the expertise of the officials assigned to operate them. Given the gaps in the local pool of

---

[5] Erik Jensen won party elections in 2021 against incumbent Kim Kielsen then Prime minister of Greenland.

[6] Quoted by Breum (2020).

human resources, the governance of Greenland is administratively dependent on agents recruited in Denmark. The latter dominate the local senior public service while political power is officially held by an indigenous elite. This "duality of power" (Gridehoj 2016) generates a relatively high level of frustration and resentment among a political staff and population aware that their territory's internal autonomy is *practically* thwarted by this two-fold, financial and technical dependence. This situation is heightened by distinct cultural differences with Denmark (Zang et al. 2021: 16). Over 90% of Greenland's population is Inuit, sharing more traits with their North American counterparts than with their fellow Danish citizens—despite spectacular changes in their way of life as a result of urban sedentarisation and the exposure of youth to cyberspace. The Greenlandic language, the relation to the collective ownership of the land and environmental preservation continue to resist quite well—for the time being—to external influences and the generational turnover. They represent the very core of collective identity. Similarly, the memory of the colonial past remains a contemporary issue. On 10 March 2022, the Prime Minister of Denmark issued a symbolic apology to the Greenlandic Inuit who had been removed from their families in the 1950s to receive a "Danish education" in Copenhagen. Seventy years later, this long-ignored episode remains a bone of contention with Denmark. In these circumstances, the recurring debate over independence in Greenlandic public life is symptomatic of the island population's attachment to their Inuit identity, and of their willingness to *effectively* manage internal affairs without hindrance from the Danish administration.

As Koci and Baar have pointed out, "*Historically, compared with Greenland, the Faroe Islands had a better position in the Danish realm but, like the Greenlanders, they never voluntarily chose to be part of it. (..) However, the advantage of acquiring autonomy earlier had enabled the Faroese to enjoy cultural rights and oppose membership of the EU. By contrast, in Greenland, accession to the EU against the will of most Greenlanders led to the awakening of nationalism in the 1970s. Compared with the beginning of the Faroe Island nationalist movement, there was a delay of almost 100 years. As the Faroese are ethnically and culturally not as different from the Danish as the Inuit are, the traditional way of life for native Greenlanders clearly suffers far more from the consequences of coloniality*" (2021: 199). In their own way, they draw attention to the risk of overstating similarities at the expense of irreducible differences between OTs that experience the same metropolitan policy. Nevertheless, in both cases but more strongly in the case of Greenland/*Kalaallit Nunaat*, the lack of an endogenous—e. g. Inuit—technocracy in sufficient numbers stirs frustrations among the political class, and thereby fuels its nationalism. Actually, political vision is but wishful thinking if it fails to translate into public policies, effectively designed and implemented by competent and loyal civil servants—ideally, drawn from the island's pool of population.

Hong Kong, the Pro-democracy Movement and Resistance to China's Political Scrutiny

In non-democratic systems, the fight for internal autonomy sometimes unfolds the other way around: the local population does not advocate for access to the same rights as their mainland peers but on the contrary, for the preservation of those inherited from its colonial past. This applies to Hong Kong, where the Chinese authorities are in the process of dismantling representative democracy through a significant reduction of public freedoms.[7] Legally, they could only start reforming the governance system as of 2047 but instead decided to launch the process in the early 2000s. In 2003, the Hong Kong government introduced a national security legislation to prohibit treason, secession, sedition, and subversion against China's mainland government. Popular protests and international criticism brought it to a temporary halt. In 2012, a new reform was submitted for Hong Kong's school curricula to promote the Chinese national identity, which many local inhabitants denounced as Chinese-led propaganda. Two years later, an electoral reform was publicly presented by the local government to restrain the pool of contenders to the position of city chief executive to a China-approved shortlist of candidates. In March 2014, additional restrictive measures were passed through Article 23, in order to strengthen China's rule over the city's rights and freedom. These pernicious moves by the PRC's central authorities and their local allies, have not only sparked international outcries, but have also given rise to strong concerns about Hong Kong's status as one of the world's most important financial centres. Hong Kong residents were very upset by the intended reform which threatened their democratic governance system, inherited from the British. Tens of thousands of protesters, among whom numerous students, took to the streets and demanded the right

---

[7] For a more in depth-analysis, refer to Michael C. Davis (2020).

to free and fair elections. These massive demonstrations are also known as the "Umbrella Movement" because the demonstrators used umbrellas to protect themselves from tear gas used by the police. The "Umbrella Movement" brought parts of the City of Hong Kong to a standstill for over two months. Once again, local authorities suspended their legislation in the aftermath of this showdown, in which the intersection of subnational, national and international issues was palpable. But that did not alter their plan to tighten the monitoring of local political life.

After a period of ups and downs, the Hong Kong authorities launched a new offensive in 2019. It began in seemingly benign ways, with an amendment to the extradition law that enabled mainland China to receive transfers of Hong Kong citizens convicted of criminal acts. In 2018, a Hong Kong resident murdered his girlfriend in Taiwan and returned to Hong Kong. After arresting him and obtaining a confession, the police could not extradite him due to the lack of relevant legal provisions. Given the mediatic impact of a murder which had made the headlines, the Hong Kong authorities decided to supplement the Fugitive Offenders Ordinance in their own special way. Introduced by the Chief Executive, the amendment to the bill in force[8] was officially aimed at establishing a mechanism for transferring fugitives not only for Taiwan, but also for mainland China and Macau. The intended reform sparked widespread criticism and condemnation, both domestically and internationally. Opposition rose from various segments of the civil society including the entrepreneurial and legal sectors as well as the media, not to mention multiple foreign governments worried about the stability of Hong Kong's legal system and business climate. Hong Kongers feared the Chinese authorities would now intervene directly in the operation of their justice system—which would jeopardise their independence and individual freedoms. Furthermore, they suspected the amendment would serve as a proxy for the Chinese government to choke any dissenting voices on the island by legally extraditing targeted individuals. In the span of a few months, individual protest actions grew into massive mobilisation which reached a million on June 9. This unprecedented level of demonstration was harshly repressed by the police, but pro-democracy activists did not give in. Protestors pressed Chief Executive Carrie Lam to resign. Pressures from major actors of the international community

---

[8] The Fugitive Offenders and Mutual Legal Assistance in Criminal Matters (Amendment) Bill 2019.

such as the European Union, the US House of Representatives and the US Senate and the UK, went increasingly. A couple of days later, Carrie Lam suspended the proposed bill but protestors demanded its withdrawal and the implementation of universal suffrage. By the end of October, the bill had been formally withdrawn after 13 weeks of protests.

The pro-democracy victory was short-lived because the Chinese authorities pursued their goal of undermining Hong Kong's democracy. The COVID-19 pandemic gave them a pretext to enact a new national security law (NSL) that came into force in June 2020. This law, which was supposedly intended to fight "separatism", "collusion with foreign forces" and "terrorism", allowed the police to arrest hundreds of pro-democracy activists and pushed thousands more into exile. In two years, dozens of civil society organisations, including Amnesty International—which kept a regional office on location—left to avoid prosecution. During the district elections held in November 2020, pro-democracy candidates scored a resounding victory. However, in March 2021, China's central authorities imposed a reform of the electoral system, which reduced the number of seats subject to universal suffrage and required "patriotic pledges" to get candidates approved. The legislation, which seriously compromises the principle of "one country, two systems", was designed and adopted by the Chinese Parliament and promulgated by President Xi Jinping. This tougher policy towards Hong Kong mirrors a two-pronged strategy. In domestic affairs, it aims to assert the Chinese Communist Party's absolute sovereignty in the special administrative regions while in global affairs, it gave evidence of its relative indifference to the international community's criticism. The island's major pro-democracy activists were arrested under any provision of the NSL. Political parties, independent media, non-governmental organisations and several unions ceased operations because of the pending legal charges threatening to fall onto their staff members. Meanwhile, Hong Kong's electoral system changed in 2021. Ever since, the candidates for public office are to be endorsed by the Chinese mainland's authorities. Other provisions of the law empower the latter with a very strong hold on the officials who govern the jurisdiction. Nevertheless, the Hong Kongers' fight for democracy never stopped, even under the tightening grip of the PRC's local allies. In his firsthand on-the-ground report (2022), Mark Clifford showed how it continues against all odds and in diverted forms, taking different paths but still striving for the same target: preserving their living conditions and shared democratic values.

A comparable political picture can be found in other overseas territories administered by People's China (Macau) and Russia (the island of Sakhalin) where the population tries taking back routes to resist pressures from the mainland. This resistance often sports ecological considerations before gaining political weight.

Conclusion

This chapter reviewed several case-studies illustrating the capacity of the OTs' inhabitants for political mobilisation when confronted with issues lying at the intersection of subnational, national and international relations. Yet, the political responsiveness of these SNIJs should neither be overestimated or underestimated, as suggested by its comparative political outcomes. Whatever the "resourcefulness" of the insular jurisdiction might be, subnational interests seldom prevail over national ones, especially when they intersect with international stakes. Of course, this is not to say that peripheral resistance is doomed to failure. It means that its political gains are frequently short-lived. In his time, Aimé Césaire used to say: "*J'ai souvent l'impression de labourer la mer (I often feel like I'm ploughing the sea)*" and he immediately used to add: "*Il faut continuer le combat pour nos droits et notre dignité parce qu'il n'a pas de fin (We must continue the fight for our rights and dignity because it never ends)*" (Delepine 2018: 187–188).

CHAPTER 9

From Environmental Issues to Health Scandals

Abstract Overseas territories are inherently vulnerable ecosystems, given their natural characteristics (Goujon, Hoarau 2015). However, their degradation has accelerated due to the public policies that their administering countries have applied and/or continue to apply them with the sole purpose of satisfying national interests (Ferdinand, Manglou 2021). In most cases, the threats they pose to the health and environment of populations are well known to political authorities when they intentionally relocate them to offshore territories. In some situations, ecological or health considerations are pushed to the background in the name of public interest. In others, different laws and/or convenient exemptions allow activities that are prohibited on the mainland to be carried out with impunity. This is why, in many overseas territories, peripheral dissent is strongly rooted in environmental and heritage claims. In territories exposed to nuclear testing, populations have mobilised to obtain the "neutralisation" of contaminated areas and reparations for the damage done. In those subjected to various forms of chemical pollution, collective struggles focus on the decontamination of ecosystems and the recognition of diseases induced by irresponsible agricultural practices. Again, the issues under consideration lie at the intersection of divergent subnational, national and international interests. They are often approached through the prism of decolonial theories, by researchers who sometimes originate from these OTs. Their scientific enquiries then become a source of inspiration and legitimacy for non-governmental and even political activism.

Keywords Radioactive liabilities of nuclear powers · Marshall Islands · Antonio Guterres · Pollution of natural environment · Dissemination of radioactive materials · Radiation-induced diseases · French Polynesia · Nuclear debt · Decontamination · Novara Zemlya · Guadeloupe · Martinique · Chemical contamination · Chlordecone · Hawaii · Health scandal · DBCD · Aruba · Curaçao · Oil refinery · Royal Dutch Shell · PVDSA

Overseas territories are inherently vulnerable ecosystems, given their natural characteristics (Goujon, Hoarau 2015). However, their degradation has accelerated due to the public policies that their administering countries have applied and/or continue to apply them with the sole purpose of satisfying national interests (Ferdinand, Manglou 2021). In most cases, the threats they pose to the health and environment of populations are well known to political authorities when they intentionally relocate them to offshore territories. In some situations, ecological or health considerations are pushed to the background in the name of public interest. In others, different laws and/or convenient exemptions allow activities that are prohibited on the mainland to be carried out with impunity. This is why, in many overseas territories, peripheral dissent is strongly rooted in environmental and heritage claims. In territories exposed to nuclear testing, populations have mobilised to obtain the "neutralization" of contaminated areas and reparations for the damage done. In those subjected to various forms of chemical pollution, collective struggles focus on the decontamination of ecosystems and the recognition of diseases induced by irresponsible agricultural practices. Again, the issues under consideration lie at the intersection of divergent subnational, national and international interests. They are often approached through the prism of decolonial theories, by researchers who sometimes originate from these OTs. Their scientific enquiries then become a source of inspiration and legitimacy for non-governmental and even political activism.

The Radioactive Liabilities of Nuclear Powers

With the exception of PRC, the nuclear powers of the UNSC have conducted a significant volume of their nuclear tests in offshore territories. Decades later, the latter still bear various stigma: from the contamination of sites to the storage of radioactive materials; from the displacement of populations to the lasting pollution of natural environments; from the destruction of corals to radiation-induced diseases. In May 2019, the UN Secretary General, Antonio Guterres, on a tour of the Pacific, raised international awareness on this irreversible damage. During his visit to the Marshall Islands, he went to a radioactive waste landfill site threatened by rising sea levels. At a press conference, he stated: *"I've just been with the President of the Marshall Islands, who is very worried because there is a risk of leaking radioactive materials that are contained in a sort of coffin in the area. A lot needs to be done with regards to the nuclear explosions that took place in the area. This has to do with consequences on health, the impact on communities and other aspects. Of course, there is a question of compensation and implementing a mechanism to mitigate these impacts"*[1] A Cold War legacy, this storage location was established in the Enewetak atoll, then under American sovereignty. In 1958, highly radioactive materials were stored there in an open crater, without any special insulation or protection. They stayed as such until 1979 when the US federal administration set up a concrete dome to lower the risk of dissemination. Still, the structure cracked in places and seawater infiltration was known to occur periodically. In 1986, the Marshall Islands gained independence but remained within the political and military fold of the United States. They were paid 800 million dollars in compensation for the damages suffered—while an arbitration court had awarded them 2 billion in that regard. In 2016, the President of the Republic of the Marshall Islands requested additional compensation due to the long-term contamination of the atolls, the persistent health effects on their residents and the acute risks of further leaks of radioactive material. During her meeting with President Trump in 2019, Mrs. Hilda Heine was met with sheer indifference—as her host was more concerned with Chinese expansionism in the Pacific than with the decontamination of the atolls. In 2021, she renewed her request to President Biden, with similar outcomes. Over 1300 miles from the Marshall Islands, Guam's domestic policy has also been paced

---

[1] Press release, Office of the UN Secretary General, 16 May 2019, online.

by the United States' "nuclear debt". Despite its status as an unincorporated territory, the population still struggles to benefit from a legislation passed by Congress in 1990 to compensate people exposed to radiation during nuclear tests (Radiation Exposure Compensation Act). At the time of its adoption and amendment—respectively in 2000 and 2017—federal law excluded Guam from its scope. Native communities interpreted this sidelining as an injustice tinged with contempt. The lobbying of the local association of radiation survivors, echoed by Governor Guerrero, invariably stumbled over the inflexibility of Congress. In the late 2000s, the association managed to prove Guam's indirect exposure to radiation (downwind areas) and the grounds for its inclusion in the federal legislation. Experts mandated by Congress confirmed its eligibility for compensations opened by the text that was already enforced in seven mainland states. In December 2021, Law H.R. 5338 enacted that eligibility status. Indigenous people can finally access the compensation that had been denied them until then. Many have died in the meantime and others will probably pass away before getting their due. But this time, justice did prevail.

This tragic story resembles in many ways that of French Polynesia, where the national authorities have also contracted a "nuclear debt" towards the indigenous population. On 2 July 2016, anti-nuclear activists gathered in Papeete under the aegis of association 193, to remember the fiftieth anniversary of the first nuclear test in Mururoa, conducted in July 1966. As Auguste Uebe-Carlson, president of this association, recalled: "*Wherever there have been nuclear tests or a nuclear disaster, such as in Hiroshima or Fukushima, the same denial takes hold: all the major nations have embraced a system that delays the dissemination of the truth.*"[2] For half a century, the military authorities and the French Atomic Energy Commission (*Commissariat à l'énergie atomique*—CEA) deliberately kept Polynesians in the dark about the environmental and health effects of these atomic experiments. Worse; they continued to argue these experiments were safe, and categorically ruled out any risk of radioactive clouds. Presidents of the French Republic all kept that fiction alive in the official discourse. Polynesians, who had been benefitting from the economic spin-offs of the activities carried out by the Pacific Experimentation Centre (CEP), widely endorsed the latter. They could not begin to fathom

---

[2] Polynésie La Première France Television, 27 July 2021 Online.

a government lie with such far-reaching consequences. However, the number of civilian and military personnel affected by radiation-induced diseases increased and their health raised nagging concerns. Associations and whistleblowers emerged such as Bruno Barillot, co-founder of the Nuclear Veterans Association (AVEN) or Ronald Oldham, president of *Mururoa e Tatou* (Mururoa and us). They filed legal suits to demand the declassification of top-secret archives. Their persistence eventually resonated with President Sarkozy, who passed the law of 5 January 2010 on compensation for victims of nuclear tests. Nonetheless, that compensation scheme—which is driven by the principle of national solidarity—demands that victims prove their case. Failure to establish a causal link between their disease and exposure to radioactivity, saw several cases dismissed by ruthless procedures. Out of nearly a thousand potential cases, barely a dozen succeeded. While campaigning for a second term, the Head of State pledged to ease those terms for compensation as part of a new decree. But he did nothing of such—while his successor, François Hollande, committed to turning the page on the nuclear testing era by revising the conditions of compensation for victims, monitoring the environmental consequences of testing cycles, creating a centre for the memory of the nuclear tests and securing Polynesia's overall autonomy budget. A few years on, promises are still slow to materialise. The remediation of nuclear sites is far from complete. Mururoa and Fangataufa remain off-limits to the public. The hospital's oncology department lacks permanent physicians. Nuclear history is nowhere to be found in school programmes. The centre for the memory of nuclear testing has yet to see the light of day. Last but not least, the Territory has yet to regain some sort of economic stability, twenty-five years after the CEP got shut down. In October 2020, the President of French Polynesia went to Paris to reactivate these pending matters and prepare the Head of State's visit to his homeland. A year later, President Macron made the trip to Papeete where he mentioned nuclear testing: on the one hand, he acknowledged "*the Nation's debt towards the Territory*" and "*launches that were not clean*"; on the other, he asserted "*that there was no lie (..) but risks that were not perfectly measured because we did not comprehend them entirely (..)*". In terms of compensation, the Head of State advertised extended deadlines to file applications, as well as a census campaign to register victims in the most remote areas. By the end of his five-year term, eighty-five people had been compensated, half of whom were Polynesian civil rights holders. For associations of nuclear veterans, these advances are not enough. Based on the results of two independent investigations (Philippe Statius, 2021 Metz 2022) conducted from archives declassified by the Ministry of Defence in 2013, they argue that scientific and military authorities had deliberately underestimated the radiological impact of nuclear launches on populations and natural environments. Indeed, the results of both studies do confirm that the military was unaware of the extent of the fallout from the very first launches, but that they then minimised the risks for the population so as to avoid having to warn of their dangerousness. Nuclear veterans also lament the fact that the decontamination of those areas has not made much progress and that the Head of State does not see the use of asking forgiveness from the Polynesian people on behalf of the nation.

In the category of environmental disasters, the radioactive pollution of Novaya Zemlya is one of a kind. A Russian nuclear test site during the Cold War, it later became an open-air radioactive waste storage site. For the Soviet authorities, this vast offshore territory located in the Far North provides an ideal stage for secret experiments. It features defined perimeters. The indigenous population was displaced *manu militari* to another section of the island. One hundred and thirty-eight aerial, ground and submarine launches took place in situ, causing lasting radioactive contamination over wide areas (Khalturin Rautian Richards Leith, 2005). After the last launch in 1990, the (already heavily contaminated) territory was converted into a landfill for radioactive equipment and materials. Soiled land was stored on location without any precaution, and wrecks of nuclear submarines were sunk in the Kara Sea. Little known until then due to its geographical remoteness and the omerta of the military authorities, the extent of this environmental disaster only showed in the wake of the policy of transparency (*glasnost*) led by Gorbachev. Environmental advocacy in the Soviet Union then focused on the effects of the Chernobyl disaster. In Novaya Zemlya, many archives relating to nuclear activities have disappeared—while the army continues to hamper access to sensitive areas. Putin's rise to power restrained the activities of environmental organisations whose positions were harshly repressed. Many suspended their activities after being classified as "foreign agents" or subjected to legal proceedings. Others like the "Russian Ecological Society" (REO)—which is a sheer creation of the government—have been fighting those that remain independent from power. Such is the case of the Russian branch of Greenpeace, which directly challenges the state-owned company in charge of the nuclear sector (ROSATOM) and the federal environmental agency (ROSGUIDROMET). It seeks to force them to decontaminate polluted sites and to create a radioactive waste reprocessing centre. These measures, which were recommended by the International Atomic Energy Agency (IAEA) in 2013, have yet to be implemented. The lobbying of Russian environmentalists runs up against the indifference of political authorities, the negligence of national bureaucracy and the military's involvement with unscrupulous investors. For the time being, the Russian authorities are fully focused on the war in Ukraine. They couldn't care less for environmental protection and public health in the Far North. And yet, the melting of the permafrost will soon release radioactive material buried in the ground, thereby aggravating an already very disturbing situation. Yet, according to a US academic team led by Jeffrey Lewis and Anne Pellegrino,[3] there are now growing concerns about whether Russia might decide to resume nuclear testing. One of their findings is that the Central Testing Ground at Novaya Zemlya is once again well kept and could, if necessary, resume nuclear testing activities.

Chemical Contamination of Island Ecosystems

Because of its scale and persistence, the chemical contamination of island ecosystems has fuelled fierce mobilisations of populations against public authorities accused of indifference, contempt and even ecocide.[4] The Environmental Justice Atlas (Temper Del Bene Martinez-Alier, 2015) lists about fifty conflicts unfolding in offshore territories, which systematically pit civil society organisations against private stakeholders and the public authorities. In 2021 and 2022, thousands of people demonstrated on the streets of Fort-de-France (Martinique) and Pointe-à-Pitre (Guadeloupe) under a shared motto: "*Arété méprizé pep là. Jigé sé Koupab la.*" (Stop looking down on the people. Judge the guilty). These umpteenth collective actions were meant to echo a legal suit for endangerment of others by poisoning that was filed in 2006 by a group of associations in Guadeloupe and Martinique, but faced dismissal on grounds

---

[3] In 2018, they launched an interactive website offering extensive information about historical and current activities at the Russian nuclear test site of Novaya Zemlya. The website is managed by the Middlebury Institute's James Martin Center for Non-proliferation Studies (NPS).

[4] In French Guiana, there is a growing concern over the contamination of rivers with mercury due to clandestine gold panning. This ongoing pollution is a human tragedy that affects Amerindian peoples in particular.

of an alleged statute of limitations. Rallying under rare consensus political parties, trade unions and environmental organisations; they expressed the demonstrators' resentment and anger towards the public authorities, accused of having failed in their duty to protect populations and their living environment.

For over twenty years (1972–1993), agricultural soils on both islands were contaminated with an organochlorine molecule (chlordecone) used as a pesticide against an insect (the weevil) that plagued banana plantations. This contamination of about 49.421 acres of land area bears catastrophic environmental and health consequences. Not only could it last several centuries depending on the level of soil impregnation, but it has also had a deep impact on both islands' ecosystems. Traces of chlordecone can thus be found in the water network including groundwater tables; in mangroves—whose crucial role in the renewal of marine fauna is well-known—as well as in certain agricultural produce and seafood. As early as 1979, however, the WHO had warned of the environmental and health risks of this carcinogenic molecule, which is banned in many countries—including the United States, one of its largest producers. France would only ban it in 1990 but the political authorities extended its use until exhaustion of stocks, at the request of the *White Creole* growers' lobby.[5] Agricultural workers (who were directly exposed) and the general population were kept in the dark about the proven hazard of this powerful pesticide.

Thirty years later, the *environmental* disaster merged with a *public health* scandal. At least one third of farmland is polluted as well as several coastal fishing areas. The consumption of contaminated products increases the frequency of premature births, neurological disorders in children and belated cognitive development—not to mention the highest rate of prostate cancers in the world. Several medical professors (Luc Murtigner, Pascal Blanchet, Dominique Belpomme)[6] drew the public authorities' attention to this proliferation of cancers related to the chemical contamination of soils. Civil society rose to the occasion. Several civil collectives emerged (*Zero Chlordecone, Objectif Zéro Poison, Matinik Lib*) which amplified the endeavours of environmental organisations. Local

---

[5] On this minority of power dubbed "Békés", refer to my chapter in Johnston Howard and Karl Watson (2000: 167–190).

[6] Among many publications, refer to Luc Montagner (2008).

deputies echoed the population's concerns. In 2008, the French government launched the first Chlordecone Plan to raise awareness among the general public, support agriculture professionals and foster research on this toxic pesticide. We are now on the fourth Plan (2021–2027) which marks a step forward compared to previous ones but still notoriously lacks sufficient funding. In a parliamentary report (2019), Justine Benin highlighted the discrepancy between the damage caused and the level of reparations considered. According to a study by *Santé Publique France* (Public Health France), 90% of both islands' populations are contaminated. Struck by the extent of this chemical pollution and compelled by the strength of mobilisation in the French Antilles, President Macron recognised that "*the State must take its full share of responsibility in dealing with this environmental scandal*" but he categorically objected to the existence of a "*public health scandal*."[7] His statement sparked an outcry in the French Antilles. For MP Serge Letchimy, "*the problem relates to how the overseas territories are treated. If pollution of similar magnitude had occurred in mainland France, the state would not have waited thirty-six years to step in. This only shows contempt, detachment, condescension, disrespect*."[8] In 2023, after 16 years of proceedings, the French justice system dismissed the chlordecone case. The dismissal, which carried significant symbolic weight, was the outcome dreaded by the elected officials and populations of Martinique and Guadeloupe, who construed it as a "denial of justice" and appealed the decision. Since the dismissal of charges, demonstrations and rallies have flourished across both islands. The case is far from closed.

Hawaii experienced a similar rift that led the local population to oppose the US giants of the fruit industry (Dole Fruit Company, Del Monte, Maui & Land and Pine). For forty years, a molecule known by the acronym DBCD was used in pineapple plantations to control worms that compromised fruit growth. According to the manufacturers, the pesticide did not theoretically pose any threat to humans or their living environment. But in reality, it contaminated groundwaters and the drinking water supply network. In 1977, DBCD was banned in California following laboratory tests and the emergence of diseases among the staff of several agricultural companies. Links of causality were established with liver and

---

[7] Press conference during his 2018 visit to Martinique.

[8] Reported in the newspaper France Antilles, 17 July, 2018.

kidney damage, which could lead to cancers. The federal Environmental Protection Agency (EPA) then required all States to ban its use by 1979 but granted the Hawaiian Association of Pineapple Producers a waiver to continue as if Hawaii were not a State like the others. Douglas Costle, its administrator, then justified this exception on grounds that the interests of Hawaii's main economic sector should prevail over the population's health. Initial studies revealed that Hawaii's soils contained ten times more pesticides and herbicides per mi2 than those of other States. This resulted in a capacity failure of the drinking water distribution system. This environmental crisis began turning into a health scandal as serious health problems started to rise among the population: kidney and liver dysfunctions, testicular atrophy and fertility disorders. The Department of Health and the Water Authority defied the Department of Agriculture and the Federal Environmental Protection Agency. The former sounded the alarm while the latter kept stalling. Environmental organisations stepped up their game to get a permanent ban on DBCD and spoke out against the authorisation agro-industrialists enjoyed to deplete their stocks. The NGOs succeeded in 1984 but legal actions were still ongoing to achieve the decontamination of sites by industrial operators. Periodic sampling showed a downward trend in DBCD levels but traces of the pesticide still remained in 2018. Environmental activists then launched a second battle against another pesticide that took over from the first; chlorpyrifos, whose ban was suspended by the Trump administration. This time, Hawaii became the first US State to forbid its use, in 2019; and to prescribe impact studies to monitor its effects over time on the population and its living environment.[9]

In the Dutch overseas territories, islanders have been waging a similar fight against the environmental and health impacts of the oil industry. In Curaçao and Aruba, which are also two hotspots of world tourism, the operations of oversized factories generated toxic emissions for decades. In the former, the *Royal Dutch Shell* oil company operated, from 1915 to 1985, one of the largest refineries in the Caribbean: the *Isla Refineria*, which processed crude oil from an offshore deposit in Venezuela. As the largest employer in the island, it attracted hundreds of workers from neighbouring countries. The Dutch hydrocarbon company thus became the epicentre of power in Curaçao, which was then a colony

---

[9] For an update, refer to Temper Del Bene and Martinez-Alier (2015).

administered by a governor. For nearly a century, the refinery released various pollutants such as carbon monoxide, fine particles and greenhouse gases into the atmosphere. These toxic emissions have caused health problems among employees and the local population. According to an impact assessment (Pulster 2015), concentrations of fine particles and sulphur oxides were among the highest in the world. Echoing the people's unrest, environmental organisations demanded that environmental protection and the health of local residents be put on the agenda. Demonstrations took place in front of the refinery's headquarters, which faced legal proceedings. The local authorities called on the Dutch government to intercede with its national champion. In 1985, Royal Dutch Shell chose to sell the plant for a symbolic guilder to the government of Curaçao rather than align it with international standards. The latter decided to entrust its management to the group *Petroleos de Venezuela* (PVDSA) which aggravated the environmental bill and put the blame on the Dutch multinational. Toxic discharges into the air continue to jeopardise the health of the 20,000 residents living near the refinery. On their behalf, the environmentalist foundation SMOC[10] sued PVDSA in court to force it into *greening* its production process and compensate the contaminated residents. The Venezuelan company escaped all sanctions until its operating contract terminated in 2019. Since the refinery was shut down, the level of air pollution has dropped considerably even though the chemical contamination of soils still remains a concern. And yet, the riparian communities did not get any compensation for the harm suffered. Just like in Aruba, which experienced a similar misfortune with US giant *EXXON*, Curaçao's environmental organisations demanded that the local authorities include drastic environmental standards in the operating contract of any potential buyer.

Conclusion

This chapter examined several case studies of collective struggles that reveal the increasing politicisation of environmental issues, and the overseas territories' ability to respond to discriminatory treatment from their administering countries. It delves into the many ways in which OTs became laboratories for all kinds of experimental and illegal activities

---

[10] In Dutch, *"Schoon Milieu op Curaçao"* which means Clean Environment in Curaçao.

prohibited in the mainlands. Furthermore, some have paid a heavy price to ensure the safety of their "motherland" thousands of miles away. Others suffered for the benefit of large metropolitan firms whose activities were relocated overseas to bypass the environmental standards applied in the mainland. These facts, some of which have been silenced for a very long time in official history, are suddenly coming to the fore and memory becomes the banner for new struggles being waged in the name of justice and dignity.

CHAPTER 10

From Memory Conflicts to Reparation Claims

Abstract The war of memories is another dimension of the overseas territories' mobilisation for *true* equality. Often branded by the stigma of slavery and colonisation, their history is either ignored or kept on the margins of national narratives. The legitimacy of these narratives is then challenged by the rise of other narratives of that shared past, brought into the public arena by minorities concerned about their inclusion in national symbolic constructs. These peripheral disputes spread to mainland capitals and take various forms. In some cases, they manifest in the reconsideration of historical figures celebrated in the public space such as in the Cook Islands, Greenland/Kalaallit Nunaat or Martinique. In others, they involve demands for land redistribution or the return to original territories such as in Easter Island, Christmas Island, Guam, the Chagos archipelago or French Polynesia. In all cases, they crystallise demands for the reparation of memorial wounds. Wherever the bites of colonial history are still raw, the struggle for *real* equality goes hand in hand with a politicisation of territorial identities (Constant 1993). This demand for cultural autonomy and respect for local cultures is another aspect of resistance to national authorities. Identity claims act as safety valves for unresolved sociopolitical tensions between islands and mainlands.

Keywords War over statues · Heroes or colonial masters? · Cook Islands · Maori cultural activists · Nuuk · Revaluation of Inuit culture · Martinique · Promotion of Black figures · Displacement of population ·

© The Author(s), under exclusive license to Springer Nature Switzerland AG 2024
F. Constant, *Overseas Territories in World Affairs*,
https://doi.org/10.1007/978-3-031-64233-3_10

Land redistribution · Easter Island · Christmas Island · Guam · Chagos · French Polynesia · Politicisation of culture · New Caledonia · Jean-Marie Tjibaou · Identity claims as safety valves

The war of memories is another dimension of the OTs' mobilisation for *true* equality. Often branded by the stigma of slavery and colonisation, their history is either ignored or kept on the margins of national narratives. The legitimacy of these narratives is then challenged by the rise of other narratives of that shared past, brought into the public arena by minorities concerned about their inclusion in national symbolic constructs. These peripheral disputes spread to mainland capitals and take various forms. In some cases, they manifest in the reconsideration of historical figures celebrated in the public space. In others, they involve demands for land redistribution or the return to original territories. In all cases, they crystallise demands for the reparation of memorial wounds.

THE WAR ON STATUES: HEROES OR EXECUTIONERS?

Statues are regularly targeted by activists who challenge the authorities on the predominance of European, colonialist and paternalistic figures in the public space. These activists demand a transformation of the statuary landscape to incorporate non-European historical figures who have embodied ideals of freedom and emancipation. While these actions of protest are nothing new, they were revived by the death of George Floyd under the knee of a White police officer in the United States (Celestine 2018). The contagion effect played its full part in that process, via social media and the overseas diasporas.

In March 2019, at the request of local customary authorities, the Government of the Cook Islands set up a commission to propose a Maori language name for their country which bears that of Captain James Cook, who is associated with British expansion in the Pacific. The commission, which has registered a hundred proposals, continues its consultations with the archipelago's fifteen islands to reach consensus on a figure or a vernacular term to honour their thousand-year language, culture and history. According to its President, a compromise could be found in the combination of a Maori name with that of Cook, as is the case of New Zealand-*Aoteaora*. Whichever solution is chosen, it must symbolise the

Polynesian identity of this overseas territory of New Zealand. On 22 May 2020, in Martinique, a handful of activists broke two statues of Victor Schoelcher, who initiated the decree of 27 April 1848 that abolished slavery. With this controversial gesture, they intended to expose the conveniently ignored role of slaves in their own liberation, and challenge the view of abolition as a generous gift from France. "*Schoelcher is not our savior*", they wrote in a statement in which they took a stand against the outdated imagery "*of a White France stroking the frizzy hair of a Black child just freed from their chains.*"[1] From their perspective, the French Republic must also celebrate Black figures who have shaped the shared history but remain oddly unknown to the general public. A few weeks later, the Norwegian missionary Hans Egede, founder of the city of Nuuk in 1728 and eponymous figure in the history of Greenland, was the target of Inuit activists. A symbol of Danish colonialism, his statue was vandalised with red paint and its base was tagged with the word "Decolonize". With this unprecedented move, they called for a reassessment of his legacy and demanded that unjustly ignored Inuit figures be brought to light. In response to this call-to-action, city authorities held a consultation of its citizens in July 2020. Sixty percent of voters chose to leave the statue at its current location while forty percent demanded the relocation of this "*symbol of colonial violence*". At the same time, Puerto Rico was experiencing a revival of activism against the presence of Spanish colonial figures in the public space. In the bull's eye: Christopher Columbus and Juan Ponce de Leon in particular. Both historical figures are charged with enslaving the indigenous populations before undertaking their near final extermination. Some of their statues were knocked down during demonstrations across the island. According to Puerto Rican activists, "*it is not the statue as such but what it represents that is unbearable; that is, the celebration of our genocide.*"[2]

These conflicts of memory resonate in the big "mainland" cities that are home to many overseas diasporas. From Los Angeles to Paris, from San Francisco to Wellington, from New York to Copenhagen; initiatives are multiplying that aim to relay advocacy from offshore territories. In the two US west coast cities, protestors unbolted the statue of Junipero Serra, a Spanish Franciscan missionary accused of contributing to the

---

[1] Reported in *Le Monde Newspaper*, 23 May, 2020 online.
[2] Reported in Wyatte Grantham-Philipps (2020) online.

subjugation of the Native Americans. In the Danish capital, activists attacked a replica of the statue of Hans Egede which they vandalised in the same way as the original in Nuuk. In Wellington, city authorities chose to remove a statue of James Cook while in Gisborne, its replica was damaged by groups demanding its removal from public space. In Paris, an anti-racist activist tagged and threw paint on Colbert's statue in front of the National Assembly. This Minister under Louis XIV, celebrated by the French Republic, was also the founder of the *Compagnie des Indes* (French West India Company) and the inspiration for the *Code Noir* (Black Code) which regulated slavery in the French colonies. This protest action crystallised a public debate that was also taking place at the same time in other capitals. The parties involved fall into three factions. The first one comprises those who demand that European figures embodying the colonial past be replaced by overseas figures who instead symbolise the anti-colonial struggle. The second rallies those who refute this radical transformation of public statuary landscapes, on the grounds that it would trigger a vicious spiral by wrecking the project of a shared national narrative. The third faction brings together those who, on the contrary, advocate a rebalancing of the statuary landscape based not on the removal of any controversial figure but on the addition of previously marginalised ones. Obviously, the heart of the debate—which does not only affect the overseas territories but is magnified by their lens—is *political*: will the acknowledgement of "minority" narratives foster social cohesion or instead, social fragmentation? For some, it would provide a salutary update to a shared history. For others, it may shatter national foundations. In any case, the debate's recurrence goes to show that the status quo is no longer sustainable (Rothberg 2013).

From Population Displacement to Land Redistribution

Many overseas territories have experienced phases of forced displacement or geographical seclusion of their populations. From French Polynesia to Guam, from Christmas Island to the Bikini and Enewetak atolls, from Easter Island to Chagos; thousands of indigenous people or long-established workers were driven *manu militari* from their territories. Induced by Reason of State, these traumatic events of the past provide their victims or their descendants with leverage to demand symbolic and financial reparations. The various judicial processes and social mobilisations that ensued, however, have not been equally successful. In French Polynesia, the forced evacuation of several atolls is still a pending matter. Despite the small size of the populations affected, no provision was made to compensate the expropriated islanders who were arbitrarily relocated to other atolls. Three thousand Mururoa natives were in that situation. Thirty years later, none of them have been able to settle back. The atoll has been classified as a "military area". About twenty soldiers take turns to monitor the site. Rather than individual compensations, the French authorities have emphasised the payment of a "nuclear annuity" to the Territory since the CEP was closed. This political sleight of hand does not match the sacrifice of these citizens who paid a personal tribute to France's nuclear independence. As one of them willingly states, *"The popaas (Whites) have soiled our fenua (Earth). They have to fix it."*[3] This determination is shared by other indigenous communities that were also brutally deprived of their property and living environment for similar motives. The aboriginal populations of Christmas and Malden Islands—expropriated because of the nuclear tests conducted by the United Kingdom with the agreement of Australia—were initially unsuccessful in the British courts. The latter rejected them on the grounds that the United Kingdom did have sovereignty over these territories at the time of those nuclear tests. The complainants then pressured the Australian authorities for about a decade. In 1995, they received compensation of 13.5 million Australian dollars for their forced displacement. In 1998, their land was finally returned to them. Controversy then shifted towards the quality of the site's decontamination and the reliability of the radioactive waste containers buried in part of the atoll.

In Guam, in the name of US security, the Chamorro people were concentrated in a section of their territory turned into a naval air base. Military facilities occupied a third of the island. Labour flew in from the Americas and the Philippines. Very quickly, the Chamorro became a minority while the extension of the military complex restricted their freedom. Criticism of Guam's militarisation peaked in 2017 when North Korean leader Kim Jong-un and Chinese President Xi Jinping announced they could destroy the island with a purpose-built missile. During a public meeting with Governor Lou Guerrero, a Chamorro directly called

---

[3] Reported by *Polynésie La Première*, Portal of News related to French OTs, 23 June 2019, online.

out to her: *"We will all die without having obtained reparation, without having been returned our land, without having saved our culture. And for what? For their national security that puts our lives at risk!"*.[4] According to the Governor, Guam's political status—as an unincorporated territory—does not allow it to be heard by Congress, which can unilaterally decide on its "assignment". That is the reason why she advocates for a statutory change that would grant its inhabitants the political power to resist the decisions made in Washington DC. But here again, the ultimate decision is the prerogative of Congress, which invariably favours the strategic security of the United States over the indigenous peoples' right to self-determination.[5]

The British Indian Ocean Territory (BIOT) is another harrowing illustration. A few years before the independence of Mauritius, the United Kingdom detached the Chagos Archipelago to build military facilities shared with the United States. The 1,500 inhabitants employed in copra plantations were then transferred to Mauritius against their will and without any compensation. Deprived of their possessions and jobs, they wound up in utter misery and dire psychological distress. At the same time, the United States was converting the largest island, Diego Garcia, into a centrepiece of its offshore military architecture, as part of a bilateral agreement with the United Kingdom. The Chagossians then engaged in a long political and judicial struggle to obtain the right to return to their homeland. Assisted by various NGOs, they brought cases before the British and US courts. In 2006, the British High Court recognised their right to return, but the English Government appealed to the Judicial Committee of the House of Lords, which ruled in its favour. US courts routinely dismissed plaintiffs while petitions to US Presidents came to no avail. The Government of Mauritius relayed the Chagossian petition to the International Court of Justice which urged the United Kingdom to *"cease its administration of the archipelago as soon as possible"*,[6] based on a United Nations resolution prohibiting the partition of colonies before their independence. The UK rejected this decision issued in 2017, on the grounds that the Diego Garcia Naval Air Station was protecting

---

[4] Reported in *Guam Daily Post*, 4 December 2017, online.

[5] For a more in-depth analysis, refer to Kruse (2018).

[6] Refer to the official decision made by the International Court of Justice and published on its website.

the entire world against *"international terrorism, crime and piracy"*.[7] After a new condemnation by the United Nations General Assembly, the British authorities this time challenged the sovereignty of Mauritius over the Chagos. These stalling manoeuvres devastated the Chagossian community. But thanks to demonstrations in Port Louis and London, they were granted, in February 2022, permission for a short visit to the archipelago—with the notable exception of Diego Garcia. And yet: the more time goes by, the less likely the prospect of a return home. Many are either dead or too old. Their descendants have built a life in exile—even as the myth of a potential return remains. Either way, it is an essential part of their collective identity that feeds an asymmetrical fight against powers concerned above all with their own strategic interests.[8] Despite appearances, these collective struggles are not completely in vain, for they highlight failures to the democratic principles that these very powers cry out for.

Territorial Identities as a Power Struggle

Wherever the bites of colonial history are still raw, the struggle for *real* equality goes hand in hand with a politicisation of territorial identities (Constant 1993). This demand for cultural autonomy and respect for local cultures is another aspect of resistance to national authorities. In their comparative approach to a sample of OTs, Malcolm Ferdinand, Gert Oostindie and Wouter Veenendaal even suggest that this requirement *"has become Plan B for communities that have suffered from colonialism and its legacy but at the same time, for practical reasons, dismiss the option of full independence."* (2020: 20). In societies characterised by strong socioracial divides, the identity debate is much more salient than in more homogeneous ones—such as Saint Barthélemy, Saint Helena or Faroe Islands—because they pit individuals perceived as distant relatives of slave-holding settlers, against others who identify as direct descendants of enslaved or colonised peoples. This colonial history, looming on the surface of general awareness, escalates even the most trivial social

---

[7] Excerpt of a press release, Office of the Prime Minister, London, 27 September 2017, online.

[8] For more arguments and facts, refer to Peter Harris (2022).

conflicts—like a ticking time bomb. In these territories marked by political and economic dependence, identity claims act as safety valves for unresolved sociopolitical tensions. Among other examples, New Caledonia, Easter Island and Curaçao are striking illustrations of how cultural grievances have been part of dynamic political compromises with mainland authorities. In the former, the Kanak awakening was fuelled by the fight against appalling socio-economic inequalities but also by a fierce desire to promote ancestral memory and culture which were threatened by folklorisation. The "*Mélanésia 2000*" festival, organised in Nouméa by Jean-Marie Tjibaou in 1975, was the event that kicked it off. For the first time, the Kanak's population publicly presented their folk arts and traditions; positing the Territory's future in terms of recognising the Kanaks as Kanaks; recalling that this land was their fathers' and that nothing sustainable could possibly be built without them. While this unprecedented cultural festival did not keep its political promises, the revival of Kanak culture remains at the core of its people's emancipation project. Having become leader of the Kanak and Socialist National Liberation Front (FNLKS), Jean-Marie Tjibaou defined the outlines of that project as follows: "*To allow Kanaks a self-projection that will enable them to discover and redefine their very identity (..) to help them gain self-confidence and regain more dignity and pride (..) to remove psychological blocks such as the inferiority complex that is largely linked to the cultural insignificance they have been reduced to*" (1996: 89). The Matignon Accords of 1988 took stock of that project with the creation of a centre devoted to the promotion of a future-oriented Melanesian culture. Designed by world-class architect Renzo Piano, its design is a modern interpretation of the traditional Kanak habitat and its ocean-oriented dimension (Bensa, 2000). Inaugurated in 1998 following the Noumea Accords, the centre epitomises the official acknowledgment of a Kanak identity open to the world. In 2010, New Caledonia adopted a distinctive flag to be displayed next to the tricolour emblem during official ceremonies. But these measures were far from unanimous. The city authorities of "*Nouméa, la blanche*" (White Nouméa) opposed the installation of a Kanak totem pole in the city centre, which would eventually be erected in a suburban district thanks to a change of majority within the council. In an anthropological study published in 2018, Caroline Graille pinpointed some relevant pending matters: in a society deeply divided along ethnic and racial lines but to a certain extent, mixed and multicultural; what traditions, heroes and symbols could possibly embody "living together" in New Caledonia's future—if it is not too late[9]?

In many regards, the *Rapa Nui* people's identity struggle resembles the Kanaks'. After an extraordinarily violent colonisation, the *Rapa Nui* were marginalised and stigmatised on their own land. Then began a long political struggle to assert their cultural rights, demanding a control of migration as well as land restitution. On the one hand, it was a matter of stopping a vicious process in which the indigenous people were minoritised by the massive immigration of mainland Chileans; on the other hand, it was a question of recovering lands that sheltered their ancestral heritage. A law was finally passed by the Chilean parliament to regulate the length of stay of nationals and international tourists; but the sacred archaeological sites occupied by demonstrators were brutally evacuated by the Chilean special forces. The representatives of the Pascuan people demanded their restitution and the co-management of the natural park that covers forty percent of the island. Their determination and pressure from international NGOs forced the Chilean authorities to meet part of these requests. Some urban and peri-urban land was indeed returned. Members of the *Rapa Nui* community were co-opted in the governance of the park which however remained property of the Chilean government. Powerful economic interests have worked behind the scenes in this measured arbitration, with international tourism now the territory's main economic pillar. One hundred and sixteen thousand people visit it every year to admire the famous monumental sculptures called *moai* that have become its "star product". This continuous surge of travellers undermines the balance of the island's ecosystem, affecting the natives' way of life in the process. Their cultural struggle reflects their political willingness to exert some control over the future of their millennial homeland. It has also led them to launch a campaign for the return of *moai* held in European museums. In 2018, a delegation of *Rapa Nui* went to the British Museum to plead for the return of the *moai Hoa Hakananai'a*—bird man—taken away by the British one hundred and fifty years earlier; but the claim did not succeed. A year later, the same approach proved more successful with a Norwegian museum. The director pledged to return the archaeological and photographic pieces collected by explorer Thor Heyerdahl during his expeditions in the mid-twentieth century—provided that

---

[9] On the same topic, I highly recommend Anthony Tutugoro's forthcoming book issued from his PhD. Dissertation in political science (Tutugoro 2024).

they be preserved in good conditions. A small victory for the *Rapa Nui* people that had little impact on domestic politics where their aspirations still take second place to the Chilean central authorities' concerns.

Opposite Easter Island, the Caribbean overseas territories display a myriad of situations where political demands are also expressed in cultural terms. In Martinique and Guadeloupe but also in Puerto Rico and Curaçao; nationalist, anti-colonial and identity upheavals have transformed vernacular languages into political instruments. Creole, Spanish and Papiamento have thus become the banner of territorial identities that politicians hold up in resistance to national political injunctions, and to let the world know *ki moun nou yé* (literally, "who we are"). In Curaçao, this identity debate is rooted in the concept of *Yu di Kòrsou* which literally means "Child of Curaçao". The question it raises is: Who is one and who is not? The answer is complex because it involves sedimented and competing identities built around unresolved historical issues, postcolonial, political and constitutional changes; and belonging to a globalised world. Originally, the term *Yu di Kòrsou* appeared to demand the civil integration of the population of African origin. For centuries, citizenship was tied to colour and religion. Legitimate citizens were White and Protestant Curacians. Afro-Curacians were excluded until the introduction of universal suffrage in 1949, when the Church advocated for their inclusion. With their gradual political awakening, *Yu di Kòrsou* became synonymous with Curacians of African descent. According to René Rosalia, an Afro-Curacian politician, "a *Yu di Kòrsou is someone who speaks and understands Papiamento (…) accepts and embraces Curaçao's multicultural context (..) recognises that elements of African origin are fundamental in the culture of Curacao.*"[10] Thus defined, *Yu di Kòrsou* excludes Curacians of European origin (*makamba*), Dutch as well as English-speaking or Spanish-speaking Caribbean immigrants residing on the island. Unlike Dutch citizenship, which legally makes every Curacian a member of the Curacao political community—as an integral part of the Kingdom of the Netherlands—*Yu di Kòrsou* connotes a subjective belonging to the population's majority socio-racial group, intensely experienced as such by those who view themselves and are recognised as such. "(..) *being Yu di Kòrsou,*" writes Rose Mary Allen, "*has a less tangible and more emotional resonance, because it involves (a sense of grounding),*

---

[10] Quoted in Rose Mary Allen (2016: 129).

connection, inclusion, unity, belonging, access, fidelity, loyalty and belonging to the place where one's umbilical cord is buried as goes the local saying" (2016: 142). This fierce desire to set a cultural identity apart from the Netherlands' multiplied tenfold with the "autonomous country" status achieved by Curaçao in 2010, and coexists with aspirations of equality with the European compatriots. The coexistence of such claims, which has been misconstrued as contradictory, is blatant in political relations with the Dutch authorities. Depending on the situation and the stakes, Curaçao sometimes plays off its position as a member of the Kingdom of the Netherlands; sometimes off its status as an OCT of the European Union; and some other times off its Caribbean and Latin American affiliation. This tactical sway between variable-geometry allegiances, which is leveraged in many other non-sovereign territories (from French Polynesia to the Faroe Islands or the Canary Islands and Sint Maarten), demonstrates the flexibility, pragmatism and even opportunism that overseas countries can display in order to get some leeway in a postcolonial and globalised context—including in international matters where some of them show remarkable diplomatic activism.

Conclusion

This chapter commented on several case-studies related to conflicts of memory and reparation claims. It demonstrated how aspirations for political empowerment can enter the cultural and identity arenas and draw from the repertoire of decolonial activism. In subnational jurisdictions whose deep divisions run along ethno-racial lines—such as New Caledonia/Kanaky or Easter Island/Rapa Nui—the struggle for local power merges with an internal fight for collective identity, ancestral memory and values. Especially in the former, it carries the dormant risk of social explosion or even civil war, given the population's split into two communities opposed to each other. One recognises France as a motherland while the other calls on Melanesian culture to self-determine as a nation in the making. These contradictory predicaments bear consequences in the international arena, which will be examined in the following section.

PART IV

An Ambivalent Status on the International Stage

« *Long-standing distinctions, both legal and diplomatic, between established sovereign states and other international actors seem to be increasingly blurred by changing practices in international relations. Sub-national island jurisdictions are among the less recognized players in conventional international relations, despite the fact that many of them are now particularly active in external representation, engaging in unexpected external relations, and acquiring means to enhance their regional and even global presence.* »
Barry Bartmann (2006: 541–542)

In theory, overseas territories do not have a legal existence in the realm of international politics. As non-sovereign jurisdictions, they are not expected to maintain autonomous international relations. And yet, some of them have indeed built relationships with third countries using either the diplomatic platform provided by central authorities, or Track-Two diplomacy based on informal interactions. While vertical relations with the administering powers still prevail on horizontal exchanges involving other territories, overseas territories continue to gradually expand their international reach through a growing range of themes, over time and according to opportunities. Initially limited to non-sovereign fields such as culture, sports or convenience stores, they now include natural disaster management, territorial connectivity, energy transition, environmental issues and climate change. This development is supported by national authorities in view of further amplifying their own diplomacy of influence via their regional overseas assets. With timelines specific to each overseas territory, this unprecedented policy has enabled transfers of powers that benefit local authorities, thereby empowering them to engage in formal relations with independent states under the more or less strict supervision of their administering nations.

Scopes of action vary considerably from one offshore land to the other. The Cook Islands and Niue boast the largest scope of action on the international stage, where they operate as independent states although they are not formally considered as such. Since 1978 and 1988, respectively, they are free to become members of multilateral and international organisations in their own names, to sign bilateral treaties with sovereign entities and to open representation offices in third countries. Another step forward was made in the 2000s when the New Zealand government officially authorised them to conduct their own foreign policy. A one-of-a-kind situation acknowledged by the United Nations, that sharply contrasts with the case of smaller territories like Saba or Anguilla; or isolated ones such as the Pitcairn Islands and Tokelau—not to mention militarised examples like Guam, where international policy remains the undisputed jurisdiction of the countries in charge of its administration. Along that spectrum lie a broad range of intermediate situations where varying degrees of power delegations allow other overseas territories to partake in the definition and sometimes, in the implementation of their administering countries' foreign policy. This applies to the Faroe Islands, French Polynesia, Curaçao, Puerto Rico and the Cayman Islands, among others.

Either way, the overseas territories' involvement in international affairs mirrors a tri-fold incentive: asserting regional identities and belonging; boosting local economic growth and promoting territorial interests when they do not coincide with the mainland's. To achieve these goals, overseas territories have embraced increasingly diverse forms of international interactions: they either complement their administering state's international policy, or seek to undermine or resist it when it conflicts with their territorial interests.

CHAPTER 11

Diverse Forms of International Interaction

Abstract In theory, overseas territories do not have a legal existence in the realm of international politics. As non-sovereign territories, they are not expected to maintain autonomous international relations. And yet, some of them have indeed built relationships with third countries using either the diplomatic platform provided by central authorities, or Track-Two diplomacy based on informal interactions. While vertical relations with the administering powers still prevail on horizontal exchanges involving other territories, overseas territories continue to gradually expand their international reach through a growing range of themes, over time and according to opportunities. Designated as paradiplomacy, it comprises all relations set on the international stage for representation purposes or the promotion of specific interests. It includes membership to regional and multilateral organisations, signing international agreements with third countries, the creation of representation offices abroad and the incorporation of ad hoc representatives to their respective state's diplomatic and consular network - or leveraging European programmes for territorial cooperation. That multilevel paradiplomacy unfolds at macro-multilateral and micro-regional scales depending on stakes, constraints, and resources. It is meant to strengthen the attractiveness and reputation of the overseas territories based on their insertion into international networks that value their assets, and the pooling of their development costs.

© The Author(s), under exclusive license to Springer Nature Switzerland AG 2024
F. Constant, *Overseas Territories in World Affairs*,
https://doi.org/10.1007/978-3-031-64233-3_11

Keywords Paradiplomacy · Association of Caribbean States · Caribbean community and common market · Cook Islands · Melanesian spearhead group · Organization of Eastern Caribbean States · Pacific Commission · Pacific Islands Forum · Indian Ocean Commission · Alliance of small and Islands States · Indian Ocean Rim Association · Common Market for Eastern and Southern Africa · United Nations Economic Commission for Latin America and the Caribbean

The type of foreign policy conducted by overseas territories—designated as paradiplomacy because it is led by subnational authorities—comprises all relations set on the international stage for representation purposes or the promotion of specific interests. It can be defined in general terms as *"(..) the outreach of non-sovereign jurisdictions to actors beyond their own borders"* (Bartmann 2006: 543). It includes membership to regional and multilateral organisations, signing international agreements with third countries, the creation of representation offices abroad and the incorporation of ad hoc representatives to their respective state's diplomatic and consular network—or leveraging European programmes for territorial cooperation. That multilevel paradiplomacy unfolds at macro-multilateral and micro-regional scales depending on stakes, constraints, and resources. It is meant to strengthen the attractiveness and reputation of the overseas territories based on their insertion into international networks that value their assets, and the pooling of their development costs (Constant 2020).

A Growing Presence in Regional and Multilateral Organisations

Apart from a few exceptions, the overseas territories are represented, under various statuses, in regional and multilateral organisations. That global, exponential trend is especially tangible in the Pacific Ocean where they leverage their multiple identities to extend their international surface area and promote their own interests. Among the twenty institutions that connect them to the countries in their regional environment,[1] five play a frontline role. The oldest one is the Community of Pacific States (CPS),

---

[1] For further historical background on regional cooperation in the South Pacific, refer to Michael Haas (1989).

a scientific and technical organisation that funds development projects. Established in 1947 at Australia's and New Zealand's joint initiative, it now includes the United States and France as well as about twenty of Oceania's countries and offshore territories. Formerly represented by their mainlands, the overseas territories affiliated to New Zealand (the Cook Islands and Niue), the United States (Guam, the Northern Mariana Islands, Samoa), France (Polynesia, New Caledonia, Wallis and Futuna) and Britain (Pitcairn) thus accessed full membership. But that status change barely altered the power balance in an arena where Western powers set the terms for discussion and contribute most of the available funding.

The frustrations of small island states and territories brought them to create the Pacific Islands Forum (PIF) which provided them with a political platform to defend and promote a vision of development, solidarity and peace, truly rooted in Oceania. Launched in 1971, the PIF, which rallied eighteen territories including Australia and New Zealand, began raising strong opposition to nuclear testing in the Pacific. The soundbox of a powerful anti-French sentiment, the PIF prompted the adoption of the Treaty of Rarotonga, establishing a nuclear-free zone. In 1986 and then again in 2013, several of its members supported the inclusion of New Caledonia, French Polynesia, Guam, Pitcairn, the American Samoa and Tokelau to the list of non-autonomous territories of the UN—thereby forcing their administering countries to report to its special commission for decolonisation (C24) in regard to their efforts to foster self-determination and development. France and its overseas territories were sidelined from the PIF until the end of nuclear tests. A normalisation phase then began that ended with the accession of New Caledonia and French Polynesia as associate members in 2006 and then as full members in 2016. Yet, some members of the PIF feared that the two French OTs could affect the balance of policy influence to benefit the Forum's former colonial powers (France, New-Zealand and Australia). These fears turned out to be unfounded: *"(..) despite their status as non-self-governing territories, New Caledonia and French Polynesia have at times successfully pursued their own interests over those of France (..). rather than acting as France's Trojan horse, (..) the two territories' membership further strengthen the Pacific canoe"*. (Leslie Prinsen 2018: 388). France and the United States share the status of Post-Forum Dialogue Partner, which keeps them from taking part in political discussions reserved to plenary members. While the PIF remains the main regional political organisation in the Pacific

Ocean, the dissatisfaction expressed by some members towards the political and financial dominance of Australia and New Zealand, has revived subregional ethnocultural identities.

In 1988, Papua New Guinea, the Solomon Islands and Vanuatu created a political alliance called the Melanesian Spearhead Group (MSG) which later went to incorporate Fidji and Indonesia. Its purpose is to promote Melanesian peoples on the global stage—starting with the political emancipation of the Kanak, and New Caledonia's independence. In that sense, it symbolically welcomed into its ranks the *Front de libération nationale Kanak et socialiste* (FLNKS—Kanak and Socialist National Liberation Front)—the only political formation to boast membership of a regional organisation. It rose in support of Western Papua's pro-independence movements while accepting Indonesia as an associate member. That inter-Melanesian solidarity also shows in the economic sector where it gave birth to an intergovernmental cooperation agreement. Backed by the PRC which established its headquarters in Port Vila, the MSG[2] has aroused suspicions among France, the United States, Australia and New Zealand, who fear the Asian giant could take a hold of New Caledonia in the event of independence. The rise of MSG created a ripple effect across both Polynesian and Micronesian subregional ensembles. In 2011, the Polynesian Leaders Group (PLG) emerged with the aim of promoting solidarity and cooperation between Oceania's peoples, and of protecting their traditions, cultures and values. Unlike the MSG, it includes a greater number of non-sovereign territories (the Cook Islands, Niue, Tokelau, the American Samoa, French Polynesia, Hawaii, Wallis and Futuna, Easter Island) than independent states (Samoa, Tonga, Tuvalu and New Zealand). In turn, five Micronesian states and territories (the Federated States of Micronesia, Kiribati, Nauru, Palau, the Marshall Islands) joined forces to make their voices heard on the regional stage. In February 2021, they initiated their withdrawal from the PIF to protest their candidate's alienation from the General Secretary position, contrary to the rule of alternate governance between all three sub regions.

Symmetrical shifts of varying extents took place in the Atlantic and Indian oceans. In the Caribbean, overseas territories began accessing regional organisations at different paces. The British territories (Anguilla, Bermuda, the British Virgin Islands, Montserrat, the Cayman Islands,

---

[2] For a more in-depth analysis, refer to Nathalie Mrgudovic (2015).

Turks and Caicos) were the first to become members of the Caribbean Community (CARICOM)[3]—the main sub regional forum with about twenty independent countries and non-sovereign territories, which succeeded in creating a free trade area in 1973 followed by a single market in 2006. Applications from the Dutch overseas territories (Aruba and Curaçao) and their French counterparts (Martinique, Guadeloupe and French Guiana) are being reviewed by an ad hoc committee. In contrast, both French island departments/regions became associate members of the Organisation of Eastern Caribbean States (OECS)[4] respectively in 2015 and 2019. Created in 1981, the OECS strives to promote the interests of the nine least developed countries and territories of CARICOM, providing them with a common economic and monetary space as well as a web of shared institutions (a Central Bank and a Supreme Court, in particular) that remain exclusive of associate members. During the accession process, the OECS delegates demanded a direct pipeline to the local elected representatives of both candidates, thereby sidelining the French authorities to stress the fact that the sole target of negotiations was the membership of those two French territories (rather than France as a nation). For that same reason, they requested that their emblems (flag, anthem, logotype) used in official bodies be different from those of the French Republic. The OECS is one of the few regional organisations that France—in contrast with some of its overseas territories—is not a member of (Byron 2015). A situation that led it to assign a dedicated ambassador in charge of pursuing its cooperation policy and monitoring interactions with its offshore territories. Finally, the Dutch, British and French overseas territories became members of the Association of Caribbean States (ACS) which rallies, to date, twenty-five countries of the Greater Caribbean—including Mexico, Panama and Colombia. Unlike the OECS, France is an associate member of ACS via French Guiana and Saint Barthélemy, while the Netherlands and the United Kingdom remain simple observers. The participation of overseas territories to ACS sessions entails previous consultations with their respective capitals, to ensure that they keep within the boundaries of their powers and jurisdictions. Ahead of these summits, negotiations take place

---

[3] For a historical retrospective on CARICOM, refer to Pasty Lewis, Terri-Ann Gilbert-Roberts and Jessica Byron (2018).

[4] For an institutional presentation of the OECS, refer to Alana Lancaster and Jill St George (2015).

between state representatives and elected representatives of the overseas, to prevent any dissonance during public meetings.

There are fewer interactions with regional organisations in the Indian Ocean. Out of the five overseas territories located in the region, only Reunion Island and Mayotte are represented in such forums—although to limited extents. The Indian Ocean Commission (IOC)[5] is their primary arena for foreign affairs. Composed of the Union of the Comoros, Mauritius, Seychelles, Madagascar and France via Reunion Island; it is an intergovernmental organisation designed to echo its member states' concerns and stances on the global stage. France stands for Reunion Island, but not Mayotte—due to the dispute opposing it to the Union of the Comoros. Neither Australia or the United Kingdom are members or observers of the organisation on behalf of their eligible overseas territories. The IOC has developed a portfolio of public policies aimed at boosting regional cooperation and integration in terms of energy and ecological transition, maritime security and even public health. The Common Market for Eastern and Southern Africa (COMESA) is the second forum leveraged by Reunion Island and Mayotte for potential interactions. With a membership of twenty-one African States, COMESA drives economic integration at a regional scale through the development of trade and investments. For the past ten years or so, it has been benefitting from a customs union and a common external tariff meant to boost domestic and cross-border trade (Girma Endale 2020). France has requested to move from its observer status towards associate membership in the name of Reunion Island. Regional authorities periodically attend the COMESA summits in view of opening up growth and employment opportunities for Reunion Island businesses looking to conquer market shares on the African mainland. For the time being, that approach has produced mixed outcomes. COMESA authorities seem to fear that Reunion Island might actually serve French interests rather than contribute to Africa's prosperity. A similar view prevails within the Indian Ocean Rim Association (IORA); a broad organisation with an economic mission that rallies countries as diverse as Iran, India, Mauritius, Tanzania or Oman. There again, France—which seats as a Dialogue Partner just like the United Kingdom - has applied for membership in the name of Reunion Island. But apparently, several member states suspect the French

---

[5] For a more detailed presentation, refer to Joy Vivek (2019).

of using Reunion Island to advance extra regional aspirations (Ogutu 2021).

That paradiplomatic approach also operates in multilateral institutions and various civil society organisations. Some overseas territories (Cook Islands or Niue) are members of several specialised agencies of the United Nations. Others are affiliated to their regional branches, as is the case of Puerto Rico, Bermuda or Guadeloupe—all are associate members of the Economic Commission for Latin America and the Caribbean (ECLAC). Others still (the American Samoa, the Dutch Antilles or Guam) are affiliated to the Alliance of Small Island States (AOSIS), which engaged in heavy lobbying at the COP 21 in view of adopting a strategy for climate change mitigation and adaptation accounting for the extreme vulnerability of island micro-states. Most of them belong to civil society organisations such as the Pacific Conference of Churches (especially New Caledonia and the Cook Islands), the International Football Federation (Curaçao, French Polynesia, the Cook Islands and Puerto Rico) or the Caribbean Tourism Organisation (Martinique, Aruba, the British Virgin Islands). All participate in cultural events such as the Caribbean Festival of Arts (CARIFESTA), the Festival of Pacific Arts & Culture (FESTPAC) or the Indian Ocean's music festival SAKIFO (SMF). All of these activities contribute to the overseas' visibility and to the convergence of their struggles. Seemingly benign, they actually carry the stakes of political recognition on to the international stage, where the overseas territories relentlessly seek partners to support their growth.

Differentiated Partnerships with the European Union

The European Union has established differentiated partnerships with twenty-two offshore territories owned by five of its member States (Spain, France, Denmark, the Netherlands and Portugal). In the aftermath of Brexit, the British Overseas Territories no longer enjoy such partnerships (Bosque 2020). Based on EU law, European overseas territories fall into two categories: the Outermost Regions (ORs) and the Overseas Countries and Territories (OCT). The former comprise the Azores, the Canary Islands, Guadeloupe, French Guiana, Martinique, Mayotte, Saint Martin, Madeira and Reunion Island—all of which are full-fledged parts of the EU. They are entirely subject to European law—with adjustments designed to accommodate their specific situations. The latter include

Aruba, Bonaire, Curaçao, Greenland, French Polynesia, New Caledonia, Saint Barthélemy, Sint Maarten, Saint Pierre and Miquelon, Wallis and Futuna and the French and Southern Arctic Lands (FSAL), which are not considered EU soil. EU law does not apply in those territories but their citizens do enjoy European citizenship—which allows them to move around freely and to work within the Union. In line with their status as EU associated territories, they are however eligible for development aid. With time, the EU seized the value of the overseas territories for its politics of influence and for promoting its strategic priorities in terms of sustainable development. That growing awareness translated into the implementation of a Territorial Cooperation Policy (TCP) to provide them with levers of growth and employment in their respective environments. Thus, the EU became the primary funder of their regional interactions.

Over the 2014–2020 period, the ORs have enjoyed a budget of 200 million euros from the European Regional Development Fund (ERDF), distributed across four operational programmes broken down into geographical zones (the Amazon region, the Caribbean, Madeira-Azores-Canary Islands, Indian Ocean). For instance, the 64 million euros allocated to the Caribbean have contributed to fund several projects involving ORs, OCTs and regional organisations. Among them, the CARIMAM project which strives to interconnect maritime protected areas devoted to the protection of sea mammals in the Greater Caribbean, received funding from the European Development Fund (EDF) to match contributions from the Dominican Republic and the US Virgin Islands. In the transport sector, the CARIBSKY project, initiated by Guadeloupe in view of optimising air travel across the Lesser Antilles, was enabled by EDF funding to Dominica and Antigua and Barbuda. In the field of entrepreneurship, the TEECA project led by Martinique and aimed at supporting medium size companies on the regional market, was backed by the OECS as well as the Caribbean Export Development Agency (CEDA). On the other hand, Madeira, the Azores and the Canary Islands have received about 100 million euros to implement cooperation projects with Cabo Verde, Senegal and Mauritania. On environmental matters, the IMPLAMAC project undertaken by the Canary Islands to assess the impacts of micro plastics and other emerging contaminants, has brought universities and research institutions together with the health authorities of the countries involved. On economic aspects, all three ORs have experimented with a model of sustainable, integrated and innovative aquaculture rooted in research and development, in the business-oriented view of producing invertebrates. Clearly, these projects contribute to the EU's influence in those parts of the world where the ORs stand as its outer borders. The latter also benefit from the resulting reinforcement of their horizontal relations—even at the cost of a new form of dependence on European funds.

Over the reference period, the OCTs have enjoyed a budget of 110 million euros from the EDF for the purpose of regional cooperation and integration. These credits were distributed between three operational programmes that cover respectively the Atlantic Ocean and the Caribbean, the Pacific, and the Indian Ocean. For example, the Pacific Territories Regional Project for Sustainable Ecosystem Management (PROTEGE), endowed with 36 million euros, seeks to foster economic development in terms of sustainability and resilience to climate change, based on biodiversity and renewable resources. Managed by the Pacific Community, it has been implemented in New Caledonia, French Polynesia, Wallis and Futuna as well as the Pitcairn Islands. However, since Brexit, the latter have lost their beneficiary status. Beneficiaries of the programme have praised it for a number of reasons. It has fostered networking among New-Caledonian, Polynesian and Wallisian professionals through training sessions addressing optimal water management, the development of the agroecology sector or sustainable forestries. These knowledge transfers coupled with the mobility of stakeholders have generated undeniable added value; but they continue to depend on EU funding, expertise and technical assistance. Greenland/Kalaallit Nunaat displays similar shortcomings. Over the 2014–2020 period, it received over 200 million euros in European financial aid in view of diversifying its economy and training young professionals both qualified and competent for the new jobs thereby created. Seven years after implementation, the results are quite uneven. In terms of education, schooling rates among the Inuit community have strongly increased but only half of students go on to secondary school. Those who leave school prematurely end up working in the fishing industry, which remains the island's main economic pillar. Economic diversification has not made much progress due to insufficient investments. As a result, Greenland/Kalaallit Nunaat—which is already structurally dependent on public funding from Denmark—is also proving increasingly dependent on European funding. In fact, the budget programmed for 2021–2027 has been incremented with the aim of anchoring it further West at a time when Russia and China are multiplying approach manœuvres in the Arctic region. In this regard, Ursula Von der Leyen, president of the European Commission, headed to Nuuk in March 2024 as part of the EU's search for materials to implement a green transition. Her visit was clearly "geopolitical" in a context of increasing international competition over strategic mineral resources. Following a partnership agreement signed in November 2023, she opened an office in the capital city despite the autonomous Danish OT not being part of the EU. In fact, Greenland/Kalaallit Nunaat has grown strategically important to Brussels, especially for its green-technology raw materials such as rare-earth elements and metals. According to experts, the world's largest OT counts 27 out of 34 strategic and critical raw materials needed by the EU to speed up its green transition (Bryant 2024).

The Overseas Countries and Territories Association (OCTA) seems less concerned about these hidden geopolitical agendas than about securing ever more funding from the EU. The obligation of means, which has grown more acute due to the impacts of the COVID-19 pandemic, has taken precedence over the demand for results. Moreover, this quest for international aid has also brought them to multiply cooperation agreements with third countries.

THE EXPONENTIAL RISE OF BILATERAL AGREEMENTS

The overseas territories that enjoy a high level of autonomy also boast a rather broad portfolio of bilateral relations. The Cook Islands stand out with a listing of fifty-two. With only eleven thousand residents and 91 mi2, this is an absolute record. There are three concentric and circular layers to its web of external relations. The first one comprises some fifteen of Oceania's countries including New Zealand and Australia, in addition to a myriad of island micro-states affiliated to the Pacific Community. The second group features a dozen Asian nations among which the People's Republic of China, India and Japan, Indonesia and the Philippines. The third layer counts with EU member states (namely, France, Belgium, Germany, Italy) and affiliated countries (Turkey and Switzerland, in particular). One of the Cook Islands' partnership agreements with Australia (2019–2024) gives them access to development aid destined to fund health, education and environmental projects. Relations with India took off in 2014 with the creation of the Forum for India-Pacific Islands Cooperation (FIPIC), which echoes their voice on matters of global warming, ocean protection or energy transition. Clearly, the leaders of these island micro-states—starting with the Cook Islands'—are flattered to be considered by a world power that, as a result, can count on their support during voting sessions at the United Nations. When it comes to France, relations follow both national and territorial tracks. With the central government, the Cook Islands—which frequently attends the France-Oceania Summits—maintains bilateral relations, especially on sovereign matters. The Armed forces of French Polynesia often take part in relief operations or joint drills. The French Embassy in New Zealand also carries out educational and cultural initiatives on location. With French Polynesia and New Caledonia, this proximity of Oceania's territories facilitates the implementation of large-scope projects: the setup of a submarine telecommunications cable rallying Tahiti and its neighbours; as well as the twinning of the maritime protected areas sheltered by both territories. These international actions displayed by the Cook Islands are supported by a rather extensive (para)diplomatic network, comprising four embassies in Wellington, Suva, Canberra and Brussels—not to mention a dozen general and honorary consulates. The office that was established in Belgium in 2002 right after the Cook Islands ratified the agreements between the EU and ACP countries, remains its only diplomatic mission outside the Pacific. Avarua, capital of the Cook Islands, hosts the embassies of New Zealand and Australia as well as twenty-four non-resident ambassadors distributed between Canberra and Wellington. The efficiency of that diplomatic setup relies not only on the convergence of views between the Cook Islands and New Zealand's national government, but also on the former's capacity to defend their own interests without hampering the latter's.

In spite of enjoying lesser autonomy, the Danish overseas have built, within the realm of their powers, official relations with third countries. The Faroe Islands maintain diplomatic relations with several states in which they have opened representation offices. Because fisheries are the territory's main source of income, they are the core pillar of Faroe's diplomatic endeavours. The archipelago's first mission abroad was set up in Brussels in 1998 to follow through on relations with the EU as a major diplomatic partner and primary market for exports. These bilateral relations were not smooth from the get go. On various occasions, the EU sanctioned the Faroese government for exceeding fishing quotas, and has provided strong incentives for banning traditional whales fishing (*grindadràp*). As they share a maritime boundary with the United

Kingdom, the Faroese authorities signed, following Brexit, a free trade commercial agreement and a framework agreement on fishing areas. With Iceland, they have established a single market (*Hoyvík Agreement*) to allow goods, services, capital and people to circulate freely. When it comes to Russia, to which they sell very lucrative fishing licences and where they export a third of their fish produce, they have been facing a dilemma since the start of the war in Ukraine: how can they preserve their commercial interests without facing the international community's criticism? Out of excuses to offer, the Faroese Parliament adopted, in May 2022, a law that provides sanctions on principle without fundamentally challenging any existing agreement in the fishing sector. The creation of a representation office in Beijing in 2019 is the direct consequence of a spectacular surge of Chinese imports in fishing produce. In anticipation of market volatility, this office was intended to secure alternative trade opportunities for a fishing industry that proves vital to the Faroe Islands. Likewise, they established another mission in Tel Aviv in 2021, to attract investors in view of diversifying their economy. The French overseas territories emulated that shift along a slightly different timeline. Thanks to the evolution of its autonomy status in 2004, French Polynesia was able to strengthen and extend its relations with its direct neighbours and with regional and extra regional powers. Its relations with the Cook Islands have materialised in high level political visits. President Édouard Fritch used to go to Avarua and his counterpart Mark Brown is a frequent visitor to Papeete. In May 2022, the agenda driving his presence included the preparation of the next Pacific Islands Forum, as well as the decision to contract Tahitian companies for the maintenance of the submarine telecommunications cable and the extension of the Cook Islands' digital infrastructure. At the same time, the French Polynesian authorities were consolidating their ties with New Zealand where Édouard Fritch also travelled on several occasions; namely in 2019 to pay tribute to the victims of the Christchurch terrorist attack. A year prior, he was in Wellington to sign a joint cooperation agreement (2018–2023) with New Zealand's Prime Minister, who inaugurated in 2021 a general consulate in Tahiti as French Polynesia became her country's third export market in the Pacific. Similar developments occurred with Australia, resulting in increased bilateral relations with French Polynesia as part of its strategic plan for the Pacific (*Pacific Step-up*). In 2021, a general consulate opened in Papeete in view of boosting cooperation in the areas of economy, trade and higher education. That paradiplomatic activity led French Polynesia's President to Easter Island and mainland Chile. In *Rapa Nui*, he celebrated the human, linguistic and cultural proximity between the two peoples. In Santiago de Chile, he tackled the protection of the Pacific Ocean and digital connectivity. On the first topic, he stressed once again the crucial matter of adapted governance and the need for a reasoned exploitation of resources. On the other, he offered President Sebastian Piñera to extend the submarine telecommunications cable from Tahiti to Chile in order to connect Oceania's southwest to South America. Finally, in Valparaiso he was welcomed at the Senate by Isabel Allende, daughter of the past President and former Chair of the Senate as well as active Senator. Back in Tahiti, Édouard Fritch received the new General Consul of the People's Republic of China, who had just entered office. With a quarter of its population claiming Chinese ancestry, French Polynesia has had a long-term relation with the Asian giant. In 2016, a PRC ambassador to France paid the French archipelago a mediatised and unprecedented visit. An adept of "wolf warfare diplomacy", Faye Lu emphasised the existing bilateral relations with the French OT and went as far as to state its significance as a pillar of diplomatic ties between China and France. A year later, a general consulate opened in Papeete as human, economic and cultural exchanges kept on thriving. As the French territory was severely hit by the COVID-19 pandemic, the Chinese authorities deployed a cargo plane with medical supplies. On the economic side, several infrastructure projects are backed by Chinese funding; which has triggered a prompt response from the French political authorities.

Conclusion

This chapter has brought evidence of the many ways in which subnational island jurisdictions interact in world affairs. Despite being non-self-governing territories by international law, some of them are actually engaged in multilateral organisations and able to maintain bilateral relations with sometimes faraway sovereign states. Nevertheless, they must navigate two pitfalls: one is being used as Trojan horses by their metropolitan power; the other is, on the contrary, openly opposing the latter's views. The first situation disqualifies them in the eyes of neighbouring states. The second one typically triggers political conflict with their administering country. In all cases, OTs are compelled to carve out a nuanced and flexible foreign policy in order to reap benefits from a multi-layered diplomacy, where every actor enters the power play with their own agenda. Under specific circumstances, clashes between OTs and their "motherland" are inevitable.

CHAPTER 12

Relays of Hardly Mutual Interests

Abstract Does the paradiplomacy conducted by the overseas territories serve their particular interests or those of the powers in charge of administering them? Is it a lever for the expansion of their respective mainland's influence or for promoting their views on the international stage? If conflict of interests there is; what is the common ground for arbitration and at whose expense? Academic literature is divided on these incidental questions. Some argue that non sovereign territories often reap a benefit from unfavourable power balances; while others consider that administering powers ultimately dominate any and all such partnerships. In reality, none of these views prevails over the other. Their relevance depends on the empirical evidence to which they are subjected. In some conflicts of interests, local authorities succeed in standing their ground. In other cases, national authorities are the ones imposing their agenda. Generally speaking, when major strategic interests are at stake, there is little room for compromise. Otherwise, any arrangement is possible. Several instances are considered such as Brexit (is it an opportunity for Global Britain or a step backwards for UKOTs?), maritime transport of nuclear waste (is it a riskless strategic activity or a major environmental threat?) or cooperation with People's Republic of China (is it mutually beneficial or potentially dangerous?).

Keywords Paradiplomacy · Linkage politics · National interest · Subnational interest · International issues · Intersectionality · Regional

© The Author(s), under exclusive license to Springer Nature Switzerland AG 2024
F. Constant, *Overseas Territories in World Affairs*,
https://doi.org/10.1007/978-3-031-64233-3_12

147

cooperation · Brexit · United Kingdom Overseas Territories · Nuclear waste · Association of Caribbean States · People's Republic of China · New Caledonia · French Polynesia

Does the paradiplomacy conducted by the overseas territories serve their particular interests or those of the powers in charge of administering them? Is it a lever for the expansion of their respective mainland's influence or for promoting their views on the international stage? If conflict of interests there is; what is the common ground for arbitration and at whose expense? Expert literature is divided on these incidental questions. Some (Prinsen 2018, Rezvani 2014) argue that non sovereign territories often reap a benefit from unfavourable power balances; while others (Aldrich, Connel 2020, Ferdinand et al. 2020) consider that administering powers ultimately dominate any and all such partnerships. In reality, none of these views prevails over the other. Their relevance depends on the empirical evidence to which they are subjected. In some conflicts of interests, local authorities succeed in standing their ground. In other cases, national authorities are the ones imposing their agenda. Generally speaking, when major strategic interests are at stake, there is little room for compromise. Otherwise, any arrangement is possible. Below are some examples that mirror a variety of key issues.

BREXIT: AN OPPORTUNITY (FOR "GLOBAL BRITAIN") OR A STEP BACKWARDS (FOR OVERSEAS TERRITORIES)?

One of the traits shared by all overseas territories is their invisibility on the national public stage of their administering countries. This was blatantly reasserted during the referendum of 2016 regarding the United Kingdom's exit from or continuance within the EU. During the election campaign, neither "*Leave*" or "*Remain*" advocates ever mentioned the matter of the British Overseas Territories (Bosque 2020). Admittedly, the consultation excluded them from voting—with the exception of Gibraltar—but their situation could have been discussed by national parties, considering their OCT status. Given their lack of representatives at the British Parliament, the United Kingdom Overseas Territory Association (UKOTA) could have been referred to. The joint Council of

Ministers that, each year, brings the national government and the overseas authorities together at the same table, only addressed the topic a year after the referendum—as part of broader discussions on post-Brexit relations. As Bishop and Clegg (2018) but also Bosque (2020) have shown, the UK has clearly disregarded its OTs' interests. More precisely, *"(..) it has prioritised its interests over these territories' interests; the UK has not been able to directly involve these territories in the withdrawal negotiations with the EU and has not been able to secure a special deal with the EU that could allow these territories to keep their current EU statuses. The UK has mechanisms such as entrustment which could have helped these territories conclude their own agreements with the EU, but the UK decided not to use them"* (Bosque 2020: 165).

Gibraltar, as a full-fledged part of the EU, was the only one to enjoy that special treatment since its citizens took part in the referendum vote. Had voters from the British Overseas Territories been granted that right, they would have most likely chosen to *"Remain"*—like their Gibraltar counterparts who gave that option its highest score across the entire nation, with 96% of votes. This electoral behaviour is easy to explain. Over the previous decades, the EU had grown to become a primary partner for the British OCTs. This entailed financial and technical support on issues as crucial as economic resilience, energy transition and even adaptation to climate change. Their citizens enjoyed full freedom of movement across the Schengen area and their products were allowed to enter the European market. In many regards, these territories were more easily heard by the EU than by the British authorities. Brexit mirrors to an even larger extent that unbalanced relation with the UK's overseas territories, which it only views through the lens of national interests. And yet, Brexit has already generated negative consequences for these OCTs, unilaterally and without any possibility of appeal or amendment. As of February 2020, they have lost their status as EU associated territories—which also implies losing access to the EDF and to technical assistance for the implementation of development projects—not to mention, relays to make their case.

For all these reasons, Brexit has revived the debate on their constitutional status. A debate that can be summed up in one question: how can they influence the decisions that affect them without directly breaking all ties with the United Kingdom? According Susie Alegre (2017), they could be empowered to sign international treaties in their own names or benefit from "safeguard clauses" when their interests fail to align with the United Kingdom's. Failing such transfers of powers, she cannot fathom a sustainable path for the British authorities to continue exerting their sovereignty over these offshore territories while still keeping them on the sidelines of public consultations that have a direct impact on their populations' living conditions. Against this backdrop, what is the value of self-determination as a core principle of the democratic creed claimed by the United Kingdom, if it is sacrificed on the altar of the nation's superior interests—a nation they are not even fully incorporated to? Furthermore, it is the very definition of sovereignty which comes into question. "*Events like Brexit,* writes Maria Bosque, *should help these territories put their feet on the ground and realise that, at crucial times, Westphalian or traditional sovereignty matters, even if these territories enjoy the greatest degree of autonomy possible. These territories have been deprived of the ability to make critical decisions regarding their present and future. While it is true that there are other forms of sovereignty, none of them provide complete independence"* (2020: 164).

Without responding to that pending matter, the Chamber of Commons requested in 2019 that the British Government compensate the end of European funding by the creation of a special fund for the overseas territories. It also recommended that these territories no longer be managed by the Ministry of Foreign Affairs, but instead by an ad hoc inter-ministerial department. For the time being, the British government does not seem open to these constitutional or administrative reforms, probably out of fear that they might establish a dangerous precedent considering its strategic interests in the Indian Ocean where it runs, alongside the United States, a military base set up on territory stolen from the people of Chagos.

Transport of Nuclear Waste: Riskless Strategic Activity or Major Environmental Threat?

With the end of nuclear tests, the deep-sea shipping of radioactive material became a highly sensitive topic. France is one of the few European countries to boast a nuclear processing plant in The Hague, which regularly delivers and receives loads of hazardous materials that travel through the Caribbean Sea and Panama's Canal, in particular. Coastal countries periodically voice their concerns regarding the environmental risks inherent in these nuclear waste shipments. At the second Summit of the Association of Caribbean States (ACS) hosted in April 1999 by the Dominican Republic, the Heads of States and Governments of the Member States adopted a final declaration in which they expressed their disapproval for the on-going maritime transport of nuclear waste across the whole region. Point 6 of the official document reads as follows: "We *consider the Caribbean Sea an invaluable asset and agree to give special priority to its preservation. We therefore deplore its ecological degradation of the Caribbean Sea and its continuous use for the transport of nuclear and toxic waste.*"[1]

France, which took part in that international meeting as an associate member through its departments in the Americas (Guadeloupe, French Guiana and Martinique) argued otherwise that these shipments were harmless and conducted in strict compliance with international standards. That official position stirred tensions among the French delegation. Antoine Karam, then President of the Regional Council of French Guiana and head of the delegation, stood his ground in the backstage against the French government's ambassador, dispatched in a hurry. The former refused to embrace the theory of harmless shipments while the latter urged him to stick to the official guidelines. One was eager to support the full declaration issued by the ACS on behalf of the French overseas territories, when the other pressured him to raise a caveat on a paragraph that indirectly targeted France. Warned by his ambassador, the French Minister of Foreign Affairs commanded President Karam to refrain from signing the document and withdrew his delegation powers. The decision further deepened the strife that opposed, within the delegation, locally elected representatives who refused to embrace a "*position contrary to the interests of the Caribbean peoples*"[2] and the national government's representative whose mission was to ensure the continuation of a very lucrative economic activity. A couple of years later, Alfred Marie-Jeanne, then President of the Regional Council of Martinique and head of the French delegation to the ACS, reiterated the French OTs' stance against the maritime transport of nuclear waste in the Caribbean. He fully approved the final declaration of the meeting held in Panama, namely article 19: "*We reaffirm the position adopted at the 3rd Summit in Margarita, where we reiterated our strenuous and forceful rejection of the continued use of the Caribbean Sea for the shipment and transshipment of nuclear material and toxic waste, given*

---

[1] ACS, Final Declaration, 2nd Summit of the Heads of States and Governments, 1999, April 17 online.

[2] Reported by *RFO Guyane*, 19 April 1999, online.

the threat that any accidental or deliberately induced spill of these materials would represent to the life and ecosystem of the region."[3]

Long before the law of 5 December 2016 came in force to expand their international jurisdiction, this French internal conflict went to show the capacity of local elected representatives to favour solidarity with Caribbean states and territories over their belonging to the French Republic, when national strategic interests do not match those of their respective territories. That resistance to national guidelines displayed overseas put a temporary hold on a nagging question raised by some member states in regard to their role within ACS: were they first and foremost the zealous stooges of the French authorities or on the contrary, unwavering allies of the Greater Caribbean? In contrast, Paris saw that same stance with the bafflement of a socialist government deemed close to regional authorities, and thereby far from anticipating such a conflict of interests - not to mention the foreseeable attitude of its head of delegation. In the aftermath of that diplomatic incident, ACS member states—endorsed by CARICOM—asked the United Nations for the creation of an international legal instrument aimed at regulating the maritime transport of nuclear materials; including compensations in the event of accidents affecting coastal states during transit. A few years later, the ACS initiated, with the support of Martinique and Guadeloupe now associate members in their own names, the proceedings required to convert the Caribbean Sea into a special international zone.

Cooperation with China: Mutually Beneficial or Potentially Dangerous?

Some overseas territories under Western sovereignty have long-standing relations with the People's Republic of China. Now a global power that claims strategic equality with the United States, the latter seeks to exert influence through development aid void of political strings. That approach to cooperation matches the eagerness of local authorities when it comes to boosting the development of their territories via additional funds to those allocated by their respective administering countries. By leveraging its diplomatic network as well as the links that bridge its diaspora and

---

[3] ACS, 4th Summit of Heads of State and/or Government, Declaration of Panama, July 29, 2005, online.

the homeland, PRC has strengthened its presence in the Pacific southwest with a proactive approach to both the bilateral and regional levels. Viewed as an intrusion in the Indo-Pacific region dominated by the United States and its allies, that diplomacy of influence stirs recurring tensions between overseas territories and their administering countries. The former view cooperation with the Asian giant as beneficial and welcome at a time when they must face multiple challenges simultaneously. Local authorities have a pragmatic stance on the matter, as it entails opportunities to broaden the scope of their international partnerships. The latter, instead, see it as a decoy to counter their own influence and impose Chinese hegemony over the Indo-Pacific region in the mid-run. From that perspective, Western powers have been calling their overseas territories back to order, persuading them to turn down partnerships with China that proved equally appealing and detrimental.

In June 2022, the Chinese Minister of Foreign Affairs toured about a dozen of small countries and territories of Oceania, to renew existing partnership agreements—including on military aspects. In the Cook Islands, Prime Minister Mark Brown suggested prioritising the tourism and education sectors in addition to infrastructures—while excluding security matters. During a press conference, Brown thanked the PRC for its long-term and massive support to the Cook Islands' development, and its selfless assistance to his country's fight against COVID-19—despite its own pandemic mitigation challenges. He highlighted the positive contributions of Chinese firms and local governments to the construction of infrastructure and improvement of people's livelihoods in the Cook Islands. He emphasised the PRC's indiscriminate approach towards small countries and its vision of mutually beneficial cooperation. His closing remarks asserted that the future of the Cook Islands is intricately linked with China, noting that the island country stands ready to push for further development of bilateral relations in the next 25 years.[4] Wang Yi responded by reiterating his country's willingness to back the Cook Islands' development efforts in exchange for mutual support on the international stage.

In Niue, Prime Minister Dalton Tagelagi reached an agreement with his Chinese counterpart to define his territory's needs over the following ten years. "*Joint initiatives with China*, he specified to the media, *such*

---

[4] Ministry of Foreign Affairs and Immigration, Press release, "Cook Islands and China Talk further Cooperation", June 19th 2022, online.

as road infrastructures or other types of investments, ultimately improve everyone's living conditions and contribute to Niue's aspiration for self-sufficiency. China heard Niue's call and we are very grateful for it.[5]" In both cases, the partnership with PRC is aimed at complementing island development without challenging special relationships with New Zealand. On the other hand, Chinese authorities refrain from openly challenging New Zealand's sovereignty over these overseas territories and instead, nurture the image of a well-meaning nation, attentive to the needs of those smaller territories. From Auckland's standpoint, however, the consolidation of this bilateral cooperation scheme jeopardises their political autonomy and exposes them to greater economic dependence. In response, then Prime Minister Jacinda Arden took the two-fold initiative of calling Western powers to action on those regional security and development issues in view of reducing the vulnerabilities of small island states likely to be fed on by the PRC; and of warning her overseas counterparts against "*obscure cooperation agreements, negotiated in a hurry and total lack of transparency*", which often comprise "*provisions that threaten their own territorial sovereignty*" and could make them "*pawns on the chessboard of China's geopolitical ambitions.*"[6] But her reach was limited to the realm of political persuasion, given their power to conduct foreign policy in their own names. Following this Pacific push from the PRC, Jacinda Ardens rushed to Washington DC to forge closer security ties with the US. For the first time,[7] she took a firmer stand in response to China's increasingly assertive stance in the Indo-Pacific.[8] For the time being, the realism exhibited by Mark Brown and Dalton Tagelagi compels them to try and combine the dividends of China's greed and the benefits of political affiliation to New Zealand.

---

[5] Reported by *Niue Star*, June 17th 2022, online.

[6] *New Zealand Herald*, July 3rd 2022, online.

[7] Historically, New Zealand was perceived as a country resisting militarisation in the region.

[8] The US and New-Zealand released a joint statement in which they "(..) *share the concern that the establishment of a persistent military presence in the Pacific by a State that does not share our values or security interests would fundamentally alter the strategic balance of the region and pose national-security concerns to both our countries.*" June 1st 2022, US State Department, online.

France is no exception in that it also faces Chinese competition in Oceania, where New Caledonia and French Polynesia maintain relations with the Asian giant without necessarily consulting or associating with national authorities (before or after the facts). Cultural exchanges nurtured by the Chinese diasporas have given way to political relations embodied by the opening of general consulates in Noumea and Papeete. The three consecutive referendums on self-determination in New Caledonia, held in 2018, 2020 and 2021 respectively, were closely monitored by the Chinese government, which objectively supported the pro-independence movement through the Sino-Caledonian Friendship Association affiliated to a branch of China's Communist Party (APCAE), whose mission is to spread the Asian power's influence worldwide. For the latter, the archipelago entails major economic and strategic value for its expansion in the South Pacific. New Caledonia is one of the largest nickel producers in the world, and PRC is its main client. With French Polynesia, bilateral relations took on a political charge about a decade ago. Local chief executives, from Gaston Flosse to Edouard Fritch - not to mention Oscar Temaru—made the trip to Beijing while high officials from China such as President Jiang Zemin or then Vice-President Xi Jinping also visited Papeete. To date, Chinese economic investments remain limited and have been focusing on the hospitality sector—in which the Hainan Group owns two of the biggest hotel establishments.

In 2013, a private Chinese investor presented a giant aquaculture farm project to the local authorities. Envisioned in a zone abandoned since the end of nuclear tests, it was initially endorsed by the French Polynesian government but its gigantic scope soon triggered suspicion among the public opinion and environmental organisations: over a billion euros over ten years, a construction over 26 thousand feet wide, fifty thousand tons of fish produced annually and half a thousand jobs created. Supported by some given its potential added value to the local economy, this industrial aquaculture project was opposed by others because of the environmental risks entailed and the fear of setting a Chinese takeover of the territory. During his visit in 2021, President Macron stressed the risks raised by that aggressive Chinese approach for geopolitical balances in the Indo-Pacific, before warning local elected representatives against the temptation of the Chinese mermaid song: "*(..) I will say this bluntly; the coming times will not favour the small, the isolated, those exposed to the influence and incursions of hegemonic powers eager to come take their fisheries, their technologies, their economic resources (..) So let me say this just as bluntly: when*

I sometimes come across projects that, if I may say so myself, can be deemed exotic, adventurous, with doubtful funding and unlikely job creation plans, odd investors? Beware! It is all but a good idea (..)."[9] Before returning to Paris, the French President mentioned the same Chinese investment project once more, at a press conference. From his perspective, national interest had to prevail: "*(...) just consider the French Republic's efforts for the French Polynesian economy without any contribution from Polynesian economic players - not even the local government - we have contributed 600 million euros, 600 million! There is no department in France where such an effort of solidarity has been made without any local input. So one cannot be French on Monday and Chinese on Tuesday. In this case, the project has no documented job creation strategy but suggests dubious investors and has raised much suspicion, especially about its source of funding (...) I'd rather see a new Adapted Military Service unit deployed, than endorse projects with no future (...)*".[10] For French Polynesian authorities, this industrial aquaculture project deserved, instead, full support if it was to truly boost the archipelago's economy. According to Edouard Fritch, realism was to prevail over preexisting positions: "*We are open to private Chinese investors just like we are open to any US, French, European, Samoan or New Zealander investor in economic activity sectors with a potential for external markets such as tourism and aquaculture*".[11] From his standpoint, the Territory had no interest opposing the Chinese "Silk Road" to the French strategy in the Indo-Pacific, but in reaping benefits from both in terms of development: "*We, Pacific countries, must consider that these two offers presented by two great powers, China and Europe, are compatible and an opportunity for each of our states or countries in the Pacific. Both initiatives are very welcome in our region. They will be welcomed as long as they support projects defined and designed by the countries of the Pacific in view of meeting their fundamental necessities or their need for economic development.*"[12] While that difference in views does not challenge the French state, it does demonstrate French Polynesia's capacity to devise an autonomous geopolitical strategy (Milhiet 2022).

---

[9] Reported in *Le Monde*, July 26th, 2021, online.

[10] Reported in *Le Monde*, July 28th, 2021, online.

[11] Reported in *Polynésie La Première*, July 29th, 2021, online.

[12] Key Address, Papeete, University of the French Polynesia, September 10th, 2021, online.

CONCLUSION

This chapter listed short but telling illustrations of clashes between OTs and their administering countries. It highlighted that *"little places (..) can throw up big principles, especially where the evolution of postcolonial relations is concerned"* (Hintjens 1995: 26). It described how the former and the latter interact from different standpoints over international issues. For metropolitan powers, the national interests defined unilaterally by central authorities must prevail at all costs. For SNIJs, local interests as defined by island authorities, should not be sacrificed on the altar of the mainland's *Raison d'Etat*. From the administering countries' perspectives, it is above all a matter of international consistency and national security. From the OTs', it is first and foremost a matter of pragmatism—i. e., the necessity to find resources wherever they are—but also one of respect and dignity. As a result, the OTs' capabilities should neither be overestimated or underestimated. When strategic issues are at stake, mainland powers usually impose their views whatever it takes. Only when these issues are not strategic, local views may prevail.

CHAPTER 13

Vulnerability as a Political Resource

Abstract There is an abundance of literature (Rezvani, 2014; Prinsen, 2018, Connel Aldrich, 2020; Ferdinand Oostindie Veenendaal, 2020; Réno 2022) documenting the ways overseas territories have leveraged their dependence politically. Far from suffering from it, local elites have sometimes managed to do so in view of resisting or influencing the external decisions imposed on them. However, little of the literature produced by the existing schools of thoughts in international relations shows identical ends to the ways overseas territories have leveraged their heteronomy. Rather than focusing on dependence only, I emphasise the notion of *vulnerability* as it conveys other characteristics of these offshore territories—such as their isolation, insularity, low surface area or substantial exposure to climate hazards. In fact, all of these criteria—beyond sheer political or economic subordination—are used, politically, by these subnational island jurisdictions as they strive to achieve their goals in the global arena. To demonstrate it, several short but illustrative case-studies are considered such as joint action from the EU's outermost regions (ORs), the overseas territories' advocacy for ocean protection, and the growing claim for more political autonomy in most democratic offshore subnational jurisdictions.

Keywords Vulnerability as a political resource · Autonomy · Self-government · Subnational interests · Peripheral resistance · Outermost regions of the European Union · The Conference of the

© The Author(s), under exclusive license to Springer Nature Switzerland AG 2024
F. Constant, *Overseas Territories in World Affairs*,
https://doi.org/10.1007/978-3-031-64233-3_13

presidents of the Outermost Regions · Azores · Madeira · Canary Islands · Guadalupe · Guiana · Martinique · Mayotte · Saint Martin · Ocean protection · French Polynesia · Edouard Fritch · Sylvia Earle · Multi-scalar paradiplomacy

When it comes to domestic policy, there is an abundance of literature (Rezvani, 2014; Prinsen, 2018, Connel Aldrich, 2020; Ferdinand Oostindie Veenendaal, 2020; Réno 2022) documenting the ways OTs have leveraged their dependence politically. Far from suffering from it, local elites have managed to do so in view of resisting or influencing the external decisions imposed on them. However, little of the literature produced by the existing schools of thoughts in international relations shows identical ends to the ways OTs have leveraged their heteronomy. Rather than focusing on dependence only, I emphasise the notion of *vulnerability* as it conveys other characteristics of these offshore territories—such as their isolation, insularity, low surface area or substantial exposure to climate hazards. In fact, all of these criteria—beyond sheer political or economic subordination—are used, politically, by the OTs as they strive to achieve their goals in the global arena. To make my case, I will examine a number of examples of joint action from the EU's outermost regions (ORs), of the OTs' advocacy for ocean protection, and of the growing claim for more political autonomy in democratic offshore territories.

The Lobbying Initiatives of Europe's Outermost Regions (ORs)

Created in 1993, the Conference of Presidents of the ORs is a political action and coordination body that rallies the authorities of the Azores, the Canary Islands, French Guiana, Guadeloupe, Madeira, Martinique, Mayotte, Reunion Island and Saint Martin. It meets at least once a year to establish and foster joint approaches to the development challenges faced by these regions far-flung from the European continent. The final declarations adopted at the end of each meeting are valuable material when it comes to monitoring the evolution of the ORs' strategic priorities and the ways in which they convert structural handicaps into levers of European funding. They also define the practical substance of the generic *outermost* notion that constitutes the base for the continuous lobbying pursued by OR authorities with the European Commission, Council and Parliament—as well as with the French, Spanish and Portuguese governments.

Initially, the OR Conference of Presidents was mostly focused on the crucial need for a strategy to catch up on the development gaps experienced by their territories in regard to the European Union's average. That focus led systematically to requests for additional funds, as shown in the closing remarks of the conference held in Pointe-à-Pitre in 1995: "*(...) [The Presidents] call for the creation of specific financial lines for the outermost regions, over and above what is provided for in the Regional Development Plan (RDP) and the Community Initiative Programme for Isolated Regions (CIP-REGIS), so as to go beyond the eligibility criteria of the Structural Funds in certain areas (energy in particular), and also to meet the requirements of European integration, in particular those arising from the single currency.*"[1] Later on, the Conference began focusing on the need to secure the legal status of all ORs in successive treaties with the EU, in view of preventing any challenge to Community acquis (*acquis communautaires*). That demand sought both the full implementation of European policy and the principle of adjusting measures according to their respective specificities. It recurred in several final declarations until the adoption of Articles 349 and 355 of the Treaty on the Functioning of the European Union (TFEU). The ORs' lobbying efforts then shifted towards the Commission's overly restrictive interpretation of these provisions. Several conferences made a strong point to highlight this, as in Fort-de-France in 2011, which lamented that "*(..) the Article 349 of the TFEU that recognizes the specificities of the outermost regions has yet to be effectively implemented by the European Commission, guardian of Treaties.*"[2] OR authorities requested the broad application of all provisions relative to the EU's outermost areas, as a *sine qua non* condition for the optimal implementation of several sectorial policies overseas. In its ordinance of 15 December 2015 relative to Mayotte, the European Court of Justice lifted the so-called legal obstacles to the inclusion of the ORs

---

[1] 2nd Conference of the Presidents of ORs, Pointe-à-Pitre, Guadeloupe, October 18th, 1995, online.

[2] 8th Conference of the Presidents of ORs, Fort-de-France, Martinique, September 18th, 2001, online.

into certain European policies, thereby dismissing the restrictive interpretations that prevailed until then. *"(..) We reassert that while this ordinance has clearly reached a legal verdict, as per the final declaration adopted in Funchal in 2016, the rest will stem from political will alone. From now on, legal clarity and political will go hand in hand."*[3]

A new narrative emerged in the European Commission's public discourse, during the 2000s. It subtly slipped from the image of Europe as *an opportunity for the overseas territories,*[4] to the overseas being increasingly depicted as *an asset for Europe*[5] and the self-representation it seeks to broadcast to the world. That noticeable shift is also mirrored in the discourse of national authorities as they became more eager to leverage their ORs' potential by echoing their claims in Brussels. The priority now advertised by OR Conferences is less to catch up on their development gaps than to seek a sustainable and inclusive path for growth that makes the most of each territory's comparative advantages. The quest for more qualitative development initiatives, designed and implemented by the local authorities, has reached the forefront of collective awareness. The European Commission made it a priority area of focus in a report released on 3 May 2022, titled *Putting people first, securing sustainable and inclusive growth, unlocking the potential of the EU's outermost regions.*[6] It states its willingness to put the local populations' well-being at the top of its concerns, pursue its tailor-made OR policy and adopt urgent, adapted and adequate measures to address challenges specific to only some of them, as they are the EU's outer boundaries. However, these guidelines took a while to come into force; so much so that the OR Conference of 2022 continued to " *wonder and therefore worry, about the failure to apply Article 349 of the TFEU, namely within the legal framework " Fit for 55" for a green transition, which jeopardizes the equal treatment of the European overseas populations."*[7] While the European Commission has yet to meet all their demands, OR authorities still succeeded in influencing

---

[3] 22nd Conference of the Presidents of ORs, Cayenne, Guiana, October 18th, 1995, online.

[4] My emphasis.

[5] My emphasis.

[6] European Commission, Office of Public Relations, Brussels, May 3rd, 2022, online.

[7] 28th Conference of the Presidents of ORs, Las Palmas, Canary Islands, November 8-9th, 2022, online.

some public policies involved in their territories' financial resources, by co-defining a new framework for their implementation.

The Battle for Ocean Protection

The battle for ocean protection has become a platform for the OTs' international action. While this is essentially a matter for sovereign powers, they have proven successful in getting their voices heard as they join international coalitions alongside sovereign nations, and speak out against their paradoxical situations as territories with little polluting responsibility but high exposure to the Anthropocene's effects. From the rise of sea levels to the acidification of oceans, from chemical and plastic contamination to overfishing; they stand on the frontline of climate urgency. There again, their political strategy consists in converting their vulnerability into a political lever to call on the United Nations and pressure major world powers into acting immediately to safeguard their living environments. The OTs of the Pacific are at the forefront of the environmental struggle as their peoples have known for millennia that their existence relies on peaceful coexistence with the ocean.

Among them, French Polynesia has undeniably had a knock-on effect on its counterparts thanks to its multi-scalar green diplomacy. In 2022, French Polynesian President Édouard Fritch committed, during the *One Ocean Summit*,[8] to dedicate a coastal area of 193,151 mi2 to small-scale and subsistence fishing, to protect over five thousand seven hundred ninety mi2 of coral reefs, and to create a new maritime protected area called *Rahui Nui* and equivalent to the total surface area of mainland France. A few months later, the Government of French Polynesia co-hosted in Papeete the *Blue Climate Summit*, an endorsed action of the United Nations Decade of Ocean Science for Sustainable Development. Conceived by world-known oceanographer Sylvia Earle, it brought together public and private institutions including NGOs involved in expanding maritime protected areas (*hope spots*) wide enough to *"save the planet's blue heart."*[9] Then, President Fritch attended the second United Nations Oceans Conference (UNOC) organised in Lisbon, where French

---

[8] A French initiative under the auspices of the United Nations, the event took place in Brest, France, on February 9–11th, 2022.

[9] As nicely stated by Sylvia Earle in her opening remarks, online.

Polynesia was praised as an example for converting, in 2018, its exclusive economic zone into a maritime protected area and a sanctuary for sea mammals. "*We, Oceania's peoples,* as Édouard Fritch likes to say, *are the guardians of the Pacific Ocean [...] The sea is our temple (Marae), the ultimate sanctuary and the world's wonder. It symbolises mystery and respect as it raises collective awareness of space.*"[10] In-between, he presided the celebration of the "World Ocean Day" in Papeete, with the participation of delegations from Micronesia and Melanesia, convinced that the OTs have a crucial message to deliver the world.

In the Arctic, Greenland/Kalaallit Nunaat, driven by its Prime Minister Múte Egede, followed a similar path when it decided, in 2021, to end offshore drilling for the sake of ocean protection and preserving the fisheries that generate most of its self-generated income. That astonishing forfeiture contrasts sharply with the realism of his predecessors and consecrated his government's environmental pledge. "*Every day, our country faces the consequences of climate change (..)* Najaa Nathanielsen argued, adding that the decision was made "*(..) for the sake of our nature, for the sake of our fishing sector, for the sake of our tourism industry and to foster a sustainable development model.*"[11] Before the Nordic Council in which they sit alongside the Faroese Islands, Finland, Denmark, Iceland, Norway and Sweden, Greenland's authorities plead in favour of a strict application of the declaration of 30 October 2019 on the ocean and climate, adopted by their Ministers of Environment. That awareness is just as strong in the Caribbean, which is home to half of the existing maritime protected areas—located in Dutch, French, US and British Overseas Territories. These initiatives are rooted in the Cartagena Convention framework for the protection and promotion of marine environments and reflect the local authorities' eagerness to act jointly to restore the ecosystems threatened by the Anthropocene. OT executives request from their respective mainland's authorities the power to engage in multiscalar environmental paradiplomacy. Based on their diverse institutional or geographical affiliations, they are eager to preserve the ecological balance of their respective territories. There again, local governance models and technical know-how determine the scope of potential initiatives.

---

[10] Speech by Edouard Fritch in Lisbon, June 29th 2018, online.

[11] In her capacity as Minister of Natural Resources, Greenland Herald, July 16th, 2021, online.

Is There any Political Alternative to Autonomy?

Except perhaps for the Faroe Islands, Greenland and New Caledonia, independence no longer appears as the OTs' go-to option. The wide majority of these territories have instead preferred varying levels of autonomy which allow them to be actively involved in local administration without challenging their belonging to broader political entities. Towards the end of his academic career, David Lowenthal—who devoted his life to comparative island studies—had forecast that development: *"At the end of the day, a certain level of autonomy is key for their development. I am not advocating for official sovereignty [...] but for sufficient autonomy so as to allow people to feel like they own their home enough to have it renovated."* (1992:28). The United Nations Special Committee on Decolonisation has confirmed autonomy's appeal for the seventeen territories whose administration by former colonial powers lies under its supervision. Several factors underlie its popularity in OTs even when they are part of democratic political systems. First of all, globalisation has strengthened interdependence between nations and thereby nuanced the very notion of independence by highlighting its limitations when it has failed to generate a satisfactory level of development—as is the case of most microstates in their vicinity. Then, the OTs realised that their political subordination does not exclude them from handling matters of common interest jointly—provided a new distribution of powers between them and their respective administering countries. From one OT to the other, power distribution schemes vary greatly but the all-around dynamic favours greater local autonomy - including in territories already empowered with broad jurisdictions.

From the Danish or French OTs to their British and US counterparts, from New Zealand's and Australia's to the Dutch or Chilean offshore lands, the notion of autonomy conveys at least a two-fold democratic demand: full involvement in the development of said territory and full recognition of its territorial identity. Finally, the flexibility and room for evolution provided by autonomy regimes are viewed as an asset by local populations and elected representatives eager, first and foremost, to enjoy "the best of both worlds" i.e. the benefits of belonging to a broad political ensemble together with the potentialities offered by simultaneously fitting into a different regional environment. In fact, these regimes of internal autonomy allow them to alternately leverage the principles of equality or identity, depending on the circumstances. Nevertheless, they fail to eradicate tensions with central authorities and popular discontent—including among mainland populations who feel like they are subsidising overseas compatriots obsessed by self-differentiation. However, they do offer a fitting mitigation framework in that all parties usually reach the consensus of redistributing the share of responsibilities. Of course, no consensus is a permanent fix. It must be reestablished periodically depending on the level of frustration it inevitably generates in the SNIJs concerned (Jack Corbett 2023).

For all these reasons, OTs celebrate their autonomy with just as much pride as their neighbours boast their independence. Wherever they take place, these festivities carry both a political and an identity charge. In the Faroe Islands, they occur on 29 July and open the new parliamentary session. They symbolise the Faroese people's eagerness for self-administration based on peaceful relations with the Danish authorities. In Greenland, festivities celebrate the autonomy status and Inuit identity at the same time. In the Cook Islands, *Te Maeva Nui* celebrates its population's ancestral cultural heritage and collective achievements. Such assertions of identity are the cement of a national sense of belonging. In French Polynesia, the *Tahua Tu Marama* rallies highlight the progress enabled by autonomy, not only to revive the Polynesian culture and languages but also to expand the territory's international reach. In New Caledonia, the strife between pro-independence advocates and those loyal to the French Republic hampers the celebration of an autonomy status with no equivalent in the national foil. The former view it as a mere stepping stone towards full sovereignty. The latter view it as the end of the road. In all cases, the overseas territories' ability to transform their vulnerability into a political resource relies as much on the foresight of professional politicians as it does on the quality of administrative governance, the level of expertise of its civil servants and their ethical compliance. In most OTs, crucially needed public policies are often hampered by clientelism, nepotism or corruption, which are closely linked to the prevalence of primordial sentiments (Geertz 1983) over citizenship (Constant 1988). Changes in political majority across local political bodies often lead to public civil leaders being hired along political lines—regardless, at times, of how suited they are for the job. In SNIJs where human resources are very limited, these political practices are counterproductive. Representation on the international stage, for instance, requires a technical capacity to design and implement multimodal and multiscalar diplomacy (Lechervy 2019), to process information rapidly from multiple sources, to anticipate and leverage sometimes unforeseeable events and to arbitrate on competing allegiances depending on the stakes at hand. From that standpoint, the OTs are all but equal. Those with the best results are not only the ones that have embraced the best political strategy but also the ones with the skills needed to implement it. No matter how it is defined, autonomy will always be wishful thinking if it does not combine political vision and technical competences. And the overseas territories are not alone in having to learn that lesson.

Conclusion

This chapter aimed at discussing vulnerability as a political resource. It briefly reviewed some illustrative aspects of the paradiplomacy conducted by OTs. From ORs lobbying the EU to the influential role of an OT-inclusive coalition for ocean protection; it showed that SNIJs can sometimes make a difference—even when their own interests diverge from their administering power's. It then went on to explain why political autonomy is by far the OTs' preferred option. First, because in the age of globalisation, independence means nothing but interdependence—especially for smaller states. Second and most importantly, autonomy encompasses varying degrees of empowerment, providing OTs with a significant level of agency to manage or co-manage their own public affairs. Last but not least, it is a status that can evolve according to local aspirations. However, successful subnational governance requires more than a foresighted leadership. It demands adequate human resources at every level of the administrative body, starting with top management positions.

Conclusion

No privileged pole or rapport.
Nil, depreciated. Yes: we are
each in this drama the overseas
of others.
Edouard Glissant (1997: 187).

At the end of this comparative review of OTs in world affairs, conducted with the blend of audacity and risk-taking inherent in such a venture; several lessons can be learned. Contrary to persistent views, OTs are full-fledged parts of their administering countries' national histories—even as they have been artificially kept on the sidelines of national narratives. Their alienation has no *political* or *scientific* legitimacy whatsoever. By-products of their colonial expansionism, these offshore lands are coveted assets disputed by these powers in their frantic quest for world domination. Since their invention, OTs have crystallised power struggles that unfold way over their heads but are the cornerstones of their fates. Shaped by administering countries that use them as pawns on the chessboard of self-interest, they are nonetheless essential to these countries' futures. In each era and each geographical area, they have provided the latter with considerable wealths, strongholds; either sharing or upsetting their goals; embracing or fighting their ideologies—though always in close relation with their fortunes and misfortunes. In the aftermath of World War II and in the age of decolonisation, new geopolitical calculations ushered in the definition of their post-colonial statuses and gave them a new rating on the stock exchange of strategic values. As advanced security and defence outposts, drivers of the fight against communist ideology, or displays of pluralist and liberal democratic models; they were actively involved in the strategic rivalry between the US and the USSR. Their exclusion from or marginal presence in history books contrasts with the key role some of them played in that chapter. It nurtures the illusion of an irrevocable separation between *mainland* powers and overseas territories that are meant to stay in the former's shadow. It fosters the dissemination of a *one-dimensional* version of a shared history much more substantial than popular opinion cares to admit and actually relevant to both the overseas territories and their administering countries. Mitigating that fact as this volume attempts to do, not only bears heuristic value but also contributes to righting some wrongs inherited from history.

Globalisation has by no means diminished the OTs' geopolitical virtues—not even those of offshore lands barely visible on a map. Contrary to commonly held interpretations, transnational dynamics and the dematerialisation of influence processes have absolutely not demonetised *territory* as a notion—despite the transformations engendered by globalisation. Regardless of their surface area, population size or administration regime; they remain on the frontline of their mainland's strategic interests. They provide power levers, especially in the maritime sector, that sometimes lead to sovereignty conflicts resulting in bitter litigations before the International Court of Justice. They keep on multiplying regional affiliations; thereby legitimising their presence in most of the world's strategic regions. Despite the mutation of transnational threats, they continue to stand as major security/defence assets—in particular for the prepositioning and dispatch of conventional forces, the deployment of air and sea-based strategies of nuclear deterrence, or the implementation of space and cyber defence doctrines. These assignments, however, typically change depending on the geopolitical context. Some overseas territories have been promoted as a result. Others, in contrast, have been somewhat derated. The strategic shift towards the Indo-Pacific, a corollary of the Sino-American competition for world leadership, has resulted in a relative depreciation of the offshore territories along the Atlantic seaboard in favour of those in the Indo-Pacific zone. Geopolitical rivalries, which are also expressed in economic terms, have been increasing the value of those areas that harbour considerable resources. At the same time, the ecological and energy transition that is gradually permeating international relations is turning others into environmental sanctuaries. Finally, culture, which is at stake in the symbolic struggles between states for control of soft power, is transforming some of them into platforms of international influence.

And yet, heteronomy does not deprive them of resources to oppose, influence or benefit from a *complex* and *nuanced* relationship characterised by relations of cooperation, competition and conflict, paced by interactions between local and national, public and private stakeholders operating at various political, administrative, economic or cultural levels. It generates resistance that transpires from their electoral choices, the symptomatic recurrence of the status debate, high intensity social mobilisations and even the use of violence. The demands it engenders invariably strive for shared decision-making powers, the redistribution of economic and financial resources, the joint design of local public policy or the sensitive matter of *subjective* belonging to the national community—not to mention that of postcolonial identities upset by unresolved historical disputes. The political dynamics that underlie them, combine a demand for *real* equality and an eagerness for *singularity*. These seemingly antagonistic aspirations also reflect in the OTs' commitment towards the protection of their environment and acknowledgement in the national narrative of their respective countries. Health scandal whistleblowing and memorial conflicts go hand in hand with claims for reparations and compensation, which are increasingly present in state contestation. In the wide majority of situations, autonomy has superseded independence and become the final political horizon. But its substance varies from one territory to another. Many continue to oppose the cumbersome supervision of central authorities regardless of the expansion of their local prerogatives. Others seek first and foremost to mitigate disregard and isolation from the mainland. Others yet have tried to contain its political interventionism in order to safeguard their local governance model. In every case, compromises are *temporary* and *reversible* because the struggle for democracy is a never ending one. It may take roundabout routes or different paths; it may show realism and even expediency but it always targets the same goal: broadening the range of possibilities—especially in the realm of international relations where the overseas territories contribute to their administering countries' politics of influence and also empower them with an archipelagic scope. For all these reasons, they should be further investigated through a geopolitical lens as they provide an original outlook onto the modern world's mutations.

* * *

Among the dozens of people interviewed throughout field surveys, one of them had a lasting impression on me. Not by the content of her remarks so much as by the poetic note of her conclusion. A retired Principal in a subnational island jurisdiction of the US, she ended up our interview with the following lines of one of Maya Angelou's most famous poems:

> *You may write me down in history*
> *With your bitter, twisted lies,*
> *You may trod me in the very dirt*
> *But still, like dust, I'll rise.*
> *You may shoot me with your words*
> *You may cut me with your eyes*
> *You may kill me with your hatefulness*
> *Still, like air, I'll rise* (1978: 25).

Epilogue

History continues to unroll its elusive scroll. It often beats the most reliable forecasts. And sometimes propels less predictable ones into the present. Here are a few flash points that have come to the fore after I put a final period to this book, and rise precisely at the intersection of subnational, national and international politics.

New Caledonia/Kanaky: Towards a Breaking Point?

Saturday, April 13th, 2024. The scene takes place in the heart of Noumea city. Thousands of people march through the streets. Some wave France's tricolour banner. Others walk under the Kanaky flag. About 35,000 make up each side. Mostly White people on the former. Mostly Kanak on the latter. The Loyalists rallied under a telling motto: "*Le dégel, c'est la démocratie*".[1] The Separatists, uttered a momentous slogan: "*Non au dégel electoral*".[2] In between, security forces were massively deployed to prevent any clashes among opposing groups of demonstrators. Could there be a clearer vision of a deeply divided society? After about 30 years of political de-escalation, how did this breaking point

---

[1] Literally, it means "Democracy Is Enlarging the Electorate" i.e. to include every person who has lived in New Caledonia for at least 10 years.

[2] No to any enlargement of the electorate (i.e., the pool of residents allowed to vote under the self-determination referendum).

© The Editor(s) (if applicable) and The Author(s), under exclusive license to Springer Nature Switzerland AG 2024
F. Constant, *Overseas Territories in World Affairs*,
https://doi.org/10.1007/978-3-031-64233-3

become so tangible? At least three governmental decisions have led to the current political deadlock, exacerbating the political divergences between loyalists and separatists. First of all, the third and last referendum on self-determination was unilaterally maintained in December 2021, even as the pro-independence parties had asked to postpone it a few weeks.[3] Despite an abstention rate of 57%—mostly from Kanaks—, the results were recognised by the central government and interpreted as the people's definitive preference for New Caledonia's belonging to the French Republic.

However, such interpretation amounts to mistaking legality for legitimacy. The consultation was perfectly legal, but not legitimate—given the massive abstentionism of the (mostly Kanak) electorate. Nevertheless, the referendum's outcome put an end to the *Accords de Nouméa* (Nouméa's political Agreement), and in particular to its underlying drive to favour consensus among stakeholders. This empowered the French government to take a second political decision with far-reaching consequences: "*unfreezing* the electorate". This ongoing reform aims at incorporating to the electorate every resident having lived in New Caledonia for at least ten years. To enable that measure, the French government and its local allies launched a constitutional amendment and postponed the local elections that were normally due to May 2024. From the pro-independence perspective, these decisions are an unacceptable setback expected to foster its political marginalisation. In fact, it would allow Loyalists to outnumber Separatists and take control of the Provincial assemblies which determine the political make-up of the Congress of New Caledonia.[4] In addition, the French State has been attempting to regain temporary control over a nickel sector in crisis through an organic law. For the pro-independence movement, this is *casus belli*. The nickel industry is considered the main economic driver of full sovereignty aspirations. Apparently, President Macron seems determined to push these reforms in order to weaken the pro-independence movement and further strengthen France's hold over New Caledonia. This political manoeuvre is obviously connected to the

---

[3] Given the devastating impact of Covid-19 among the Kanak community and the period of mourning that followed.

[4] Furthermore, this political marginalisation would not be consistent with international law and the resolutions of UN C24, which require the administering countries to make sure that demographic changes originating from outside territories would not alter the exercise of self-determination for the peoples concerned.

French Republic's growing involvement in the Indo-Pacific under the US' lead, to contain the PRC's global influence.

Greenland/Kalaallit Nunaat: Increasing Autonomy, Postponing Independence?

Wednesday, February 21st, 2023. Vivian Motzfeldt, Minister of Foreign Affairs and Independence, presents Greenland/Kalaallit Nunaat's new foreign policy strategy (2024–2033), speaking only in Greenlandic. One line in particular pinpoints the strategy's objective: *"Nothing about us, without us"*.[5] It carefully reflects the vision of connecting the Danish OT to the outside world. As the Minister puts it: *"We are working to achieve independence, and achieving independence means being able to take on every challenge."*[6] Given its large size and small population, Greenland/Kalaallit Nunaat seeks cooperation to tackle its many challenges. It is actively looking for strategic partners in the Arctic, North America and China. The idea is to attract any country willing to work for the benefit of Greenlanders, without excluding any prospects on ideological grounds. The prospect is then to engage with the US, Canada or Iceland and the PRC as far as it serves the development of the SNIJ. This pragmatic approach stems first and foremost from its relationship with Denmark. The latter remains its primary partner; especially in the realm of preparedness and security. Pragmatism and flexibility prevail on both sides. Contrary to the process of re-centralisation currently affecting New Caledonia, the Danish authorities are, on the contrary, keen to increase Greenland/Kalaallit Nunaat's autonomy in the Kingdom. For instance, they waited for the Greenlanders to adopt their Arctic policy before releasing their own, emphasising the importance of the former to guide the latter's orientations. Unlike France Vs. New Caledonia, no deadline was imposed on the Greenlandic government. More to the point, Danish Prime Minister Mette Frederiksen decided to give Greenland/Kalaallit Nunaat—and the Faroe Islands—a "front seat" in the Arctic Council. This high-level forum composed of 8 countries—including the United States and Russia—is dedicated to promoting cooperation on Arctic issues with

---

[5] Ole Ellekrog "Call for Arctic Cooperation in Greenland's New Foreign Policy Strategy" *Polar Journal*, February 2nd, 2024, online.
[6] Ibid.

the exception of security. It is now agreed that in the Arctic Council, Greenland/Kalaallit Nunaat's Prime Minister will be able to conduct its own foreign-affairs policy. For the Danish Prime Minister, "*This a reflection that the world changes, and the kingdom must change and evolves with it*".[7]

Of course, Greenland's growing foreign-policy autonomy serves Denmark's interests. First, because without its former colony, the Kingdom of Denmark would hardly be an Arctic nation. Second, and most importantly, increasing Greenland/Kalaallit Nunaat's self-governing capacity is definitively, for the time being, the most adequate way of keeping it in the fold of the Danish Kingdom. Greenland/Kalaallit Nunaat's political journey does not imply that aspirations for full sovereignty have gone. It surely highlights new insights on the never-ending debate over decolonisation and sovereignty. It stresses that politics are all about contingency. It shows why and how pragmatism is usually a key word for leaders of subnational island jurisdictions.

Mayotte: The Misfortunes of a Postcolonial Conundrum

Tuesday, February 13th, 2024. Thousands of Mahorans paralysed once again all activities in France's poorest *département*.[8] Most of the main roads were restricted by roadblocks. Protestors rose against continuous and massive waves of clandestine immigration associated with insecurity. Half of the local population of 310,000 inhabitants was not born on the island. 95% of these *undesirable* immigrants originate from the Comoros archipelago which Mayotte belonged to until 1975. Mahorans feel abandoned and discarded by the French authorities. They have been relentlessly calling on the State to take sound and firm actions—in vain. This feeling of frustration and of not being taken seriously, has led Mahoran electors to award Marine Lepen[9] with unprecedented scores (48% and 59%) in the first and second rounds of the presidential elections

---

[7] Kevin MacGwin "Denmark Gives up Arctic Status, Says 'Greenland first'", *Polar Journal*, June 11th, 2021, online.

[8] In addition, since the end of April 2024, a cholera epidemic has been spreading in Mayotte, apparently imported by Comorian migrants.

[9] Leader of the *Rassemblement National*, France's far-right and populist political party, historically based in the mainland.

of 2022. However paradoxical this might seem, the vote was rooted in a form of despair, from not being heard by the central French government.

Unsurprisingly, the French Minister for home affairs launched, in 2023, a spectacular and highly mediatised police operation—called *Wuambushu* ("Regaining constrol") in Shimaore. It aimed at deporting illegal aliens, destroying slums and fighting crime. Obviously, it was far from resolving the situation. An unprecedented wave of violence ensued. One year later, *Wuambushu II* unfolded over a period of eleven weeks. Security forces, including one elite police squadron, were sent to Mayotte in that view. A curfew was enforced in certain areas. In addition, President Macron committed to a reform of nationality rights to deter undocumented migrants from coming to Mayotte. He wants the Constitution to be amended in order to abolish the right of the soil in this specific *département*. This constitutional revision on such a major topic, which would undermine the principle of indivisibility of the French Republic, sparked a national debate. On the one hand, some support the measure on grounds that it would be limited to one overseas territory and because they believe it is the best way to solve the crisis. In contrast, others oppose it because it would jeopardise one of the cornerstones of the French Constitution, and because it would not respond efficiently to Mayotte's cross-sectional crisis. In fact, Comorians do not come to Mayotte to obtain French citizenship. They leave their homeland *en masse* first and foremost to flee a hopeless situation. Even if Mayotte is the poorest *département* in France, it still enjoys far better living conditions than any Comoro Island. As a result, law and order cannot suffice to address the crisis adequately. Today's inextricable situation is the predictable outcome of past political choices (Roinsard 2022), precisely when Mayotte was artificially separated from the Comoros after the referendum on self-determination. It reflects a postcolonial conflict left unsolved. It would certainly take a multi-dimensional package of public policies to curb the issues at hand; a combination of domestic measures designed for Mayotte, and increased international cooperation with the Comoros. Reducing migratory pressure on Mayotte can only be achieved by further supporting the development of the Comoros namely in the island of Anjouan. There is no use in multiplying police operations to charter back illegal migrants.

Indeed, OTs mirror some of the core principles underlying our democracies. Rather than double standard politics, they deserve to be treated like any other part of the national ensembles they officially belong to. No more, no less. Democracy goes beyond the logo map.

Bibliography

ACKREN M. (2006) "The Faroe Islands: Options for Independence", *Island Studies Journal* 1 (2), 223–238.
ACKREN M. JAKOBSEN U. (2015) "Reenland as a Self-governing Sub-national Territory in International Relations: Past, Current and Future Perspectives", *Polar Record* 51 (4) 404–412.
ADLER-NISSEN R. PRAM GAD U. (2013) *European Integration and Postcolonial Sovereignty Games. The EU Overseas Countries and Territories*, Londres, Routledge.
ALDECOA F. KEATING M. eds. (1999) *Paradiplomacy in Action: The Foreign Relations of Subnational Governments*, London, Frank Cass.
ALDRICH R. CONNEL J. (1992) *France's Overseas Frontier*, Cambridge, Cambridge University Press.
ALDRICH R. CONNELL J. (1998) *The Last Colonies*, Londres, Cambridge University Press.
ALLEN R. M. (2016) «Yu di Korsu, a matter of negociation: an anthropological exploration of the identity work of Afro-Curaçaons» dans Duyvendak J. W. Geschiere P. Tonkers E. dir. *The Culturalization of Citizenship. Belonging and Polarization in the Global world*, Londres, Palgrave MacMillan, 137–160.
AL WARDI S. REGNAULT J. M. eds. (2021) *L'Indo-Pacifique et les Nouvelles Routes de la Soie*, Papeete, Api Tahiti éditions et diffusion.
ANON. (2017) "Why the Faroe Islands Want Independence from Denmark?" *The Economist*, August 12.
ANGELOU M. (1978) *And Still I Rise*, New-York, Random House.

ANSES SANTE PUBLIQUE France. (2018) *Evaluation des expositions au Chlordécone et autres pesticides en Martinique et en Guadeloupe*, Paris, Octobre.

AVELLANEDA C. N. BELLO-GOMEZ R. A. eds. (2024) *Handbook on Subnational Governments and Governance*, Cheltenham, Edward Elgar Publishing Limited.

BADIE B. (2023) *Pour Une Approche Subjective des Relations Internationales*, Paris, éditions Odile Jacob.

BALDACCHINO G. MILNE D. eds. (2000) *Lessons from the Political Economy of Small Islands: The Resourcefulness of Jurisdiction*. Basingstoke and New York, Macmillan and St. Martin's Press, in Association with Institute of Islands Studies, UPEI.

BALDACCHINO G. MILNE D. (2006) "Exploring Sub-national Island Jurisdictions: An Editorial Introduction", *The Round Table*, (95) 348, 487–502.

BALDACCHINO G. (2008) "Islands in Between: Martin Garcia and Other Geopolitical Flashpoints", *Islands Studies Journal* 3 (2), 211–224.

BALDACCHINO G. MILNE D. eds. (2009) *The Case for Non-sovereignty. Lessons from Sub-national Jurisdictions*, Londres, Routledge.

BALDACCHINO G. (2010) *Islands Enclaves: Offshoring Strategies, Creative Governance, and Subnational Island Jurisdictions*, MacGill-Queen's University Press.

BALDACCHINO G. (2018) "Mainstreaming the Study of Small States and Territories", *Small States and Territories Journal* 1 (1), 3–16.

BALDACCHINO G. WIVEL A. eds. (2020) *Handbook on the Politics of Small States*, Cheltenham, Edward Elgar Publishing.

BALDACCHINO G. ANTAT S. (2023) "Degrees of Success: The Alliance of Small Island States at the 2015 Paris Climate Change Conference", in BALDACCHINO G. ed. *The Success of Small States in International Relations*, London, Routledge, 124–135.

BARTMANN B. (2006) "In or Out: Subnational Island Jurisdictions and the Antechamber of Paradiplomacy", *The Round Table*, 95 (386) 541–559.

BENIN J. (2019) *Rapport de la commission d'enquête sur l'impact économique, sanitaire et environnemental de l'utilisation du chlordécone (..) en Guadeloupe et Martinique, sur les responsabilités publiques et privées dans la prolongation de leur autorisation et évaluant la nécessité et les modalités d'une indemnisation des préjudices des victimes et de ces territoires*, Paris, Assemblée Nationale.

BENWELL M. C. CLEGG P. HARMER N. PINKERTON A. (2022) "Guest Editorial Introduction: Overseas Territories & Crown Dependencies: What Future in 'Global Britain'?" *Small States & Territories* 5 (1), 3–12.

BENSA A. (2000) *Ethnologie et architecture: Nouméa, Nouvelle-Calédonie, Le Centre culturel Jean-Marie Tjibaou*, Paris, Biro.

BERNAL R. L. (2017) *The Influence of Small States on Superpowers. Jamaica and Us Foreign Policy*, Kingston, Ian Randle Publishers.

BIRNBAUM P. (1979) *Le Peuple et les Gros. Histoire d'un Mythe*, Paris, Grasset.

BISHOP M. CLEGG P. (2018) "Brexit: Challenges and Opportunities for Small States and Territories", *The Round Table*, 107 (3) 329–339.

BISHOP M. BYRON-REID J. CORBETT J. VEENENDAAL W. (2022) "Secession, Territorial Integrity and (Non)-Sovereignty: Why do Some Separatist Movements in the Caribbean Succeed and Others Fail?", *Ethnopolitics* 21 (5), 538–560.

BONILLA Y. (2015) *Non-sovereign Futures: French Caribbean Politics in the Wake of Disenchantment*, Chicago, Chicago University Press.

BOSQUE M. M. (2020) "The Sovereignty of the Crown Dependencies and the British Overseas Territories in the Age of Brexit", *The Round Table*, 15 (1), 151–168.

BRENDON P. (1997) *The Decline and Fall of the British Empire 1781–1997*, London, Vintage.

BREUM M. (2020) "New Political Leader in Greenland: 'We are on the Path Towards Independence'", *High North News*, November 30, online.

BRYANT M. (2024) "Von der Leyen Heads to Greenland as EU Seeks Materials for Green Transition", *Polar Journal*, 14 March, online.

BYRON J. (2017) "Martinique's Accession to the Organization of Eastern Caribbean States: A New Chapter in Caribbean Regionalism?", The Round Table, Published Online 21 June.

CAWLEY C. (2015) *Colonies in Conflict: The History of the British Overseas Territories*, Cambridge, Cambridge Scholars Publishing.

CELESTINE A. (2018) «Comparaison n'est pas raison? A propos des mobilisations pour George Floyd et Adama Traoré», Analyse Opinion Critique (A.O.C), June 8th, Online.

CHAMOISEAU P. (2022) «Pour en finir avec l'Outre-mer», *Le Monde*, September 7th, online.

CHAUVIN S. CLEGG P. COUSIN B. eds. (2018) *Euro-Caribbean Societies in the Twenty-First Century: Offshore Finance, Local Élites and Contentious Politics*, Londres, Routledge.

CLEGG P. PANTOJAS-GARCIA E. eds. (2009) *Governance in the Non-independent Caribbean. Challenges and Opportunities in the Twenty-First Century*, Kingston, Ian Randle.

CLEGG P. (2018) "The United Kingdom and its Overseas Territories: No Longer a 'Benevolent' Patron?", *Small States & Territories* 1 (2), 149–168.

COGNEAU D. (2023) *Un Empire bon marché. Histoire et économie politique de la colonisation française, XIXe–XXIe siècle*, Paris, Seuil.

CONNELL J. ALDRICH R. (2020) *The Ends of Empire. The Last Colonies Revisited*, Palgrave Macmillan, Singapore.

CONSTANT F. (1988) *La Retraite aux Flambeaux. Politique et Société en Martinique*, Paris, Editions Caribéennes.

CONSTANT F. (1992) "Alternative forms of decolonisation in the East Caribbean", dans HINTJENS H. et NEWIT M., eds. *The Political Economy of Small Tropical Islands*, Exeter, Exeter University Press, 1992, 51–64.

CONSTANT F. (1992) «La Régulation Politico-Institutionnelle de la Migration Antillaise en France», in DOMENACH H. PICOUET M. eds. *La Dimension Migratoire des Antilles*, Paris, Editions Economica, 79–109.

CONSTANT F. (2000) "French Republicanism Under Challenge: White Minority 'Béké' Power in Martinique and Guadeloupe" in HOWARD J. WATSON K. *The White Minority of Power in the Caribbean*, Kingston, Ian Randle Publishers, 167–190.

CONSTANT F. (2001) "The French Antilles in the 1990s: Between European Unification and Political Territorialisation", in RAMOS G. A. RIVERA ORTIZ A. I. eds. *Islands at the Crosswords: Politics in the Non-independent Caribbean*, Kingston, Ian Randle Publishers, 80–95.

CONSTANT F. (2020) «Pour une géopolitique des outre-mer. Plaidoyer pour la reconnaissance et la valorisation de territoires à forte valeur stratégique» dans PASQUIET-BRIAND T. dir. *Spicilegium Juris Politici. Mélanges offerts à Philippe Lauvaux*, 332–355.

CONSTANT F. (2021) «Les Outre-mer et la République: légitimité politique et visibilité médiatique» dans DANIEL D. et DAVID C. dir. *75 ans après. Quel avenir pour les collectivités d'Outre-mer ?* Paris, L'Harmattan, collection du GRALE, 125–152.

CONSTANT F. (2023a) *Géopolitique des Outre-mer. Entre déclassement et (re)valorisation*, Paris, Editions Le Cavalier Bleu.

CONSTANT F. (2023b) «Les Outre-mer français: des atouts stratégiques convoités qui pourraient être davantage valorisés», *Diplomatie. Affaires stratégiques et relations internationales*, 75 (3), 36–40.

CONSTANT F. (2023c) «Les Outre-mer: quelle valeur géopolitique aujourd'hui ?», *Revue Constructif*, 65 (2), 19–25.

CONSTANT F. (2024) «Emmanuel Macron et «l'Autre France». Des irritants du passé récent aux défis du futur proche», *Revue Esprit*, n 305–306, 131–141.

COOPER A. F. STOLER A. L. eds. (1997) "Between Metropole and Colony: Rethinking a Research Agenda", in COOPER A. F. STOLER A. L. *Tensions of Empire. Colonial Cultures in a Bourgeois World*, Oakland, University of California Press, 1–56.

COOPER A. F. SHAW T. M. eds. (2009) *The Diplomacies of Small States. Between Vulnerability and Resilience*, Houndsmill, Basingstoke, Palgrave Macmillan.

CORBETT J. (2023) *Statehood à la carte in the Caribbean and in the Pacific. Secession, Regionalism, and Postcolonial Politics*, Oxford, Oxford University Press.
CORBETT J. VENENDAAL W. (2018) *Democracy in Small States: Persisting Against All Odds*, Oxford, Oxford University Press.
CORBETT J. (2015) *Being Political: Leadership and Democracy in the Pacific Islands*, University of Hawai'i Press.
CORBIN C. (2001) "Direct Participation of Non-independent Caribbean Countries in the United Nations: A Method for Self-determination", in RAMOS A. G. RIVERA A. I. eds. *Islands at the Crossroads: Politics in the Non-Independent Caribbean*, Kingston, Ian Randle Publishers, 136–159.
CORBIN C. (2009) "Dependency Governance and Future Political Development in the Non-independent Caribbean", in COOPER A. F. SHAW T. M. eds. *The Diplomacies of Small States. Between Vulnerability and Resilience*, Basingstoke, U.K., Palgrave Macmillan, 81–95.
CLIFFORD M. L. (2022) *Today Hong Kong, Tomorrow the World: What China's Crackdown Reveals About Its Plan to End Freedom Everywhere*, New York, Saint Martin's Press Inc.
CRIEKEMANS D. (2020) "Protodiplomacy: Sub-state Diplomacy and Wannabe States", in BALDACCHINO G. WIVEL A. eds. (2020) *Handbook on the Politics of Small States*, Cheltenham, Edward Elgar Publishing, 395–411.
CRUSOL J. (2007) «Les ruptures politiques d'après-guerre : la bipolarisation du monde et les voies divergentes de décolonisation insulaire dans» LAMBOURDIERE E. *Les Caraïbes dans la géopolitique mondiale*, Paris, Editions Ellipses, 11–47.
DAVID C. (2019) "The Road to Sovereignty for New Caledonia? Analysis of the November 2018 Consultation on Self-determination", *Small States & Territories*, 2 (2), 141–156.
DAVIS M. C. (2020) *Making Hong Kong China: The Rollback of Human Rights and the Rule of Law*, Anna Arbor, MI., Asia Short Book Serie.
DELEPINE E. (2018) *Aimé Césaire. Ecrits politiques. 1957–1971*, Paris, Editions Jean-Michel Place.
DOYLE T. RUMLEY D. (2019) "The US "Pivot" in the Indo-Pacific" in DOYLE T. RUMLEY D. *The Rise and Return of the Indo-Pacific*, Oxford, Oxford University Press, 68–84.
DOUMENGE J. P. (2000) *L'Outre-mer français*, Paris, Armand Colin.
DUARNY J. (2017) *Puerto Rico: What Everyone Needs to Know*, Oxford, Oxford University Press.
DUARNY J. (2023) "Puerto Rico has Been Part of the US for 125 Years, But Its Future Remains Contested", *The Conversation*, July 13th, online.
DUKE S. (2019) *Will Brexit Damage our Security and Defense? The Impact on UK and the EU*, London, Palgrave Macmillan.

ELLEKROG O. (2024) "Call for Artic Cooperation in Greenland's New Foreign Policy Strategy", *Polar Journal*, March 24, online.

FABRY, M. (2000) "Sovereignty, Territory and Referendum: A Commentary on the Paper Presented by Prof. Jean Laponce", ISA Convention Workshop 'Globalization and Democracy', Los Angeles, March 14.

FABRY M. (2010) *Recognizing States. International Society and the Establishment of New States Since 1776*, Oxford, Oxford University Press, 147–179.

FERDINAND M. OOSTINDIE G. VEENENDAAL W. (2020) "A Global Comparison of Non-sovereign Islands Territories: The Search for 'True Equality'", *Island Studies Journal* 15 (1), 43–66.

FERDINAND M. MANGLOU M. (2021) «Penser l'écologie politique depuis les Outre-mer français», *Ecologie & Politique* 2 (63), 11–26.

FERRY J. (1885) *Les Fondements de la Politique Coloniale*, Discours du 25 juillet, Paris, Archives de l'Assemblée Nationale.

FRY E. G. TARTE S. Eds. (2015) *The New Pacific Diplomacy*, Sydney, The Australian National University Press.

FOUCAULT M. (1969) *L'Archéologie du Savoir*, Paris, Gallimard.

GAY J. C. (2021) *La France d'Outre-mer. Terres éparses, sociétés vivantes*, Paris, Armand Colin.

GEERTZ C. (1983) *Local Knowledge. Further Essays in Interpretative Anthropology*, New York, Basic Books.

GIRMA S. ENDALE A. (2020) "COMESA: Prospects and Possibilities for Regional Trade Integration", *International Affairs and Global Strategy*, 76, 15–21.

GLISSANT E. (1990) *Poétique de la Relation*, Paris, Gallimard.

GO J. (2011) *Patterns of Empire: The British and the American Empires, 1688 to the Present* Cambridge, Cambridge University Press.

GOUJON M. HOARAU J.F. (2015) *Vulnérabilités au changement climatique des Outre-mer et des petits Etats insulaires*, Paris, Agence Française de Développement (AFD).

GRAILLE C. (2018) «Passions identitaires et communauté de destin: une utopie calédonienne?» (Identity-related passion and common destiny: A Caledonian utopia?), *Journal de la Société des Océanistes* 147, 351–364.

GRANTHAM-PHILIPPS W. (2020) "Not Just Confederate Statues: Indigenous Activists Want Spanish Conquistadors, Missionaries Removed", *USA Today*, June 29th, online.

GRYDEHOJ A. (2016) "Navigating the Binaries of Island Independence and Dependence in Greenland: Decolonisation, Political Culture and Strategic Services", *Political Geography*, 55, 102–122.

GRYDEHOJ A. (2018) "Decolonizing the Economy in Micropolitics: Rents, Governments Spending and Infrastructures Development in Kalaallit Nunaat (Greenland)", *Small States &Territories Journal*, 1 (1), 69–94.

GRYDEHOJ A. NADARAJAH Y. MARKUSSEN U. (2020) "Islands of Indigeneity: Cultural Distinction, Indigenous Territory and Island Spatiality", *Area* 52 (1), 14–22.

HARRIS P. (2022) "The Chagos Dispute: When Rights Makes Might" *Third World Quartely*, 44 (2), 359–404.

HAAS M. (1989) *The Pacific Way: Regional Cooperation in the South Pacific*, New York, London, Praeger.

HAU'OFA E. (1994) "Our Sea of Islands", *The Contemporary Pacific* 6 (1), 147–161.

HINTJENS H. (1995) *Alternatives to Independence: Explorations in Post-colonial Relations*, Adelshot, U.K., Dartmouth Publishing.

HINTJENS H. NEWITT M. eds. (1992) *The Political Economy of Small Tropical Islands: The Importance of Being Small*, Exeter, U.K., University of Exeter Press.

HOLT R. T. TURNER J. E. (1969) "Insular Polities", in ROSENAU J. *Linkage Politics: Essays on the Convergence of National and International Systems*, New York, The Free Press, 199–237.

HOPKINS A. G. (2018) *American Empire. A Global History*, New Jersey, Princeton University Press.

IMMERWAHR D. (2019) *How to Hide an Empire? A History of the Greater United States*, New York, Farrar Straus & Giroux.

INGEBRITSEN C. (2006) "Conclusion: Learning from Lilliput", in INGEBRITSEN C. NEUMANN I. GSTÖHL S. BEYER J. *Small States in International Relations*, Washington, University of Washington Press, 286–292.

JACKSON A. (2013) *The British Empire. A Very Short Introduction*, Oxford, Oxford University Press, 53–70.

JAMES L. (1997) *The Rise and Fall of the British Empire*, New York: St Martin's Griffin Publishing Group.

JEGO Y. (2009) *15 Mois et 5 Jours. Entre Faux Gentils et Vrais Méchants*, Paris, Grasset.

JONES S. (2009) "UK Seizes Control of Turks and Caicos Over Sleaze Allegations", *The Guardian*, online edition.

KHALTHURIN V. I. RAUTIAN T. G. RICHARDS P. G. LEITH W. S. (2005) "A Review of Nuclear Testing by the Soviet Union at Novaya Zemlya, 1955–1990", *Science & Global Security* 13 (1–2), 1–42.

KAISER R. (2000) "Subnational Governments in International Arenas. Paradiplomacy and Multi-Level Governance in Europe and North America", 5th IPSA Symposium on Globalization, Nations and Multi-Level Governance: Strategies and Challenges, Montreal, 24–26 October.

KEATON D. T. (2023) *#You Know You're Black in France When...The Fact of Everyday Antiblackness*, Cambridge, MA, The MIT Press.

KIPLE K. (2012) "Biology and African Slavery", in SMITH M. PAQUETTE R. eds. *The Oxford Handbook on Slavery in the Americas*, Oxford, Oxford University Press, 293-311.

KILLLINGRAY D. TAYLOR D. eds. (2005) *The United Kingdom Overseas Territories: Past, Present and Future*. London, University of London, Institute of Commonwealth Studies.

KOCI A. BAAR V. (2021) "Greenland and the Faroe Islands: Denmark's Autonomous Territories from Postcolonial Perspectives", *Norsk Geografisk Tidsskrift-Norwegian Journal of Geography*, (75), 189-202.

KRUSE L. M. (2018) *The Pacific Insular Case of American Samoa. Land Rights and Law in Unincorporated US Territories*, New York, Palgrave Macmillan.

LAFRANCE S. (2021) "Russo-Japanese Territorial Dispute over Sakhalin and Kuril Islands", in GRAY K. W. eds. *Global Encyclopedia of Territorial Rights*, Springer, Cham.

LANCASTER A. St. GEORGE J. (2015) "The Organization of Eastern Caribbean States", in ODELLO M. SEATZU F. *Latin American and Caribbean International Institutional Law*, The Hague, T.M.C Asser Press, 231-250.

LASSERRE F. CHOQUET A. et ESCUDE-JOFFRE C. (2021) *Géopolitique des Pôles. Vers une appropriation des espaces polaires ?* Paris, Editions Le Cavalier Bleu.

LECHERVY C. (2019) «La place des outre-mer océaniens dans la politique Indo-Pacifique de la France», *Revue Défense Nationale*, 823 (Octobre 2019), 12-17.

LESLIE H. PRINSEN G. (2018) «French Territories in the Forum: Trojan Horse or Paddles for the Pacific canoe?» *Asia Pacific Viewpoint* 59 (3), 384-390.

LEVINE S. ed. (2016) *Pacific Ways: Government and Politics in the Pacific Islands*, Melbourne, Victoria University Press.

LEWIS P. GILBERT-ROBERTS T. A. BYRON J. (2018) *Pan-Caribbean Integration. Beyond CARICOM,* London, Routledge & Taylor Francis Group.

LIMTIACO S. (2023) "Guam Back to the Drawing Board on Political Status Vote", Pacific Daily News, March 8th, online.

LISINKA M. (2019) "The Falkland Dispute and the Argentine-British War", in LISINKA M. *Foreign Policy during the Military Dictatorship (1976-1983)*, London, Palgrave Macmillan, 89-120.

LOCKLEY T. (2010) "Race and Slavery", in SMITH M. PAQUETTE R. eds. *The Oxford Handbook on Slavery in the Americas*, Oxford, Oxford University Press, 336-356.

LOWENTHAL D. (1992) "Small Tropical Islands: A General Overview" dans HINTJENS H. NEWITT M. *The Political Economy of Small Tropical Islands. The Importance of Being Small*, Exeter, University of Exeter Press, 18-30.

MACGILL K. (2021) "Denmark Gives Up Artic Status, Says Greenland First", *Polar Journal*, June 11, online.
MAHAN A. T. (1890) *The Influence of Sea Power upon History 1660–1783*, London, Dover Publications (revised edition, 1987).
MALTBY W. S. (2008) *The Rise and Fall of The Spanish Empire*, New York, London, Bloomsbury Publishing.
MARSH K. G. TAITANO T. J. (2016) in LEVINE S ed. *Pacific Ways: Government and Politics in the Pacific Islands*, Melbourne: Victoria University Press, 90–107.
MENCE-CASTER C. (2023) «L'abandon du mot « métropole », ou la remise en question d'une forme de néo-colonisation», *Le portail des Outre-mer*, May 26th, online.
METZ R. VRIGNON A. eds. (2022) *Des Bombes en Polynésie. Les essais nucléaires français dans le Pacifique*, Paris, Editions Vendémiaire.
MILHIET P. (2022) *Géopolitique de l'Indo-Pacifique. Enjeux internationaux, perspectives françaises*, Paris, Editions Le Cavalier Bleu.
MONAGHAN C. (2023) "The Fight to Achieve Full Decolonisation. Mauritius Versus the United Kingdom" in BALDACCHINO G. ed. *The Success of Small States in International Relations*, London, Routledge, 148–169.
MONTAGNER L. (2008) *Pesticides et Cancer de la Prostate*, Paris, INSERM.
MOSLIMANI M. NOE-BUSTAMANTE L SHAH S. (2023) *Facts of Hispanics of Puerto Rican Origins in the United States, 2021*, New York, Pew Research Center, online.
MRGUDOVIC N. (2015) «Le Groupe du Fer de Lance mélanésien face à ses défis (The Melanesian Spearhead Group and its challenges)», *Journal de la Société des Océanistes* 140 (1), 59–74.
MURDOCH A. H. ed. (2021) *The Struggle of Non-sovereign Caribbean*, Rutgers, The State University of New Jersey.
NIQUET V. (2022) *Taïwan face à la Chine. Face à la guerre ?* Paris, Editions Taillandier.
NYE J. S. (2004) *Soft Power. The Means to Success in World Politics*, New York, Public Affairs.
ODIN P. (2019) *Pwofitasyon. Luttes syndicales et anticolonialisme en Guadeloupe et en Martinique*, Paris, Editions La Découverte.
OGUTU M. O. (2021) "The Indian Ocean Rim Association: Lessons from this Regional Cooperation Model", *South African Journal of International Affairs*, 71–92.
OOSTINDIE G. J. KLINKERS I. (2003) *Decolonizing the Caribbean: Dutch Policies in a comparative Perspective*, Amsterdam, Amsterdam University Press.
OOSTINDIE G. (2006) "Dependence and Autonomy in Sub-national Island Jurisdictions: The Case of the Kingdom of the Netherlands", *The Round Table* 95 (386), 609–626.

OOSTINDIE G. J. (2011) *Postcolonial Netherlands. Sixty Years of Forgetting, Commemorating, Silencing*, Amsterdam, Presses de l'Université d'Amsterdam.

ORTOLLAND D. PIRAT J. P. dir. (2010) *Atlas géopolitique des espaces maritimes*, Paris, Editions Technip, 2ème édition.

PATTIEU S. SIBEUD E. STOVALL T. (2022) *The Black Populations of France. Histories from Metropole to Colony*, Lincoln NE, University of Nebraska Press.

PRINSEN G. BLAISE S. (2017) "An Emerging "Islandian" Sovereignty of Non-sovereign Islands", *International Journal* 72 (1), 56–78.

PRINSEN G. (2018) "This Is Who We Are": Non-Self-governing Islands Crafting a New Sovereignty Through Five Mechanisms and Four Drivers", *Annual Report on Global Islands 2017*, 143–164.

QUINCE C. (2019) *The Exclusive Economic Zone*, Wilmington DE., Vernon Press.

QUINN C. (2021) "Greenland Rare-Earth Elections", *Foreign Policy*, April 6.

RAMOS A. (2022) "Puerto Rico and US Virgin Islands", in DANIEL D. DAVID C. *75 ans après. Quel avenir pour les collectivités d'Outre-mer ?* Paris, L'Harmattan, collection du GRALE, 2022, 509–525.

RENO F. (2022) "Dependency as a Strategy", in HENKE H. RENO F. (dir.) *New Political Culture in the Caribbean*, Kingston, The University of the West Indies Press, 17–37.

REUTERS (2021) "Greenland Ends Unsuccessful 50 Years-Bid to Produce Oil", Copenhagen (desk), July 16.

REZVANI D. (2014) *Surpassing the Sovereign State: The Wealth Self-rule and Security Advantages of Partially Independent Territories*, Oxford, Oxford University Press.

ROBERTS B. R. STEPHENS M. A. eds. (2017) *Archipelagic American Studies*, Durham and London, Duke University Press.

ROINSARD N. (2022) *Une Situation Postcoloniale. Mayotte ou le Gouvernement des Marges*, Paris, éditions du CNRS.

ROSENAU J. N. ed. (1969) *Linkage Politics: Essays on the Convergence of National and International Systems*, New York, The Free Press.

ROTHBERG M. (2013) "Remembering Back: Cultural Memory, Colonial legacy, and Postcolonial Studies", in HUGGAN B. ed. *The Oxford Handbook of Postcolonial Studies*, Oxford, Oxford University Press, 359–379.

SAVIANA A. (2024) «La redoutable stratégie de la Russie et de la Chine pour déstabiliser la France en Outre-mer», *L'Express*, 26 mars, online.

SINGARAVELOU P. (2023) «Renouer nos Histoires (XXIe siècle/XVe siècle)», in SINGARAVELOU P. ed. *Colonialisme. Notre Histoire*, Paris, Seuil, 7–17.

TAN F. VALLE S. (2022) «Exxon declares force majeure on Russian Sakahlin-1 operation», *Reuters*, April 28.

THOMAS M. THOMPSON A. eds. (2017) *The Oxford Handbook of The Ends of Empire*, Oxford, Oxford University Press.

TJIBAOU J. M. (1996) *La Présence Kanak*, Paris, éditions Odile Jacob.
TEMPER L. DEL BENE D. MARTINEZ-ALIER J. (2015) "Mapping the Frontiers and Front Lines of Global Environmental Justice: The EJAtlas", *Journal of Political Ecology* 22 (1), 255–278.
TROUILLOT M. R. (1995) *Silencing the Past. Power and the Production of History*, Boston, Beacon Press Books.
TURPIN (2017) *Jacques Foccard. Dans l'ombre du pouvoir*, Paris, Editions du CNRS.
TUTUGORO A. (2024) *Analyse des stratégies de reconquête de souveraineté par le mouvement indépendantiste en Nouvelle-Calédonie*, PhD. Dissertation in Political Science, Nouméa, University of New Caledonia, March 12, 815.
VEENENDAAL W. OOSTINDIE G. (2018) "Head versus Heart: The Ambiguities of Non-sovereignty in the Dutch Caribbean", *Regional & Federal Studies* 28 (1), 25–45.
VEENENDAAL W. CORBETT J. (2015) "Why Small States Offer Important Answers to Large Questions?" *Comparative Political Studies* 48 (4), 527–549.
VIVEK J. (2019) "Indian Ocean Commission", *Yearbook of International Environmental Law* 30 (1), 511–517.
ZANG Y. WEI Z. GRYDEHOJ A. (2021) "Electoral Politics, Party Performance, and Governance in Greenland: Parties, Personalities and Cleavages in an Autonomous Subnational Island Jurisdiction", *Island Studies Journal* 1–30.
ZUCMAN G. (2015) The Hidden Wealth of Nations. The Scourge of Tax Havens, Chicago, Chicagso University Press.

Index

A
Alliance of Small and Island States (AOSIS), 139
Antarctic International Treaty (ATS), 39
Aruba, 24, 43, 100, 116, 117, 137, 139, 140
Association of Caribbean States (ACS), 137, 150–152
Australia, 4, 11, 43, 44, 62, 71, 74, 85, 123, 135, 136, 138, 142, 143, 165

B
Balearic Islands, 12, 21, 33, 48, 84
Bikini and Enewetak, 122
Bonaire, 24, 43, 140
British Antarctic Territory (BAT), 38, 39, 86
British Dependent Territories (BDT), 34
British Foreign, Commonwealth and Development Office (FCDO), 39
British Indian Ocean Territory (BIOT), 12, 38, 124
British Overseas Territories (BOT), 22, 34, 50, 139, 148, 149, 164
British Overseas Territory Citizenship, 34
British Virgin Islands (BVI), 22, 84, 136, 139

C
Canary Islands, 12, 21, 22, 33, 48, 84, 129, 139, 140, 160, 162
Caribbean Community and Common Market (CARICOM), 137, 152
Cayman Islands, 12, 83, 84, 136
Ceuta and Melilla, 21, 33
Chagos archipelago, 63, 86, 124
Christmas Island, 73, 122
Cocos Islands, xvi
Cook Islands, 12, 57, 100, 120, 135, 136, 139, 142–144, 153, 166
Curaçao, 13, 24, 43, 47, 50, 88, 97, 116, 117, 126, 128, 129, 137, 139, 140

D

Decolonisation, 2, 10, 14, 15, 26, 30, 31, 33, 40, 51, 135, 165, 169, 176
Denmark, 4, 11, 12, 24–26, 42, 44, 48, 57, 81, 86–88, 101, 102, 139, 141, 164, 175, 176
Desventuradas Islands, 39
Diaoyu Dao/Senkaku Islands, 12, 26, 58
Diego Garcia, 39, 43, 68, 69, 124, 125

E

Easter Island (Rapa Nui), 12, 25, 87, 122, 127–129, 145
European Union (EU), 4, 33, 70, 81, 85, 105, 129, 139–143, 149, 160–162, 167
Exclusive Economic Zone (EEZ), 6, 56, 57, 59, 70, 71

F

Faroe Islands, 2, 24, 57, 101, 102, 125, 129, 143, 144, 165, 166, 175
Federated States of Micronesia, 136
France, 2, 4–6, 11–13, 21, 22, 24–26, 31, 32, 36, 39, 43, 44, 46, 47, 51, 56, 57, 62, 63, 70, 71, 74, 75, 83, 85, 97, 99, 100, 110, 114, 115, 121, 123, 135, 137–139, 145, 150, 155, 163, 175–177
Franz Joseph Land (Russia), xix
French Polynesia, 2, 7, 36, 43, 44, 57, 62, 63, 74, 84, 85, 100, 110, 111, 122, 123, 129, 135, 136, 140, 141, 143–145, 155, 156, 163, 164, 166

French Southern and Antarctic Lands (TAAF), 39, 62

G

Greenland/*Kalaallit Nunaat*, 2, 12, 24, 81, 87, 88, 100, 101, 103, 141, 142, 175, 176
Guadeloupe, 12, 15, 24, 31, 46, 85, 97–99, 113, 115, 128, 137, 139, 140, 152, 160, 161
Guam, 4, 12, 23, 35, 43, 44, 69, 77, 109, 110, 123, 124, 135, 139
Guantánamo, 23, 43
Guyane, 151

H

Hawaii, 12, 23, 25, 32, 33, 35, 43–45, 69, 77, 84, 97, 115, 116, 136
Hong Kong (HK), 3, 12, 26, 27, 36, 37, 64, 83, 88, 103–105

J

Japan, 11–13, 25, 26, 58, 59, 63

L

La Réunion, xxiv

K

Kiribati, 63, 73, 74, 136
Kuril Islands (Russia), 12, 13, 59

M

Macau, 12, 26, 36, 37, 84, 85, 104, 106
Marshall Islands, 72, 109, 136

INDEX

Martinique, 4, 5, 12, 24, 31, 46, 47, 50, 51, 97, 113, 115, 121, 128, 137, 139, 151, 152, 160, 161
Mayotte, 3, 25, 32, 62, 71, 100, 138, 160, 161, 176, 177
Melanesian Spearhead Group (MSG), 136

N

Netherlands Antilles (NA), 50, 85
New Caledonia/Kanaky, 2, 12, 24, 36, 43, 62, 71, 82, 100, 126, 129, 135, 136, 140, 143, 155, 165, 173–175
New Siberia Islands (Russia), 64, 77, 86
New Zealand (NZ), 4, 12, 43, 44, 57, 62, 71, 74, 120, 121, 135, 136, 142–144, 154, 165
Niue, 12, 57, 135, 136, 139, 153, 154
North Atlantic Treaty Organization (NATO), 42, 48, 68, 77
Norway and Svalbard, 39
Novaya Zemlya (Russia), 12, 24, 64, 73, 77, 86, 112, 113

O

Offshore Finance Centre (OFC), xxiv
Organization of Eastern Caribbean States (OECS), 137, 140
Overseas Countries and Territories Association (OCTA), 142

P

Pacific Islands Forum (PIF), 135, 136, 144
Paracel Islands, xvi, 4, 12, 58
Paradiplomacy, 134, 148, 164, 167

People's Republic of China (PRC), xvi, xviii, 3, 4, 11, 12, 26, 58, 59, 64, 70, 76, 85, 105, 136, 153–155, 175
Portugal, xviii, 4, 12, 22, 24, 33, 42, 48, 57, 139
Puerto Rico, xvi, 3, 12, 13, 23, 33, 35, 43–45, 49, 68, 88, 94–97, 121, 128, 139

R

Russia, xvii, xix, 12, 13, 26, 64, 77, 81, 82, 86, 106, 113, 142, 175

S

Saba, xviii, 24
Saint Barthélemy, xvii, 25, 26, 36, 125, 137, 140
Saint Martin, xvii, 139, 160
Saint Thomas, 24
Sakhalin (Russia), xix, 12, 59, 64, 80, 81, 106
Sint Eustatius, xviii, 24
Sint Maarten, xviii, 12, 24, 97, 129, 140
Special administrative regions (SAR), 36, 37, 105
Spratly Islands, xvi, 58, 70
Subnational (Island) Juridictions (SNIJs), 7, 8, 145, 172, 176

T

Turks and Caicos (TCI), 12, 34, 50, 137

U

United Kingdom Overseas Territories (UKOTs), 148
United Kingdom (UK), xviii, 4, 5, 11, 12, 25, 34, 49, 60–63, 69,

83, 86, 123, 124, 138, 144, 149, 150
United Nations Education, Scientific and Cultural Organisation (UNESCO), 85–88
United Nations (UN), 30, 72, 124, 135, 143, 152, 163, 174
United States (US), xvi, 4, 11, 12, 20, 21, 23–26, 32, 33, 35, 38, 42–44, 46, 48, 49, 56, 58, 59, 62, 63, 65, 68, 72, 73, 77, 86, 96, 109, 114, 124, 135, 150, 153, 175
UN Security Council (UNSC), 4, 77, 109
UN Special Committee on Decolonization (C24), 135, 174
US incorporated unorganized territories, 38
US Minor Outlying Islands, 38
US unincorporated and non-organized territories, 38

V
Vieques, Puerto Rico, 43, 49, 68

W
Wallis and Futuna, 12, 25, 36, 62, 135, 136, 140, 141